Michael Feeney Callan is a screenwriter and director. Born in Dublin, he joined BBC television as a story editor, then went on to write for international TV series like *The Professionals*. He also directed *My Riviera*, starring Joan Collins and Roger Moore, as well as the acclaimed documentary *The Beach Boys Today* in 1992.

He has published a number of books of which the most recent is *Richard Harris – A Sporting Life*.

Sean Connery
The Untouchable Hero

Michael Feeney Callan

For my parents,
Michael Callan and Margaret Feeney,
who gave me the movies and the belief

This revised edition first published in Great Britain
in 1993 by
Virgin Books
a division of Virgin Publishing Ltd
332 Ladbroke Grove
London W10 5AH

First published in Great Britain as *Sean Connery: His Life
and Films* in 1983 by W.H. Allen & Co Ltd

A catalogue record for this book is available from the
British Library

ISBN 0 86369 755 0

Typeset by Phoenix Photosetting, Chatham
Printed and bound in Great Britain

Contents

Illustrations

Foreword
by John Boorman

Sean and I made a film together: *Zardoz*. Not a big hit, although it paid its way. It was an ambitious, labyrinthine piece, an exercise in movie metaphysics expressed in sci-fi spectacle. For Connery (as for me), it was risky and daring. My script required him to spend eight weeks in a scarlet diaper in an Irish spring (Arctic), to daub his body in white clay (it plucked out his considerable body hair when removed), to rape, pillage, dress as a bride (white organza), quote T.S. Eliot, ride a horse and – a final ordeal – endure days of complex make-up for a final sequence in which we see him age, wither and die.

The picture was thick with special effects which are slow and tedious for an actor. We made the film for one million, one hundred dollars. Sean took almost no fee, contenting himself with a piece of the profits (as I did).

Sean said 'yes'. In the movie business 'yes' is hedged round with 'buts' and 'maybes'. Not so with Connery. He stayed at my side. When the going got tough he got stronger. He is loyal and true. His masculine power is so evident that it gives him the confidence to expose his poetic, feminine side. He is a complete man, standing alone, making his own judgements, realised and balanced.

There is no bitterness about his deprived childhood. He looks upon it as an enriching experience. He suffered the customary humiliations of the British class system, but today moves up and down classes with tolerance and, above all, without modifying his own behaviour.

How did he achieve this? If this book throws light only on that, then it will be worth reading.

I believe that Connery touches us because he personifies the best qualities that came out of the post-war upheavals in Britain. Such changes as the reform of education and the busting of the BBC's monopoly allowed a lot of talent to flourish. There was revolution in the theatre, in popular music with the Beatles, and in other fields. Much of it has withered and disappointed. But Connery is an archetype of what was best in those times. And that is his power. But like all archetypes, he also represents something timeless. His persona reaches back and touches a tradition in British life. I can best define that by suggesting characters that he could play better than anyone else: Captain Cook; W.G. Grace; Thomas Hardy; Keir Hardie; Isambard Kingdom Brunel; Sir Francis Drake . . .

John Boorman
Co. Wicklow
Ireland

Introduction and Acknowledgements

Balding, reputedly parsimonious, unquestionably hard-hitting, occasionally litigious, often grumpy and unsmiling, Sean Connery is considered by many the Sexiest Man Alive. In a magazine poll American women voted him just that, though Connery preferred the long overdue Oscar awarded the same year, 1987, for *The Untouchables*. In a business of manufactured mystique Connery alone, it seems, has the onion-layered complexity of a genuine enigma. He is uncompromising and that adds to the enduring mystery. When he is annoyed the world knows about it. When he is pleased, the world knows. He is not a man for half-truths but, clear to all, he is above all a man who craves privacy. Ergo, approaching a definitive biography one confronts enormous obstacles. Unlike almost every other star performer Connery has no publicist, hasn't had since the early Bond days. Maintaining personal contact with him is well nigh impossible for all writers – as witness the experience of *Sunday Times* journalist Russell Miller. In his pursuit of a comprehensive article on Connery's work in the movie of Le Carré's *The Russia House*, he endeavoured to contact Michael Ovitz, the legendary Creative Artists agent who represents him in Los Angeles. Miller found that Ovitz was 'far too important to bother about returning calls'. When he eventually winkled out the fact that Jay Maloney effectively handles Connery's affairs he succeeded, albeit briefly, in getting him on the phone. 'He seemed both terrified and appalled at the prospect of answering questions. . . . Inexplicably the line went dead at that moment and when I immediately called back, what do you know? He was in a meeting.' Miller did not report attempts to contact the elusive superstar at his home, the low-slung tile-and-stucco Casa Malibu in the village of San Pedro de Alcantara, beside Marbella, in Spain. Had he done so he would have had the polite parrying of the resident Connery secretary, Maha, and probably not much else. His friend Ian Bannen told me: 'Sean talks to the press when he wants to – not the other way around.'

The reasons for Connery's obsession with privacy are complex and vary according to the source you choose to plumb. Terence Young, director of *Dr No* and a number of early Connery films, cites without hesitation the betrayals of early journalist coverage. In the beginning, he contends, the press was snide with Connery, seeing absurdity in the portrayal of Ian Fleming's high-bred gadabout by an Edinburgh slum kid. After a year or two of Bond, when Connery was the world's number one box-office draw, he punished the press with silence. Young often stepped into the breech with a forthright explanation to the swarming press brigade. At the time of *Thunderball* he told them: 'Sean is not unpleasant. *You* started it. You tried to make a monkey out of him and now he doesn't need you.' Connery himself sardonically avoided analysis of his reasons, saying to American journalist Allyson Sloane, 'It's a known fact that most people come out of Scotland with vast superiority complexes.'

Connery has consciously endeavoured to let his work speak for itself, which is no bad thing, considering the body of diverse fine playing he has delivered over 35 years in movies. His attitude has been that he owes no one any more than a full day on the set, total professionalism, unequivocal commitment. Within the industry, undoubtedly, he is widely venerated – 'a *huge* personality,' in the words of the late John Huston. Actors of his calibre – in the first rank with the Hoffmans, De Niros and Newmans – commonly attract petty jealousies among their peers; but Connery seems impervious to this. As Michael Caine says, 'When Sean won that oscar he got *two* standing ovations. I'd never seen that in my life – for any performer. It is a measure of how many friends he has in the industry, and how honestly he is admired.'

And yet there seems a naivety in Connery's resistance to press grilling and his indifference towards journalists. The writer George Feifer, reporting on Connery's attitude to money and Hollywood lawsuits, opined that he 'shows scant understanding that he himself exploits – in the sense that the entire industry does – as well as suffers exploitation.' Robert Henderson, the actor-coach to whom Connery attributes his initial career momentum, once described Connery to me as 'a sweet, sweet man' but went on: 'He might often be misunderstood because he recognises no need to reaffirm his persona. He is what he is. He is an actor. He is good at what he does. What more is there to say?'

Writing about Connery is challenging and fulfilling on two counts. First, his achievement as a British star actor is unmatched in the history of movies. Olivier was awarded greater accolades and produced sporadically better work. Cary Grant, if his teenage departure from Britain still qualifies him, enjoyed a first-league success over a broader span of years. But Connery was the backbone of the most successful series of films in the history of cinema – films that have grossed more than *$2 billion*. He has skipped through the genres effortlessly – from period classics, to farce, to pop thrillers, to sci-fi. Few British actors have embraced so wide an audience and, today, no British actor in Hollywood is paid more than Connery. (This is quite simply demonstrable: for *Highlander II* he received $3½ million for nine days' work.) Analysing the choices he has made, and the public impact of those choices, has a value beyond simple biography. It offers an insight into the mechanism of movie-making and describes a new era in the seventh art, far removed from the studio system days, when individualism and independence distinguish all leading artists and is often the seminal source of major work.

Second is the joy of unpeeling the onion layers and finding the man. Connery throws smokescreens, mostly unwittingly, but he's glad to have them just the same. 'After Bond,' says Honor Blackman, 'he needed space. It's like the Beatles, say. You've got to imagine what that invasion of privacy was like.' As I write I know that at least three other Connery biographies are in the making. An Edinburgh friend of Connery's tells me: 'He's furious about them, mostly because he gets agitated when journalists hound him – and some of these fellows are hounding him. So he just puts up the wall.'

I was lucky. Twelve years ago I began my investigation of Sean Connery, man and myth. At the outset I had the cool but kindly good wishes of Sean Connery via a key mutual friend, and I had the copious assistance of a vast array of Connery intimates, from his brother Neil to his directors like Fred Zinnemann, Richard Lester, Lewis Gilbert, Guy Hamilton. My book was published in 1983, and in this updated version I have re-evaluated the hours of recorded interviews and, yes, re-addressed my own points of view. Regrettably, many crucial contributors and witnesses to the early Connery years have passed on. Robert Henderson is no longer with us; nor is his wonderful wife Estelle Winwood. Alfie Bass is gone, as are a number of background players. My exchanges with them were brief, but they are all fondly remembered.

In the intervening years I have met and worked with other essential participants in the Connery story, among them his first wife Diane Cilento, and his 007 successor Roger Moore. Though they did not specifically contribute to this updated text, their tangential influence here and there is significant. Conversation with them helped me round off a fresh new view of Connery and his work.

A considerable army of people directly supported this work and I am deeply grateful to them all. Some chose to remain anonymous and of course I have honoured their wishes. But I am delighted to be able to thank: Neil Connery, Kieron Moore, Michael O'Herlihy, Robert Hardy, Michael Caine, Shay Hennessy, Anne Hennessy, John

Brady, Craigie Veitch, Estelle Winwood, Robert Henderson, Alfie Bass, Ross Wilson, Ian Bannen, Fred Zinnemann, Johnny Wallis, Ian Porteous, Guy Hamilton, Honor Blackman, Denis Selinger, Zena Marshall, Richard Lester, Tony Crawley, Ivan Waterman, Frederick Albert Levy, Brian Doyle, John Clive, Jack Vinestock, Harry Band (United Artists), Paul Higginson (Twentieth Century-Fox), Andrew Fyall, Karen Cook, Alistair Sutcliffe, Marjorie Bilbow, Sammi Finneran, Bill Bryson, Fiona Perdesatt, Lewis Gilbert, Michael Hayes, Alvin Rakoff, Philip Hinchliffe, Jane Judge, Anne Marie Glennon, Mary Louise Glennon, Bill Brady, Sheamus Smith, John Boorman, translators Marianne McGeehan and Clodagh Hourigan, Conor Hourigan, Jackie Ross, Pat Perilli and the staff of the Information Section of the British Film Institute, Gilbert Gibson, Mrs J.W. Gregson of British Actors' Equity, the library staff of *Screen International*, *Playboy*, the *Guardian*, the BBC and Westminster Central Library and the Academy of Motion Picture Arts and Sciences. Among the main journals consulted were *The New York Times*, the *Los Angeles Times*, *The Times* of London, the *People*, the *Daily Express*, the *Hollywood Reporter*, *Picturegoer*, *Time*, the *Spectator*, *Punch*, *Woman's Own*, *TV Guide*, *The Sunday Times*, *Rolling Stone*, *Variety*, *Starfix* (Paris), *Photoplay* and *Films and Filming*. Grateful acknowledgment also to the various diarists and reviewers who kept pace with Connery's comings and goings and who opened their files to me. Fond thanks, too, to my editors (spanning ten years) Hilary Muray, Sally Holloway and Karin Leite. And to Jay, who always keeps the goal in sight.

Special thanks to Ree, Corey and Paris, movie lovers I love.

1

Edinburgh For Ever

It was the summer of 1991. Ross Wilson, an accomplished documentary director for Scottish TV, was looking forward to this foreign film assignment. 'It crept up on me,' he said. 'Like everyone else, I grew up with this implacable vision of heroism, of what men should be, called James Bond. And being Scottish – though from west of the promised land of Edinburgh – I took a special interest in Sean Connery. So I was keen to meet him.' Karen Cook, Wilson's researcher, was even more eager. 'I mean, for women everywhere he has become this dream figure. Still. Even twenty years after Bond. The Perfection of Man.' Andrew Fyall, who was to be the Connery insider on the production team, and who has known him for over ten years, was equally enthusiastic – but a little wary. 'Sean is very straight,' he says phlegmatically. 'That's the way his Scottishness works. We had been friends for a while. He made the Edinburgh promotional film for me ten years ago. He calls me whenever he's coming home, to say: Do this for me, or check out that. So I felt I would have his co-operation in this film documentary, and it was vital we had it. Because it was all about celebrating his coming home. You see, he had been given the keys of the city, he was a Freeman of Edinburgh. It was *the* crowning moment, I believe, maybe even beyond that Oscar. This was where Sean Connery *arrived*. This was where he made history.'

Connery himself echoed the sentiment. He said, 'When I was first approached I didn't realise the significance of it. It started in 1495. [The honour has been given] to people like admirals, kings, queens, princes. Names like David Livingstone, Ben Franklin, Ben Jonson . . . it's an amazing list.'

Connery called Fyall from Mexico to outline his agreement to do the programme and suggested that he, Wilson and the crew flew straight to Spain. This access to the inner sanctum was, in effect, the breakthrough. It was popular knowledge that the Connerys – Sean and second wife Micheline – carefully guarded the privacy of the Casa Malibu, their retreat near Marbella. Only twice before had film crews been given the run of the Connery homestead – and neither were of the Robin Leech 'Rich and Famous' persuasion.

After weeks of transatlantic talk Fyall and Cook had the deal done. Ross Wilson balanced the budget, booked the air fares and got ready for the assignment of a young Scots life.

Momentarily there was disillusion. Though Connery's office had arranged the accommodation in a local hotel, Wilson and the production team found themselves adrift in the bars and bistros of trendy Marbella, awaiting the court summons. When finally it came Wilson encountered a Connery he hadn't expected. 'He was very rough and real. He had just returned from this horrendous foreign shoot [*Medicine Man*] and accordingly looked rough. He had a cold sore on his lip, his hair was long and tousled, he had an attitude of *I couldn't give a damn.*' Wilson was wary, but Fyall understood. 'Sean never really compromised, that's the secret. He never changed. I can't think of many who've had his kind of fame and been so separated from their humble beginnings and yet remained so . . . in touch. So grounded.'

The shoot was frantic and fast and Connery sat on the plump white settee in his Malibu-white lounge, under an eighties portrait of him by Micheline, which depicts bristling, tufted, near-naked masculinity beneath a delicate intellectual face, and gave his all. 'It was extraordinarily frank,' says Wilson. 'He didn't censor us. One had these preconceptions of the difficult interview – but this time he was ready for it.' Tom Carlisle, a Bond era publicist, once said of Connery, 'He is considered the best three-second interview in the business.' Fyall says, 'He isn't a pushover. You don't get from Sean anything other than what he wants to give.' And now, in this programme that would celebrate his Edinburgh homecoming, he seemed ready for unusual candour.

Paradoxes abounded – only to be dispelled in the overview of the developing Bigger Picture. He had opinions about everything but, it emerged quickly, personal calm and security mattered most to him – especially the security of sound finance. And yet he was not interested in material possessions. He had not, he told Fyall, even bothered to retain keepsakes from the Bond years. 'Jackie Collins asked me what I did with the original scripts,' he said. 'I told her I didn't have them. I never kept those things.' (Up till the late sixties Connery never owned a new car; his current runabout in Spain is a small Renault van.) He had Micheline's home-building nature to thank for the infrastructure of comfortable domesticity. These hard-earned comforts were appreciated, but his joy in them was absent-minded and childlike. When Micheline decided to surprise him with a very special Christmas present in 1987 – a room extension on his favourite haven, the bathroom – his response had been typically understated. 'I decided to make a happening for him while he was in Chicago filming *The Untouchables*,' said Micheline. 'So when he arrived from the airport I brought him in [to the bedroom] and I had covered the door with ribbon. I said, "There's your present, open it," and he said, "Oh, it's a door," and then he opened it . . . and he was like a child.'

Connery's inner sanctum was a symbolic contrast to the deprivations of his tenement childhood. It was a golden sunshine room ('He spends hours in the bathroom,' says Micheline) with glass shelves carrying his Oscar and the two BAFTAs and a host of other awards, side by side with golfing manuals and his favoured simple toiletries. 'A far, far cry from Edinburgh,' comments Fyall, 'where the bathroom was a tub by the fireplace.'

Shortly before, in a more conventionally brief interview with film writer Marjorie Bilbow, Connery defined his sense of fulfilment in terms of his financial independence. 'I mean, one certainly has to strive for it . . . one really has to fight. Coming from my background I was always very conscious of the fact that I could never lift the phone, there was nobody at the other end [to help]. In some ways I've always found it very difficult to ask anyone for anything . . .'

The ensuing proud-loner individualism – 'his kinder brand of Thatcherism', in the words of writer Sean Fitzsullivan – seems manifestly the product of a tough youth environment and an acceptance of the responsibility to grow. A bastardised version of Chekhov's born-alone-live-alone-die-alone philosophy has always been pivotal to Connery and, in its purity of expression, has fathered many of the misconceptions about Connery the Hard Man, Connery the Aggressor, Connery the Bigot, Connery the Litigant.

Interview revelations apart, producer Ross Wilson initially found Connery true to reputed form and tending to gruffness. 'You certainly wouldn't call him a pussycat . . . I was nervous about directing him. I remember asking him to walk from the house across the garden to this outbuilding where Micheline had built him a private den. I didn't think it was quite right so I asked him to do it again. I expected a growl, but he just said, "Oh, right-o" . . . He was obliging but he worked to his own time frame. . . . Later I wanted to film him getting geared up for his golf. As soon as I mentioned it he went into another mind set and seemed to be thinking only of the golf. We did one shot, then set the camera position outside the gates, where we would shoot him driving off for a game of golf. I gave a bit of a rundown on the scene and called Action and – zoom! – he was gone, exit, cheerio, no time for retakes or discussion. It was all a bit ferocious.'

Back in Scotland Wilson saw, in stages, a different man, whose sentimentality belied the legends and defined the core. At Bruntsfield Primary School he was happy to mix with the children of a gentler, socially softer Edinburgh and to co-operate in answering the most intimate of questions as he rarely did with the media elite. Wilson was amused to see that he drew the line just once: when a bright-eyed boy asked him how much he earned per year. 'Since nobody had any interest in my yearly earnings when I was on the brew here, I never discuss it with anybody [now],' was Connery's blunt reply. Later, as a camera followed him and Micheline through the suburbs and he saw, for the first time in years, the revision of his old home town, he was smiling but subdued. Later still, at the formal reception at the Usher Hall when the presentation was made, he was – for minutes – overcome. Andrew Fyall says, 'I hadn't seen him like that since the BAFTA tribute two years before.' There [at BAFTA], in the presence of Princess Anne, he became quite emotional when he spoke of the gaps in his life, and all he had missed out on in friendships by burying himself away in Spain. His son Jason says he needs the seclusion, that he overworks and burns out and he opts for the peace of Spain to repair himself. But Michael Caine also feels he cuts himself off, sometimes to his detriment, that it isn't good for him emotionally in some ways. At BAFTA he was emotional and lost his voice for a minute. It was moving and revealing. But at the Freedom of Edinburgh bash he was positively fazed. You saw it in an instant in his eyes. The crowd was giving him a splendid ovation and he had made his speech. His eyes went round the hall, at all the Edinburgh faces of old . . . Edinburgh reaching out for the long-lost son . . . and it was all too much for one instant.'

Virility and sentiment. Aggression and responsibility. Ambition and integrity. Fatalism and dream-fulfilment . . . Connery mythology has thrived for three decades on the contrasts and contradictions. It seems inevitable perhaps that a paragon hero, supertuned and invincible as James Bond was, would incite the detractors and expose feet of clay. Fleming's Bond was debonair, Etonian, smooth as the Beluga best; Connery was the product of an Edinburgh slum. Curiously, the combination created a symbiotic dynamic that touched all classes all across the world. A billion people saw Connery play Bond. A million hacks went after both of them.

Unlike glad-handed Bond, it appeared, Connery was penurious. By his own admission many of the movies he had made pre-Bond were 'rather dreadful'. But for *Dr No*, producers Cubby Broccoli and Harry Saltzman paid him £25,000. By the time of *Goldfinger*, just two movies later, his fee was doubled and fattened by a percentage of the box-office gross. Still, as early as *Goldfinger*, he wanted more, more, more, more. As recently as 1983 his lawyers were actively hounding Broccoli for unpaid Bond monies. Broccoli defended himself: 'All I ever did to Sean Connery was make him rich and make him an international star.' Elsewhere – and frequently, spikily, in the tabloids – the accusation of plain Scots meanness was made. A bit-part actor on the Casper Wrede movie *Ransom* (1974) expressed puzzlement when describing his working relationship with the mega-rich superstar: 'I found Connery fine – courteous, tending to moodiness but very professional. Not, as many people find him, intimidating at all. Then there was an incident in a restaurant in Oslo. There was a break in shooting and I came in with a girl I wanted to impress. I didn't know Connery was lunching, but there he was with a lady friend and he got up and beckoned us over. We had a good meal and he was quite extravagant and very open-handed and we were all very flattered. Then when the meal ended – his meal, that is – he called for the bill and right in front of us all started to divide it up. "Let's see . . . you had the fish, I had the veal . . ." Well, we hadn't *asked* to join him and maybe I'm assuming too much, but you'd imagine a guy with his fortune . . .?'

Director John Boorman, who has remained close to Connery since *Zardoz* and who often entertains the actor at his County Wicklow home, refutes such implied self-centredness. For him, once again, the roots of Connery's penny-consciousness go back to tenement Edinburgh. 'Sean's surprisingly fussy about small matters,' says Boorman. 'When he stays with me he'll be the perfect house guest: graceful, attentive to others, often the last up to bed. Then he'll go round the house checking each light switch, making sure everything's properly off . . . but then he is an incredibly generous man too.' Boorman quickly reminds you of Connery's generosity in donating his entire advance earnings of a million dollars from *Diamonds Are Forever* to the Scottish International Education Trust, a charity designed by him to sponsor the underprivileged.

John Brady, who grew up with Connery and shared the deprivations and pressures of tenement poverty, is emphatic about Connery's fairness with money. 'He was fair to a fault. Careful with his money, as we all had to be then. But when it was his turn for a round at the Fountain Bar, he was fast to his pocket. He didn't like meanness.'

In the media perception Connery is also a compulsive litigant. He himself boldly boasts of having sued *every* Hollywood studio and bankrupted one but, again, Boorman counterclaims, reminding you of Connery's oft quoted adage: 'I've never stolen from anyone in my life, and I expect no one to steal from me.' In fact, Connery's litigious energies have almost exclusively been aimed at the movie industry, an institution known for its excesses and manipulative accounting. Though the tabloid illusion suggests otherwise, Connery has only ever been involved in one major magazine lawsuit – against a French journal which claimed he had gone bald, become fat and was losing screen opportunities because of diminished sex appeal. With the key evidence of a tailor's affidavit that his 1970s waistline was just one inch larger than that of his measurement in *Dr No*, Connery won the case, and damages and, one suspects, a good laugh. 'He is,' says his friend Michael Caine, 'undoubtedly the world's number one bullshit detector. He is also the funniest man alive.'

Connery's legendary bad-moodedness ranks alongside accusations of meanness and malice in the courts. On the recent *Medicine Man* he attracted a bad press by complaining about the Mexican jungle conditions during the four-month shoot. An article in the respected *Premiere* magazine panned him for self-indulgence, but the film's producer Andrew G. Vanja responded angrily in his defence: 'To subjectively assert that Connery was grouchy in the midst of nearly intolerable conditions and to suggest that he left the production early in an amateurish tantrum is to insult his professional reputation and integrity. Let me assure you that at all times Connery displayed the highest calibre of ethics and conduct. In fact, he was responsible for keeping up the spirits of the crew.'

During the filming of *The Untouchables* Connery raised some hackles by mooning around the New York sets moaning of the newer actors: 'Is that as good as it gets?' – but the director, Brian De Palma, later confessed he conspired with Connery in rousing the tyros. Sheamus Smith, former managing director of Ireland's Ardmore Studios where *The First Great Train Robbery* was made, recalls 'very few mood episodes . . . and those that did happen arose from Sean's impatience with incompetence. He is so utterly professional, so well prepared in his work, that incompetence really bugs him, that's all.' Michael Winner, director of the *Death Wish* movies, had cause to appreciate his inspired good humour following the tabloid uproar caused by revelations by young actress Simone Hyams that Winner had bedded her. In the *Sunday Times* Winner pointed out that, since he was a bachelor in a free society, his affairs were his own business. The phoneyed-up 'scandal' depressed him but Sean Connery put it all in perspective: at a London function well attended by Fleet Street photographers Connery, Winner recalls, 'suddenly grasped my head in his hands and held it there for a second, then planted a firm lip-to-lip kiss upon me. "That'll give them something to talk about," he said.'

The paradoxes disperse but leave a resonance as mysterious and provocative as black holes. 'With Sean it's a roller coaster of preconception, anticipation, discovery, appreciation and continuing quest,' says director Richard Lester. 'It's the old joke of just when you think you know him . . . he remains elusive. Not, I think for commercial reasons or tactical reasons but because he's a painfully honest man and he's more concerned with his own self-discovery than any public visions of his fame and fortune.' Andrew Fyall backs this up: 'He told me he's been offered $6 million for his memoirs. But he couldn't give a damn. He won't do it because, first, he says, it would mean telling stories about other people, and secondly, he doesn't need the money.'

Connery himself has alluded to internal turmoil. He admitted in the seventies to flirtations with R.D. Laing and has been reported visiting Norway to consult a senior follower of Wilheim Reich, the once-fashionable founder of the orgone box. Ross Wilson continues to find the disparities intriguing. 'Like this sudden new pursuit of the role of executive producer. Twenty years ago his alter ego wanted to be a director. Now it is executive producer, the function he served on *Medicine Man*, and he's serving now on his new LA movie [*Rising Sun*, directed by Philip Kaufman]. Maybe it was inevitable, the coming together of his business interests, that natural fascination with finance, and his moviemaking. It certainly is interesting in terms of what, artistically, it produces. As executive producer he can say what happens and when. Effectively, what gets seen on screen. In the past he has blamed producers for failing him. Now he can do it all himself. So what will his new movies look like? *The Hunt for Red October* was a passionate choice of his and it made a killing at the box office and proved his instincts. *Indiana Jones* did it too. But they were for other producers. Now it's for himself. One wonders, can he muster up a quality picture to match Bond?'

Bond. Like Mickey Rooney and Andy Hardy, Gable and Rhett, it will always come back to Bond. Andrew Fyall admits to Connery's continuing unease, if not terminal boredom, with the subject. But in 1991 Wilson and Fyall found him fluent on the subject. 'All that bothered him was the media exposure, which really was too much. It was overkill.'

Some years ago I was working on a screenplay for US television with playwright Anthony Shaffer, and had the opportunity to spend a few social hours with his wife, Connery's ex, Diane Cilento. She knew I had written extensively about her former husband and we studiously avoided talk of the past. She had recently been touring in *Agnes of God* around Australia (where the Shaffers live) but her conversation gravitated towards movies mainly. I recalled, apropos of the vagaries of Hollywood choices, that she was the one who urged Connery, then a struggling 31-year-old, to take on Bond. I suggested that the popular cinema had been changed by the fusion of quality script and playing in an all-action medium and that every thriller since measures itself against Connery-Bond. She resisted the compliment but expressed utter disdain for 'where Hollywood is taking us'. Bond has spoiled us, I offered. She wouldn't be drawn but said, '*Rambo* – all that rubbish – it stifles the brain, makes one despair for the future of film-making.'

Later Shaffer told me, 'Bond was a class act, no doubt. When it started [with *Dr No*] it was special. And a lot of that specialness was Sean. Maybe all of it was Sean.'

The year 1993 seems momentous because the Bond era, the thirty-year phenomenon, is finally laid to rest. Broccoli, the remaining producer-architect, has put Bond up for sale, and a TV series – the retirement pasture for all movie megastars – is in planning. In the eighties, Connery moved against his original intuition and did his bittersweet swansong *Never Say Never Again* . . . but that nightmare can now be filed for ever among the memories. There may never be another big-screen Bond, but that doesn't mean the memories are buried. Nor their legacies lost.

'I find him more reflective and calm now,' says Andrew Fyall. 'But still tending to push himself to the limits. The other day I talked to him. He was back in Spain after seventeen weeks' shooting in San Francisco [on *Rising Sun*]. He wanted to come to Scotland for the Dunhill Cup golf but he was just too tired. So he decided to stay in the sun, hidden away, recovering. Knowing Sean, that process won't last long.'

After his initial documentary film, Ross Wilson was keen to talk with him again, to prepare a new, deeper documentary profile. 'Our tribute film for the Freeman of Edinburgh was really a classy home video for him. But it *marked* something. He has distanced himself from the tedious aspects of his past career. He has earned his rewards. I think it's nurturing for him to go back to Scotland, to come home, to remember what he did and why he did it and just how rocky the road was. To define himself against the passage of time and people and place. To see his character as a product of that experience. Bond is a fighter and, by jingo, so is Sean. You understand it all, all the harmony between Sean and his creations – be it Bond or whoever – by looking back. Edinburgh is where it begins.'

2

Fountainbridge, Fife and a Feeling for Freedom

Auld Reekie – Old Smokey – the nickname given to Edinburgh in the eighteenth century, remained particularly appropriate to Fountainbridge, an unprepossessing slab of industrial red rock that lay in the valley fringing the south-western slopes of Old Edinburgh. Then, in the twenties and thirties, Fountainbridge lived up to the nickname, giving refuge to the factories and steam-driven businesses the town proper did not want.

Developed in the eighteenth century and expanded with the Industrial Revolution, Fountainbridge was an anomaly in a city which prided itself in being professional-orientated, rather than industrial, where even the railways are conscientiously hidden away. High-living Edinburgh folk adverted to the city's auspicious past – the links with Allan Ramsay, David Hume, Oliver Goldsmith, Sir Walter Scott and R.L. Stevenson; but the hardy folk of Fountainbridge merely spat out the black dust of the district's innumerable chimneys, knuckled down and coursed on with the tough life. Underprivileged they may have been, but they didn't – and with hindsight, still don't – recognise that. For the dwellers of the scattered residential blocks life had an isolated tribal closeness, a special sense of autonomy and was governed by a rule-of-thumb morality. Children of Fountainbridge were Fountainbridgers for ever.

Today the area which took its name from the main, 30-yards-wide thoroughfare is a saw-spined, forlorn semi-wilderness, its pell-mell destruction checked by Edinburgh's Housing Action Programme. But pointers to the past stand stout and proud, and it is still easy to cross a busy cobbled street, through the close of a tenement, through dustbins and unchanged charred rubble, and imagine what it was like sixty-five years ago when Joe Connery took his twenty-year-old bride across the threshold of number 176 Fountainbridge (now partly demolished) and set up home. The ground-floor wall of 176 behind which the Connerys lived when they first married still stands, and the view from the front window, were it not bricked up, remains as was: the sprawl of McEwans Brewery, punctuated by the friendly face of the Fountain Bar, the Saturday night hot-spot. Down the road the rubber works that gave so much employment to the locals is gone, and the Clanhouse Dance Hall now sells fancy goods to wayward tourists and passers-through. But enough remains to draw Sean Connery back occasionally and to evoke affectionate, though sometimes oddly mixed, memories.

Joe Connery's settling in Fountainbridge in the twenties was a shrewd and necessary move, because the kind of work he needed, unskilled labouring, was most readily available in an area of concentrated industry. His father, remembered only as Baldy by grandsons Sean and Neil, was a giant of an Irishman – Catholic and part-tinker – from County Wexford, who came to Scotland at the end of the last century, married an Edinburgh girl and found employment as an arithmetically unreliable bookie's runner. More often than not Joe totted the bookie's accounts. Neither Joe nor his father was the kind of man given to poetic whimsicality about remembering the past but Joe took some small rebel pride in his Irish ancestry. Had he delved into parish and civic records (something Neil has been threatening to do on behalf of himself and his brother for many years) he might have found an ancestral link with the prestigious Ó Conraoi or Mac Conraoi clans of County Galway, of which the most famous modern writer in the

Irish language, Padraic Ó Conaire, is a descendant; though more probably he would have unearthed association with a quite separate sept, the Ó Conaires (specifically anglicised as Connery) of Munster. Smith's *History of County Waterford* records the O'Connerys as principal inhabitants of Waterford and environs around the end of the sixteenth century.

Joe was a simple, straight-from-the-shoulder man with a gravelly singing voice he chose to air loud and often. He liked beer first, whisky second and hard toil third and was engaged, and valued, by the North British Rubber Works as a £2-a-week labourer. The rubber mill had good working conditions and such small security afforded Joe the opportunity to contemplate marriage. He proposed to his first and life-long love, Euphemia (Effie) Maclean, an Edinburgh lass, and married her the same year. The ceremony and ensuing boozy, Christmassy celebrations on 28 December 1928 were attended by the roisterous Macleans and the less outgoing Connerys in full numbers and, in the way of these affairs, a fine time was had by all. Joe took Effie home to a two-room Fountainbridge tenement with a lightless, damp-smelling hallway and outside toilet. He bought some sturdy ship's linoleum for the floor from the Forces Surplus Store round the corner in Grove Street and geared himself to carve out a comfortable life for a future growing family in the smoky tranquillity of factory-land. The encroaching Depression, recognised and gloomily discussed every night in the Grove or the Fountain Bar, didn't affect the young couple: 5 foot 8 inches tall, Joe was 180 pounds of taut, bursting muscle, fit as a fiddle and work-hungry, like his father; they had a roof over their heads and rent for the landlord and, as soon as Effie got her hands on the rubber mill's pay-packet, the makings of a savings account. Physical stamina was Joe's forte, thriftiness Effie's. Together they made a formidable pair, close and resilient as the stained red brickwork of No. 176, and much admired by their neighbours in 'the stairs', as the tenements were known.

A neighbour from nearby Brandfield Street which

boasted a different type of stair, but of identical proportions (twelve to fourteen families per house), remembers: 'The Connerys were poor for a time, that's to say they had no children. Big families were usual round Fountainbridge. It was the sort of place where the sounds of children, with the paper-thin walls and all the rest, kept a fair pace with the noise of industry.'

But by Christmas '29 Effie was pregnant. Joe, in his enthusiastic, responsible way, took whatever overtime he could find – so much in fact that he was more often out of the stair than in, setting a home routine that was to stretch into the war years. On a muggy, late summer's day, 25 August 1930, with Joe standing by for once to mark the occasion with a whisky at the Fountain, Effie gave birth to a 10½-pound child whose name she had already decided upon: Thomas, later to become Sean.

Thomas Connery was a child of the Depression, arriving on the scene just as purse strings all over the country tightened, money vanished into mist and unemployment soared. Joe, like a thousand other unskilled workers in Fountainbridge, clung to his job tenaciously, accepted cutbacks where he had to and, for the first time, considered emergency contingency options for work outside Edinburgh, even abroad. But Effie, less practical perhaps but just as obdurate, was not about to give in. 'I had wonderful neighbours and good times in Fountainbridge,' she later declared, explaining pithily her reluctance to bolt for greener pastures.

In spite of Joe's energies and Effie's care with money, young Tommy's first awareness was of a grimly restricted world. The cramped flat consisted of a bedroom and a combined living-room-kitchen called in Scotland a butt-and-ben. An alcove off the living area housed the kitchen – a cast-iron coal fireplace with two side ovens and a top-plate, a cold-water stone sink with wooden drain 'bunker' and, above, a pulley arrangement screwed to the ceiling for drying clothes when it was too wet to use the outdoors drying green. Tommy slept in his parents' bedroom, in the bottom drawer of the wardrobe, a quite regular cot for newcomers. Later he graduated to the bed-settee in the butt-and-ben, a hunk of a kid at five with gypsy-black hair and piercing chocolate eyes. Even then he was, as his mother recalled, 'different from Neil, who came along much later – impulsive, independent, ambitious'. He had Joe's restless energy, a flair for games and a passion for comic strips which quickly led, his friend John Brady remembers, to 'an interest in all kinds of reading matter'. At five he was quite ready for the strictly disciplined primary school that was his destiny, but at the same time more than a little dismayed at leaving the full freedom of the streets. His playing world was bordered east and west by factories, north and south by a rough-hewn recreation ground and the basins of the Grand Union Canal. The canal was officially out of bounds to the very young, but Tommy was never deterred by threats of authority. He fished for tiddlers with the older kids, using the end of one of his mother's nylon stockings, and boated on the lower basin at some risk. Altogether a safer proposition and far more significant in his young life was the playground behind his stair, popularly called 'the biggie'. Here, with John Brady, Michael O'Sullivan and others he discovered the challenge of soccer for the first time, bruising toes, scuffing elbows and scoring the odd bleeding nose. 'He was football wild from very early,' says Brady. 'Not especially good,' says another friend of the period, 'more useful.'

Bruntsfield Primary School, an imposing Georgian building that even today exudes a finger-wagging earnestness, swallowed up most of the five-to-eleven-year-olds from Fountainbridge and attempted to displace that endemic braggart street-wisdom with academic ABCs. Here, surprisingly, young Connery was somewhat out of place. By five he could read and write and was proficient at mental arithmetic, a knack handed down from Joe. He was in trouble often for totting sums too fast, or lapsing into loud-mouthed boredom when half the class was fumbling over A-is-for-Apple. Effie scolded him in the evenings, just as she did every other weekend when he slunk off adventurously to the canal, or tackled shins relentlessly in the biggie; Joe, fighting for family survival as job lay-offs threatened every factory in the area, was seldom round long enough to observe or object.

'My background was harsh,' Connery has said. 'We were poor, but I never knew how poor till years after.' It was impossible for a youngster to be objective about the situation but Tommy sensed Joe's deepening inability to cope, despite Effie's efforts. The birth of Neil in 1938 when the home financial situation was at its worst complicated matters not a little. So at nine Tommy decided, fully on his own account, to stop off at 'the store' – St Cuthbert's (then Kennedy's) Dairy Stables in Grove Street – on his way home from school and ask for a job. He was precocious, alert and willing and, in spite of the jobs pinch, a place was found for him on a delivery dray. Thus began an eight-year on-off spell with St Cuthbert's. The early days, for sure, were the most strenuous. 'I was up at dawn,' Connery recollects, 'then through a milk round before school.' There followed the long, dull school day then, after a while – an almost unbelievable self-inflicted punishment for a sporty, freedom-loving boy – an evening shift as a butcher's helper. Effie, naturally, was proud of him. 'With two jobs he was bringing me home £3 a week' she glowed, 'and that was before the war. He gave me every penny he earned and I banked savings for him.'

The main reason Tommy chose the milk round rested, truthfully, in a love for horses. 'He was horse daft in those days,' Effie recalled for the Scottish *Sunday Express* in 1964. 'Always taking my dusters to rub down the milk horse. And he loved driving the cart.' Connery's own memories broadly concur but over the years in varied interviews a barb of deeper insight has revealed itself. He told *Playboy* magazine: 'One's parents left one free to make one's own way. When I was nine my mother caught me smoking and she said, "Don't let your father find out, because if he does he'll beat you so hard he'll break your bottom." From the time I started working I always paid my share of the rent, and the attitude at home was the prevalent one in Scotland – you make your own bed and so you have to lie on it. I didn't ask for advice and I didn't get it. I had to make it on my own or not at all.' The implication, borne out in later interviews, was that Tommy learned to take care of himself and that his life was fully in his own hands. There was only so much Joe could provide – good example and a relatively stable home – after that Tommy had to find his own niche, and pay his way.

Others have spoken of young Tommy's topsy-turvy relationship with both parents. A respectful and generally obedient son, he was also, according to some, wary of his mother and tried, above all, to please her. 'I wouldn't go so far as to say he was afraid of Effie,' says a friend from Edinburgh, 'but she was the binding force in the family and she subtly dominated everyone and everything. In the rocky tough times Joe did what he could, but it was Effie's strength that held the family. She was the glue and Tommy – and Joe and Neil – never forgot it. I believe that all his life Sean lived under Effie's influence. The hardness in him is her.'

There followed a period of educational disruption. As the effects of the Second World War reached Edinburgh school buildings were temporarily closed and, for many months, the children of working-class families like the Connerys were farmed out to the spacious homes of the wealthy for daytime 'grinds'. Connery reflects sourly on this experience. 'It was an eye-opener. These people wanted us to deliver coal and what have you – but they didn't want us in their homes. We were too lowly for them.' As Neil remembers it, this period of 'outside schooling' didn't last long and Sean eventually returned to Bruntsfield where he sat the customary qualifying examination and was passed out. By now the war in Europe was raging, rationing was on and Joe was pursuing the tack he always guessed lay before him – working for Rolls-Royce in Glasgow, travelling home at weekends only. Tommy seems to have taken ominous warning from his father's experience and clenched his hold on his part-time job even though the obligatory two-year course of secondary education now lay before him. A contemporary of that time, Craigie Veitch, remembers facing the prospect of second-level, career-orientated education: 'Fountainbridge children had two main avenues open to them. Those who had the aptitude, or won scholarships as a result of their qualifying exams, went to Boroughmuir School. Boroughmuir had commercial ends in mind, and that's where people learnt languages – French and Italian – or economics. The second choice, the second best for many, was Darroch, a school that gave you a good basic technical education, where you learnt science and metalwork and craft. In some ways, I suppose, the measure of a man's learning capacity was which school he ended up in. Sean, of course, ended up – with me – at Darroch.'

Connery entered Darroch Secondary determined, by his own account, to fail. What is more likely, in perspective, is that his exhausting extra-curricular activities did not allow him to succeed. At any rate, John Brady says, he proved himself 'a fair scholar'. Craigie Veitch painted a compelling picture in an article he published in the Edinburgh *Evening News*:

A gaunt, grey building, Darroch was staffed by no-nonsense teachers with strong right arms, the better to belt you with, and attended by plus-12 girls in print dresses and rough-and-ready boys whose school uniform was a woolly pullover and short trousers with a shirt tail peeping through, topped off in winter with a balaclava helmet. Pop Hendry, our English teacher, always insisted that the well-rounded man must be accurate in his spelling and he kept to hand a largish *Chambers Dictionary* which he would bounce on the head of any boy thick enough to think that seize was 'sieze' . . .

We were versed in poetry too, but I cannot recall Connery ever being called to the front of the class to recite lines from three epic poems which happened to be in vogue in the Forties: 'Splendour Falls on Castle Walls' . . . 'A Wet Sheet and a Flowing Sea' . . . and something about a slave having a dream with his matted hair buried in sand . . .

There was nothing of the long-haired poet about schoolboy Connery. He was big and he was as hard as nails in an easygoing way and anyone at school who messed him about got a thick ear and a black eye; one torrid encounter, Connery v. Anderson, going the best part of 12 bloody rounds in the playground before the janitor and two teachers managed to break it up.

Though Neil says Tommy was inclined to be 'over-sensitive' in some regards, it is apparent he was also quite tough and ready for whatever trouble came his way – a by-product no doubt of his already well-developed physique and the fit agility forced on him by early-morning rising and, now, an evening newspaper round. Neil remembers Tommy had little sense of his own strength. 'He had, too, a precocious talent for melodrama.' Once, unthinkingly, he squeezed the fancy glass handle of his parents' bedroom door so fiercely that it shattered in his grip. In shock, and a shade of black humour perhaps, Tommy danced round the room, screaming so shrilly that Joe was convinced he was clowning. When he calmed down and everyone saw the blood pouring from his hand, they were at last stirred to first-aid action. 'They had quite a job digging all the glass splinters out of him,' Neil says. Later there was a sledging accident in the snows of a particularly bad winter. Tommy hammered up a makeshift contraption in the walled back drying green and christened it 'The Coffin' in his typically wry way. He crossed Tollcross to the Meadows, a huge public park half a mile from 176. The park was full of snow-crazed kids playing recklessly safe but Tommy wanted to test real risk. He found the steepest slope, padded up, mounted his rickety sledge and hurtled down. Flushed with success and the admiration of the weaker-spined, he tried again. This time the inevitable mischance befell him. The sledge went out of control and thundered into a tree. Tommy met the bole head first, but recovered enough to fling the sledge on his back and stagger home. At first Effie noticed nothing wrong and raged at the boy for being late for tea. Then his pallor and unusual quietness took her attention. He claimed he was fine – fully cool – but when he went to the sink to wash up she noticed the blood spilling down the back of his neck. The injury to his skull, Neil says, was 'huge'. Joe was in Glasgow at the time, so Effie called on her next-door neighbour for help. The neighbour ran to a telephone for an ambulance and Tommy, wide-eyed and stoical – underplaying his obvious condition dramatically – was rushed off to hospital. Thirty-two stitches in a jagged wound was Connery's reward for his casual daring. 'He was five days in hospital, ten days convalescent after that . . . and a day or two after he came home was away again to the Meadows with that sledge,' Neil grins.

Whatever histrionic facility Connery developed during his early teens found plenty to feed on in Fountainbridge. As the spreading war effort injected life back into the factories that had been foundering, vacated stairs filled up again, dormant businesses awoke to churn out dirt, smoke and rowdy men. A neighbour who lived off Freer Street, down the road from the Connerys says: 'Everything there was dominated by the smell, such a mixed blend. You had the sweetie factory, MacKay's, just fifty yards up from the Connerys, gushing out a sickly stuff, then the acrid rubber smell, then the yeasty smell from the brewery opposite . . . at times it was overpowering. Especially to newcomers. But people flocked in, looking for work. The men's lodging house in Grove Street did great business . . . and the bars did a bit too. There was plenty of drama, what with Saturday night rowing and all the rest.' Wherever immigrant workers – most Irish, some English – came to swell the slums, trickster troubadours followed, begging for scraps. A noisy busker from nowhere, weighed down with instruments he could barely coordinate, was a favourite with the stair children. He would park outside the men's lodging house or Sammy's Ice Cream Parlour, right next door to 176, and rattle off free rubbish. A crooning drifter called, inevitably, 'Bing' was another Fountainbridge favourite. His repertoire included 'South of the Border down Texaco Way'. Bing's inability to remember five lines of any song, combined with his entrancing habit of muffling one ear, closing his eyes and singing into a bean can, inspired the children especially with pure joy. Asa Wass, a wizened Jew with a huckster shop of sorts in a close beside Freer Street, was a kind of children's – and adults' – hero. By dint of turning unneeded clothing and ornaments into hard cash, Asa won Fountainbridge's devotion. He was gruff but good with children and on a few occasions Tommy was despatched with the booties of spring cleaning to make a deal. Sixpence for a cast-off jersey of Joe's was fair money and Tommy had exactly the kind of hulking inscrutability to clinch six when fivepence-halfpenny might be more to Asa's thinking. Tommy was, by all accounts, a popular choice to be sent on bargaining errands.

Outside school, work and the distractions of Fountainbridge drifters, Tommy's main and increasingly important interest was football. In an overpopulated district where space was at a premium, it was the most natural thing in the world that games which could comfortably accommodate two twenty-man sides, with a ref thrown in, would reign paramount. Connery had the advantage of being genuinely . . . well, capable. He was also, apparently, sensible enough to recognise the advantages of the game's huge popularity. 'We didn't carry coshes or bicycle chains or knives,' he points out keenly. 'We spent all our energy on football. I was football mad. That's why I left school when I was thirteen, because they played rugger at the grammar school. I set out to fail the qualifying examination, and I made it.'

There are varying stories about the abrupt conclusion of Connery's scholastic stretch. The precise facts, as Craigie Veitch said, went 'down with the ship'. No school rolls or records of Darroch for the period survive, probably mercifully. The lingering, symbolically significant memory of those who served with Connery in that unpretentious throng is of morning assembly in the big hall. 'Hail Darroch!' was the school song, drilled out pitilessly every morning at nine sharp. One line rang 'Darroch ways are honest ways' (ironic, Veitch suggests, because quite a few of their numbers were residing in Borstal at the time).

Connery aired his lungs with enthusiasm on that song. 'He was nothing as a scholar,' another Darroch boy claims, 'but he was straight as the day's long.'

Survival, with the necessary hard work it entailed, was, it seems, Tommy Connery's preoccupation. Schooling, he judged, offered him no good rung on any worthwhile ladder. Fitness and football on the other hand offered benefits – if not in the direction of self-improvement and success, then at least in terms of some fun.

Fun and freedom for Tommy were largely connected with life away from Fountainbridge. In this he was, comparatively, privileged. Neil and Helen Maclean, the grandparents, were in their sixties; worldwise, clever, fun-loving people, utterly at ease with children and passionate in particular about their grandsons. Grandfather Neil was a plasterer who rose to public works foreman before retiring to a peaceful house in Gorgie, Edinburgh, but Gorgie satisfied this open-air fanatic's needs only for a short time. Upping roots, the Macleans moved to a country cottage north of Kirkcaldy, Fife, where they bred pigs and kept chickens. It was here, on summer holidays during and after the war, that the Connery youngsters came and Tommy found a slice of heaven somewhat larger than the biggie. The shock of pleasure he experienced on first encountering 'wild' farm animals and wide, open skies would, Neil hints, have been worth witnessing. 'There was no running water and we washed at the spring. First thing each morning Granny would give us a pitcher and Sean and I would go down the road to the farm for milk, still fresh and warm from the cow . . . There was a pond where we fished for tadpoles, newts and frogs . . . and a huge Clydesdale horse on the farm, a real whopper.' In contrast to jam-packed, airless Fountainbridge, the country life took on magical aspects. Here were the luxuries of real space and free time. There was room to kick a ball crazily, with no concern for close-ranked neighbours' windows, and time to idle, time to think. For Tommy, temporarily relieved of the responsibilities of wage-earning, the chance to play kid again was precious. In Fife he discovered things about himself that had been buried under the rush to grow up. He found he liked his own company, liked to indulge his fantasies about being a cowboy riding the range. The big Clydesdale horse came in useful, far better, wilder, than anything back at St Cuthbert's. It was actually possible to mount the Clydesdale horse and romp over prairie-like meadows – with never a fear of admonition. Day in, day out, almost as if freedom had no boundaries.

Neil Maclean was an inspiration too. He was big, tough, whisky-loving, a Scottish John Wayne who could lift the kitchen table single-handed and down raw eggs for breakfast without the blink of an eye. His purpose, in a nutshell, was to get the best out of life by living brave and uncompromisingly. Tommy spun boyish fantasies around him, and cherished them into adulthood. As late as 1963 he was talking about 'this 86-year-old grandfather who drinks a bottle of scotch a day, and he's in great shape because he always eats with it'. Neil Maclean's receipt for a long life, Connery claimed, centred on cold food, and plenty of alcohol. In a newspaper interview in 1964 the old man laughingly dismissed his grandson's remarks. Exercise, he insisted, was the secret of a healthy long life. Neil Connery remembers his grandfather's dying request – for 'a drop of the hard stuff'. Neil's greatest regret is that the request was never fulfilled; having checked with nursing staff at the Edinburgh Infirmary where the old man lay dying – at the age of 93 – Neil himself undertook to bring the whisky; by the time he arrived with the half-full bottle from the dresser in his grandfather's room, the old man was dead.

Most important of all, Fife threw fresh light on life in Fountainbridge. It represented the other, unexpected, side of the coin. An attainable alternative, a sweeter, cleaner life. All right, one might have to work fifty-odd years to achieve this fulfilling freedom. But it was remotely possible, Tommy supposed, that such freedom and retirement did not necessarily go hand-in-hand. Some way, some time, there might be a short cut to Fife.

Tommy Connery, the slum kid, just might not be a Fountainbridger for ever.

3

'He'd No' Have Made It as a Milkman . . .'

During the Second World War the British cinema thrived. British film-making, which had hiccupped with the requisitioning of thirteen out of twenty-two studios and the call-up of two-thirds of its technicians, started an upswing. J. Arthur Rank, the future hero of the industry, started his meteoric rise in 1942 with his first major film, the morally starchy *The Great Mr. Handel*, and within two years the dam had burst and production of entertainments as opposed to morale-boosting documentaries was flowing again. Annual audience attendances were steadily moving towards their 1946 all-time high of 1,635 million. Though restrictions continued – film stock was in short supply, individual theatres played to limited hours, etc – an estimated thirty million cinema-goers were regularly entertained in some five thousand cinemas. In 1944 in Edinburgh, as across the country, they flocked to see Pressburger and Powell's cheeky *The Life and Death of Colonel Blimp*, Carol Reed's *The Way Ahead* and, among the swarm of irresistible Hollywood imports, Billy Wilder's *Double Indemnity*.

One of Tommy Connery's main local cinemas was called, romantically, The Blue Halls. It stood on the northern border of Fountainbridge and was known to the slum kids as 'the gaff'. 'It was,' an old Fountainbridge boy recalls, 'everything flea-pits are cracked up to be.' The place was

25

constantly the butt of spiky jokes, few requiring imaginative exaggeration. The standard piece of irreverence, well and truly meant, was 'you go to the gaff with a cardigan and come out with a jumper' (jumpers being fleas). Tommy was not, perhaps, as movie-addicted as his father, but he liked the rainy Saturday afternoon at the gaff, watching a good Hitchcock – or maybe Ralph Richardson in Brian Desmond Hurst's *On the Night of the Fire*, a thriller scripted by Terence Young, a man who would eventually play a major role in his life. Admission often only cost a jam-jar or two, but by the time Tommy was in charge of baby brother Neil the price had risen to 2*d*. each. Both brothers enjoyed the serial adventures of Flash Gordon but Tommy, rich with his memories of Fife and his love for the old milk cart dobbins, had a particular fondness for westerns. Tough men living gritty, heel-kicking lives on the range – men like grandfather Neil – appealed to him. When he first breached the film business in the late fifties Connery expressed his desire to make westerns. He did eventually make the notable British western *Shalako* (1968) – a not altogether happy experience – but Neil for one is surprised that he has not tackled more. 'He never lost that early craze for westerns, which was tied up with his love for horses,' Neil says.

With Darroch ingloriously behind him, horses were playing a much larger part in Connery's life. Milk delivery work for the store became his full-time occupation, horses a near obsession. For a time he was helper on Danny Fraser's dray – Connery fourteen, Fraser the senior at fifteen – then he was assigned his own route, the rounds of Cramond and Davidson's Mains, and his own cart. His horse was Tich, smallest of the several score at the store, but cosseted like none other. The restlessness that was to mark the later part of his teens might have been more evident now had it not been for the fact that Joe was out of work, having smashed a wrist and crushed his nose in a machinery accident in Glasgow. Effie was at work, 'charring in the rich houses quite a bit away from Fountainbridge', in John Brady's words, earning thirty shillings a week, but not managing to make ends meet. The pressures of supplementing the income to keep the family together fell squarely on young Tommy. He laboured like a Trojan during this time, handing £2.10s. to Effie every Thursday night but still finding means, through his newspaper round, to maintain a personal Post Office Savings account, building on the shillings Effie had banked for him during his schooldays.

The fashionable Fountainbridge vision of a working man's lot was the common one: a man simply works to live. Tommy Connery was unusual in that part of his psyche could not accept that standard. Denied the perpetual bliss of Fife, his independent spirit demanded recompense. One sweated to gain, he decided. So, keeping the family was accepted for the trial it was – but conditionally. A hundred per cent work effort would be augmented by another ten, and in the end Tommy would walk away from his chores with a swag that would justify the effort. These 'spoils of war' were calculatedly decided upon, and in due course won. One Christmas, Neil remembers, Tommy canvassed for and earned the vast sum of £16 in tips. By the time he was sixteen, with Joe cautiously back at work after an eighteen-month lay-off – this time employed as van driver for Duncan's Removals of Gilmore Place – he had £75 in his Post Office account. The noose of responsibility no longer tight round his throat, Connery mulled over the practical value of this wealth. £75 wouldn't buy him a smallholding in Fife or a horse and a stable of his own, but it might open a door out of Fountainbridge.

'What do you want to buy, son?' Joe asked as they faced each other across the dim-lit table in the single-end, young Connery poring over the yellowed savings booklet.

'A motorbike.'

'You're not getting a bike. Forget that.' Joe was adamant: he was suspicious, mistakenly, of Tommy's motives. Fountainbridge was full of pubescent punks, gangs like the Valdors, with their rust-rotted high-power bikes and tight-skirted tarts. Teenage warfare was rare, but from time to time it spilled in from tougher areas. On top of that, Joe was concerned about road accident risk, because of his own bitter experience. Tommy, he judged, was developing too fast. He was too big for his age, too bold, the bread-earner too early. It is likely, for that short time, Joe felt stifled by his elder son's precocity. At any rate in Effie's words, he put down his foot and 'that was that. No arguments. In those days you could tell a youngster what to do.'

Tommy didn't brood too long over this impasse. He resumed his milk round, ambled down to the gaff and chewed it over. Within a couple of days he had resolved the matter to his own quirky liking: out of the blue a fine second-hand piano, all of £56 10s.' worth, was delivered to 176. The neighbours were impressed and so was Effie, but Joe was nonplussed. Nobody in the stair could play the damned piano, least of all Tommy. 'I'll get lessons,' Tommy reassured them – but the likelihood of his finding time for study, everyone knew, was next to non-existent. As it was, he was spending no more than an hour before every bedtime in the stair: from dawn till three in the afternoon was taken up with the milk round, early evening went on the newspaper deliveries, later in the evenings it was either back to the store to brush up Tich or across the Meadows to Tollcross for properly organised football with Grove Vale Juveniles. Joe wanted the space-cramping piano to be removed at first, but Tommy in his cunning, obstinate way, resisted. He wanted some tangible evidence of his cruelly strenuous work, some representative image that reached beyond the grim monotone of Fountain-bridge. The piano idea, a friend today guesses, probably rose out of some saga of swish life Connery saw at the Blue Halls. Eventually Joe was appeased by Tommy's snatches of seriousness. Every so often, just when family patience began to run out, Tommy would sit by the gleaming mon-strosity and bash out a one-fingered 'Bluebells of Scotland' or 'Annie Laurie'. Effie was transported to ecstasy and Joe's savage breast, intermittently at least, was soothed. Never before, one suspects, was a bad piano played with such staggeringly sardonic – and brave – irony.

Though Connery had, in his own words, 'no sense of the future then', by early 1947 it was apparent to his friends that he would quit Fountainbridge within a short time. Among casual acquaintances there were boys who had worked as merchant navymen and others who had served with the Forces; and, secretly, Connery had already decided his way out: he would not settle for half-measures – what had Glasgow given Joe but a few shillings' accident compensation and a one-way ticket home? – instead he would cross the Firth of Forth, find a ship and sail abroad. It might seem fitting, in view of his later artistic develoment, to see this decision in terms of romantic idealism – the search for a perennial Fife – but earthier considerations weighed heavily too. As he neared seventeen and matured the unacceptable aspects of Fountainbridge life became clearly indentifiable to him. He wanted to leave but 'it wasn't because of an unhappy home life. Quite the reverse. I suppose I felt that a hard job like my father's, or the milk round . . . would never let me use body and mind to the full. And I think anything less is a waste of a human being.'

The realities of the Connerys' poverty were suddenly manifest. Even in the face of hard work, minor luxuries were unknown. The family diet was as basic as could be: porridge, bread and potatoes, milk, Irish stew. Cakes were unknown, clothes almost always second-hand. In order to acquire money for football boots, or new laces for that matter, a twelve-hour working day had to stretch to fourteen, thereby forging the old vicious circle: if a person must toil so hard for the smallest freedoms, then where lay everyman's due, the relaxed fulfilment of outgoing pleasures? At sixteen, for example, Tommy Connery was a big local hit with the girls – 'he did better than most of us, without trying,' says John Brady – but the pressures on his time afforded him no more than a night a week 'scouting for talent'. The worst part of being poor and reaching his teens, Connery claims, was that 'Life was completely governed by economics. You didn't leave the light on when you didn't actually need it because it cost money. You had to count up tram fares. You couldn't have a bath when you felt like it – there was the price of a plunge at the public baths to think of. I wanted to do something with my life. I wanted to have pride in it, feel the joy of it. There was far too little joy about.'

Effie herself was slightly restless in the stair now, speculating inwardly on the fortunes of those who had left during the ebb of the Depression and were, reputedly, finding all they dreamt of in less fettered environments. She began tossing round progressive ideas for Tommy, suggesting Edinburgh jobs – jobs beyond Fountainbridge – with better prospects. But Tommy's stock answer even to his mother whom he hated to disappoint, was: 'Don't put me to a trade. Give me a chance to find out what I want.'

The milk round was a stopgap – something the gruff and flinty Mr Marshall, the store's manager, would not have appreciated knowing. The beloved Tich was still Connery's bond with the store. Highlight of the year was entering Tich for the 'Best Horse & Cart' competition at the stables. Connery spent hours polishing the brasswork of the harness and plaiting tail and mane. For his troubles he received an embossed Highly Commended card, treasured and displayed in the stairs and at the Meadows till it fell apart.

Not everyone remembers Connery the milkman as an asset to the store. Today, as a division of Scottish Co-Op Dairies, St Cuthbert's stables have altered considerably. The days of dairy horses are over, but until very recently many of the old faces of the forties remained. One roundsman, Jimmy, who has worked Rose Street, Silverknowes, Craigmillar and Corstorphine for as long as he can recall, knew Connery as a fitfully enthusiastic worker, not always 'using his brain'. An incident with a fully-laden dray in the heart of the city lingers with Jimmy. Connery had just commenced his round when, in a busy street, the bridle bit broke, rendering the harness control on the horse useless. Connery panicked and instead of improvising or summoning aid from passers-by he abandoned the cart and walked back to the store. Jimmy was appalled when he was informed that a full cart and lone horse had been deserted. Connery stood before him, helpless, hands in pockets, mouth agape. Jimmy was ordered to retrieve the dray immediately, and went running. Fortunately most of the contents of the crates were still intact. Looking back with a wry, humorous grin Jimmy reflects, 'It's as well he made it as an actor – he'd no' have made it as a milkman.'

John Brady was not surprised when the end of the dairy job loomed. 'Tommy always gave the impression he'd better things in store. I was serving my time as a painter-decorator. But Tommy had something extra, and he was kind of bursting with drive.' Excess energy was still mainly worked off with Grove Vale Juveniles or, later, Oxgangs Rovers. Tommy's style was improving all the time. He was strong and deceptively fast on his feet, an ideal forward player. He smoked a bit, drank a bit, but was, says Brady, 'never the boozy type. Tommy's whole image was outdoors.' 'He ran everywhere,' says another friend, 'giving you the impression Fountainbridge was a training track, and he was limbering to get out.'

When finally he made the decisive move Connery did so in a characteristic gust of inflexible wilfulness – alone. He took a tram across to the firth then made his way on foot to HMS *Lochniver* at the Naval shore base of South Queensferry and there filled out the recruitment forms. He signed for seven years' active service, and a further five in the Volunteer Reserve. Returning home, he surprised his friends and this time shocked not Joe, but Effie. According to Neil, Effie was 'upset' by the suddenness of her son's action. Joe resigned himself quickly: the Forces kept a lad out of trouble; the Navy was an honourable job, with adequate pay – not as good perhaps as the post office, where all the shrewdest lads tied down lifelong, pension-safe posts, but quite acceptable from every angle. Conceivably too, Joe was relieved that his biggest boy was properly and safely out of the way: now there would be more room in 176, the butt-and-ben need only house Neil; Joe would be the sole 'man about the house' again, his view unchallenged by wit or wiles. Effie's point of view was different. Tommy's departure spelt a smaller house purse, less financial input, less to save.

Connery sees his rush to the Navy as an elementary case of escapism – and a mistake. The negative aspects of

Fountainbridge were too great, he says, his ever-growing responsibilities unbearable. 'It was the kind of conditioning that led me to think, "Wow – the Navy – abroad – China!"' As it happened, he never saw China, indeed he rarely roamed far from British coastal waters. Butlaw Camp, next door to Lochniver, was his first unexciting port of call, where he began training. In rapid, undramatic succession he was trainee with a gunnery school, boy seaman member of an anti-aircraft squadron, then able seaman assigned, Neil remembers, to HMS *Formidable* out of Portsmouth. From the start Connery was neither a very active nor interested seaman. Neil cannot recollect any postcards home from exotic ports, nor do his Fountainbridge mates recall much enthusing during the shore leaves. One casual friend says, 'He made no big deal about his uniform or anything like that and anyway, after the war there were uniforms galore in Fountainbridge. The Clanhouse Dancehall [next door to St Cuthbert's] was virtually a Forces dancehall . . . Tommy gave the general impression that the Navy was a dull job best not talking about.'

Portsmouth had its moments, though. With his wiry iron build Connery was nominated for and elected onto the Navy boxing team. He fought a few battles, enjoyed the release of pent-up energies and earned a new muscle or two to match the bruises. He also awarded himself the basic naval honour – twin tattoos inked on his right forearm in a dockside dive. Both bellowed the mindless, conceited chauvinism of the young – '*Scotland Forever*' inside a bleeding knife-pierced heart and 'Mum & Dad' scrolled in a bird's mouth – yet hints of a sensitivity in his outlook at this time suggest a possible truer feeling.

Inside the space of a year rumbling stomach cramps became chronic localised duodenal discomfort. He was sent to see the MO and, after tests, hospitalised. The diagnosis was ulcers, the prognosis fine – provided that stress and the regular mess diet were avoided. In a word, the MO was giving Able-Seaman Connery, aged nineteen, the passport to a premature pension.

Though he had been a Sea Cadet in his early teens,

Connery is quite emphatic about his unsuitability for Naval life. Within months of enlisting, he claims, he realised sourly that he 'didn't have the equipment for the task. No scholastic training as such.' The ulcers, he believes, developed from 'the growing knowledge that the seafaring life wasn't all that one had fantasised it to be. I was a boy seaman, and there was an ordinary seaman above me, and if you reached his status there was a naval seaman and beyond that a leading seaman, and then a petty officer and a chief petty officer – and I was aware that I had not done enough to make this kind of progress.' The dilemma – this conflict between the dream of manly escape and the reality – caused the anxiety which led to nervous ulcers. Connery also by his own account resisted the Navy's paternalist authority. For a time, he said, he had been 'conscious of keeping myself emotionally in check, never permitting an outburst'. The end result of such stringent emotional control put him in hospital for eight weeks (after which time the ulcers had, apparently, gone away) and back onto civvy street less than three years after he had signed up.

Back in Edinburgh he celebrated his discharge – and his 6s. 8d. disability pension – with a drink with friends at the Fountain Bar. John Brady says that he looked fine on discharge. Another acquaintance hints he looked too fine and mentions he was also 'a resourceful chappie'. The inference might be that, like so many other immature dreamers who sign their lives away to the Colours and Reserves, Connery's disillusionment inspired the ruse of an ulcer. But against this one must consider the fussiness and intelligence of the Forces' medical personnel, and indeed the fact that ulcers seem to run in the Connery family. Both Joe and Neil suffered stomach complaints. And the actor Ian Bannen reckons Sean never really shook off that 'ulcer-ish uptightness'. Bannen observes Connery today in company of 'chit-chatting women or boring people' at parties – 'You can sense it flaring, this ulcer thing. Sean tightens up and you see it in his face. You just know he wants to be elsewhere.'

Elsewhere in 1949 was nowhere. Whatever the exact

circumstances of his release from the Navy it is evident that the man who returned to the stair was considerably different in temperament from the boy who left. Outwardly, to street pals like Michael O'Sullivan and Brady, he was the same humorous, tearaway Tommy, but privately he was, very seriously, at war with himself. No matter which way one interpreted his service record it was, in his eyes, a catalogue of failure. He had seen little travel, achieved nothing in rank and, despite his brawn, ended up with an invalid's discharge chit. He had not made any close friends and his options in terms of places to run to were nil. With a face of bravado that barely concealed wounded self-esteem, he reluctantly moved back into the butt-and-ben, squeezing back into Joe's territory and taking a shake-down bed opposite Neil's settee. Effie did not need to hear the gossip along the stairs; she knew Tommy was desperately unhappy about his return. The Navy had certainly helped hatch him out into manhood, but the maturer Tommy was difficult, sharp-tongued and uneasy as a cornered cat. Joe was working on long-distance lorry runs, usually absent from the house from nine in the morning till nine at night, but the strain of cramped living and the heart-sickening gloom of near-poverty were unchanged. Without much planning, Tommy decided to go back to work – tackling any job he could get, except the milk round; it was essential he retained some dignity, some sense of having moved on.

Effie was quick to enquire after and suggest jobs, but Tommy had decided a course in his own mind. He wanted breathing space, time to find a direction and work that would not commit him to a Fountainbridge existence. 'Give me room,' he implored. 'I'm going to keep on going from job to job till I find the right one – and the right money. I'm not going to be like Dad and work for sweeties all my life.'

By Christmas he had torn up his medical diet card and flung himself into a routine of physically gruelling, pointless, but reasonably well-paying jobs. He was a coal-delivery man for three weeks, a steelworker for eight, a corporation road worker, an any-hours odd-job man. There was, friends suggest, almost an element of self-humiliation about the fury of effort Connery applied to some of these jobs; there was, too, his usual contemptuous wryness; the Navy débâcle had not suppressed all his old spirit. 'Money was all that really concerned him,' a labourer acquaintance says. 'He didn't give two hoots about quality of work or anything else. He just wanted cash to splash out on girls, to do things with.' His 20 per cent disability rating didn't slow him down. He worked plenty of overtime, netting a princely £10–£11 per week, 'splashing out' on beer at the Fountain and, now, further afield, up the glamorous West End, on girls. Navy life had taught him the facts of love, and with his Latinate louche looks he had no trouble pulling the girls he wanted. 'He had no strict preferences in girls,' says Brady laughingly. 'Tommy went for all women.'

The casual relationships with the opposite sex did not provide enough distraction though, and, in his own words, Connery found himself 'dissatisfied with everything' within a year. Then, out of the blue, the British Legion came to the rescue. Founded in 1921 to lend assistance to ex-servicemen, the Legion was especially active in schemes to help the young disabled. Qualifying with his minor 'disability', Connery was granted a scholarship to a trade training course. 'You could become a tailor or a barber or a plasterer or a plumber,' Connery says, 'and I chose to be a French polisher. The whole training school practised on one another. You had to go and let some of them cut your hair, and others make suits for you.' Connery polished the ramshackle furniture of tenement Edinburgh, a lusty, energy-consuming task, before being landed in the Craighouse Gardens cabinet works of Jack Vinestock in the summer of 1951. He was taken on at £7 a week – a sizeable drop in earnings – but then, to Effie's thinking, he was learning a worthwhile trade. His hours were 8 a.m. till 5.30 p.m., five days a week, and the working conditions were good. 'There was a staff of about sixty then,' Jack Jr, son of the company's founder, recounts, 'and a jolly atmosphere. We hadn't been allowed to manufacture household furniture during the war, of course, and by '51 the rush on utility stuff was finished. People were going in for a better grade of contemporary designs. We prided ourselves and worked to a high standard, and Tommy was an assistant, doing everything from dressers to wardrobes to coffins. He was a lively fellow who was tremendously popular with many of the workforce, but there wasn't a lot of time for fun-making because we were working fast and under some pressure.' Vinestock adds that he was 'very physical, and he laughed a lot . . . but he wasn't really a French polisher, he had no talent for it.' Co-workers William Strain and Johnny Wallis found him to be a relentless prankster and, as Wallis recalls, 'very wild'.

Earlier it was easy to interpret Connery's unstoppable energy and wit as carefree wildness, but now it was the open manifestation of his resentment of the trap in which Fountainbridge and his failure in the Navy seemed to have caught him. He was never the most candid of people, and some of his friends found him at this stage unfathomable. He talked idly about great ambitions – intentions to travel the world, to go to Glasgow, even to London. But his future, it was clear to Wallis and others, was entirely shapeless. One day it was speculation about the high life down south, the next he was railing against Vinestock wages and planning a resumption of road labour work.

Then John Hogg, an experienced cabinet-maker at the works, posed an idea which caught Connery's interest. It was nearing Christmas, and the King's Theatre in Leven Street, that hallowed bastion of upper-crust entertainment, needed backstage help for the busy season. Hogg, now deceased, worked nights as a dresser and naturally, enjoyed the pocket-money as much as the smell of the greasepaint. As they sweated side-by-side over a high-gloss finish on a table bound for a rich man's home, Hogg told Connery about the easy-money world of the theatre. He was, he said, quite sure he could secure for Connery a job as dresser-assistant. All that was necessary was an introduction to the stage manager. Connery had never been in a theatre in his life but the next evening after work he went along with Hogg to the King's and spoke to the manager. A few nights later he was backstage, and employed, part of the theatrical group, looking after wardrobe and sets.

He enjoyed the atmosphere and the money in equal measure and for the few weeks of his engagement his wildness and recalcitrance were, in part anyway, tamed. Here at last he had found blood brothers, respected bohemians who lived by their wits, roamed endlessly, freely and were, incredibly, related to the stout-hearted riders of the gaff range.

4

A Scottish
Schwarzenegger in
South Pacific

'I don't know when I first envisioned myself as a sort of muscle-boy, a Scottish Arnold Schwarzenegger, but it must have been in my mid-teens. Teenagers are very conscious of their bodies anyway, and the rugged jobs I'd held helped build up those muscles . . .'

Despite his height – 6 foot 2 inches at eighteen – and beefy shoulders, Tommy was, by Neil's reckoning, 'skinny' when he came out of the Navy. He was also, after a period of readjustment to the tenement cage, socially hyperactive and aggressively girl-hungry. As a prominent football player he enjoyed the fan following for Fet-Lor Amateurs, the boy's club team sponsored by the wealthy patrons, and former pupils of Fettes College and Loretto Public School in the old part of the city. In 1950 Fet-Lor's victory in a newspaper cup competition won him a medal and, more valuably, the adulation of a handful of free 'n' easy girl supporters. Later, having demonstrated a definite burgeoning flair that was at last being applauded as talent, he was voted into Bonnyrigg Rose, the junior-league mining-village team. Once again his speed and strength were noted, this time arousing the interest of the celebrated East Fife. Fife sent scouts to watch Connery play and offered him a £25 signing fee which he declined but which,

Neil surmises, jolted him into thinking about professional football as a possible escape route from Vinestock and the grind. 'The football business was always in the background,' John Brady says. 'Tommy was showing constant improvement as he got fitter and eventually Celtic gave him a trial. But something held him back, he didn't seem to want to latch to it as a career'.

By his own admission Connery turned seriously towards body-building 'to look good and get the girls'. 'Jimmy Laurie was the man he idolised,' says a Fet-Lor team mate. 'At the end of the Meadows there was a tin shed place called the Dunedin Amateur Weightlifting Club and Jimmy was the star member. Jimmy himself was only five foot six and a half, but he was built powerfully and he became a Mr Scotland. Jimmy became Tommy's coach and friend. He saw great potential in Tommy's independent determination.' Entrance to the club cost Connery 15 shillings, and he wasn't about to throw that fortune away lightly. Once promised to Laurie's back-breaking course, he settled to a three-night-a-week unshakable schedule, interrupting football training, girl-hunting and Vinestock overtime.

The records and accounts of Craighouse Cabinet Works were destroyed in the early eighties but there is a pervasive suspicion that Connery got the sack. Vinestock is foggy about the details but Wallis, who had been called up for National Service late in 1951, says he would not have been surprised. Either way, Connery left Vinestock's in the spring of '52, took a one-penny tram ride down Princes Street and offered himself as a lifeguard at the huge Portobello Pool, one of the largest salt-water pools in Britain, just as the season started. A strong swimmer since Joe taught him at the Dalry Baths when he was five, Connery was a sound and conscientious guard, only ever distracted by the flattering attention of corset-suited sylphs. His physique, thanks to the dumb-bells and chest expanders he had brought home to the stair, had improved massively. That hot summer, John Brady swears, Connery 'caught more birds than any man deserves'. Popularity at Bonnyrigg, Portobello Pool, afternoon picnics at Gullane Beach, the dips and swells of complaisant girls seduced by a sailor's yarns and the ripple of tanned muscle . . . after countless years of grey clouds the silver lining was sparkling through. Those halcyon days reaped all sorts of unexpected bonuses. At the Dunedin Club a former Mr Scotland, Archie Brennan, was encouraging Connery to take up competitive weight-lifting and model work. Like Laurie, he believed Connery's fortune lay in his strength and swarthy looks. The Navy pension-payers were offering a fat once-and-for-all settlement of £90 – taken, and spent on (at last, and without Joe's objection) a motorcycle. There was even a chance to earn good money, part-time, for doing . . . nothing. At the Edinburgh College of Art, posing only in a pouch G-string, Connery earned 6s. 8d. an hour, standing on a dais ('The girls always wanted to sketch me up close, it was embarrassing') and reclining on a bare-wood couch that had probably found its way from Vinestock's. Norfolk-based artist Martin MacKeown, now moderately successful, once studied at the college and cherishes hazy memories of the casual model. 'I can remember that I felt very sorry for him. He had a dead-end job with no future while I was busy working to become a Great Artist. Well, look how wrong one can be . . .!'

Best bonus of all, stumbled upon like everything else in a headlong venture to rebuild ego and find purpose to life, was a chance in the autumn to return to the stage – this time flexing muscles in front of the props. An advertisement in the Edinburgh *Evening News* attracted Connery to the poorly paid vacancies of the background 'spear-carriers' for the touring play *The Glorious Years*, due at the Empire Theatre in Nicolson Street (now gone) for a five-week run. Anna Neagle, first lady of British films who had hit starry heights with such bracing potboilers as *Nurse Edith Cavell* (1939) and *Piccadilly Incident* (1946), was the star, the production had been a major West End success and there was every reason to believe it would break records at the Empire.

Connery applied for and got the job as a guardsman in a crowd scene solely because of his height. The show was a hit – not that that affected Connery's career, or his pocket. Crowd parts do not exactly establish good or bad performers. But Connery got a kick out of roughing it with the other actors, and enjoyed the excitement of the make-believe, the audience expectation and the applause more than anything he had yet done. Overriding everything, of course, was the accepted transience of the whole thing – an aspect that brought back the joys of the King's at Christmas and impressed itself now very strongly on Connery. Here in the theatre there was no need to pretend allegiance in perpetuity. One accepted that the make-believe was part-time, tomorrow was another day, another problem perhaps but – most precious to so many actors – another town. Actors, it seemed to Connery, were imprisoned only by their temporary fantasy lives. Their nights were busy but their days were free, and their futures fantastically mysterious. For once in his museful analysis of a job's potential, money didn't come into it. The theatre was, simply, curious fun.

No efforts were made to persuade friends or lovers along to the Empire to watch the brief moments of public glory. 'To me it was just another of his casual jobs,' Brady says. 'He didn't talk about it any more than he talked about life-saving at the pool. It just happened, and a few weeks later it was over. Tommy was back playing billiards at the Lothian Hall, back exercising at his club.'

The kind of restless, moody stirrings that foretold his escape to the Royal Navy were not now evident, even though his days in Edinburgh were numbered. On the face of it he appeared to be contenting himself with a new weekly ritual divided between French polishing (the Portobello pool had closed for the season), working-out at the club, a bit of modelling and Saturday nights at the Palais de Danse, Fountainbridge's main dancehall. For a short time he was a bouncer at the hall, and for a long time the regular boyfriend of Isa Farmer, a well-brought-up girl from the Grass Market, behind Edinburgh Castle. Isa, a tiny dark-haired good-looker, was the only girl Connery ever took home to Effie, and there was serious talk of marriage but, because of the competition at the Palais and Connery's fast-roving eye, the affair petered out. 'The Palais de Danse was mecca at the weekends,' says Craigie Veitch. 'It had the finest, biggest floor in Scotland and regularly took upwards of two thousand people. On Friday and Saturday nights there was this tremendous, electric atmosphere – like everyone had struggled through another hard week in the smoke and were now out to make the best of hard-earned money. Connery had developed into a fine hunk of a fellow, all shoulders, and he had this notable, trendy style of dress. He appeared to be doing well. He was making money and spending it on nifty clothes. The average get-up then was pretty awful – hacking jackets and what have you. Connery – or "Big Tam", as he was known by then – wore classy semidrapes, slim-fitting, single-button suits and shiny shoes. He was an eye-catcher, and he had no shortage of dance partners, that's for certain.' His appetite for ever-changing partners – a blonde this week, a redhead next – was, others suggest, insatiable. But he carried on his affairs with discretion and a dignity that bordered on freakishness in Fountainbridge terms. There were the gropings in alleys behind the sweetie factory and all the rest, of course, but he was not averse to meeting an elegant lady at Binn's Corner beneath the famous store clock, and taking her for a decent meal in reasonable surroundings, up in the post West End.

'Money was no problem.' Brady says, 'because Tommy always found a way to boost his pocket. Around this time he was biking down to Vince Studios in Manchester – they published photo-magazines for musclemen. Tommy did modelling for them, and earned quite a bit. He'd dive down, do a session, then motor back the same day.' Next morning he'd be back in some small-time furniture-restorers', scrubbing away with sandpaper and oils, topping up his week's earnings. At home, the pressure of contributing heavily to the family purse was reduced. By now the family was living on the second floor, with a little more room in a broader butt-and-ben and Joe was finding overtime easier to cope with. Neil too was working, having graduated, resolved to follow the hero-grandfather

Maclean after whom he had been named (Neil's full name is Neil Maclean Connery) into full-time plastering.

With two happy and successful years recovering from the Navy failure behind him, Connery found himself, in the winter of '52, primed for a change. All the uncompromising pluckiness that had been knocked from him during the first flight from Fountainbridge had returned. He felt good, looked good, had trustworthy friends in Jimmy Laurie, John Brady and others. Now more than ever he was ruthless about excising from his life anything that he disliked. A spell polishing for a coffin-maker depressed him. 'The boss was a remarkable man. He knew everyone and as soon as he heard that anyone was ill he would nip around and look them over as they lay weakly in bed. With his eye he measured them for the coffin. Then he'd come back, and get us to make a coffin. Sometimes they cheated him and lived.' Connery 'retired' from coffin-making and took a heartier job, something more akin to Vinestock's, which he had enjoyed. He went to work in the printing-press room of the Edinburgh *Evening News*, becoming a greasy-faced, cloth-capped machine help – but winning Effie's beaming admiration. 'My lad works on the *News*.' The declaration had a fine, north-of-Fountainbridge ring to it, an apparent respectability to match the Post Office and in her tirelessly optimistic mother-hen way Effie might have hoped the *News* would be the turning point in Tommy's life. There were plenty of cases of assiduous workers who built up from careers in the machine room to become reception, sales or editorial staff. Craigie Veitch himself worked up to sports editorial. But Connery, as his new work mates learnt from the start, had no intention of pinning his colours to the *News* mast indefinitely. His staple conversational favourite, when the drone of the presses abated and seriousness crept into the talk, was emigration.

It was Jimmy Laurie's practicality and not some pipe dream of promise that led Connery away from Fountainbridge for the second – and final – time. Laurie was many years Connery's senior but he shared much in common with his protégé. He was intelligent, ambitious beyond

Fountainbridge, dedicated to fitness, and possessed a discerning eye. 'Jimmy Laurie wanted Tommy to try his luck in competition,' Brady says. 'Tommy was Dunedin's new star pupil, no question. When it came to discipline in training no one was like Tommy. And the training wasn't confined to the club.' As Connery saw the dividends of following Laurie's advice – at very least the value of rippling biceps when trying to impress the birds – he extended his work-outs. Ray Ellington, the popular bandleader, was another fitness fanatic. Every Trader's Holiday, when industry enjoyed its fortnight's summer let-off, Ellington's band graced the Palais stage. Tommy, who had always been popular and friendly with the management (which led to his bouncer's job), hit it off with the mercurial Ellington. Together, after Ellington's shows, the pair practised backstage. 'It was almost funny to see them, chalk and cheese, very dissimilar fellows but both obsessed by "toning up". Ellington brought equipment with him, and they shared the dumb-bells and weights.'

Connery had purchased a tracksuit too and ran regularly round the Meadows, regardless of weather conditions. Connery was 22, and Dunedin judged him to be near his athletic peak. After training one Friday Laurie put a proposal to Connery: each year a variety of 'body-beautiful' contests took place in London, most open to all comers from recognised health and fitness clubs; many were valueless indulgent exercises but one or two carried prestige; the Mr Universe contest, Laurie believed, meant something – contenders always received some press attention and winners took away more than gold medals. Connery, Laurie said, was ripe for a try. In his junior category he would romp home. The title would bring acclaim to the Dunedin Club and the ground-plan of a new, more meaningful career to Connery.

At first the suggestion seemed too preposterous to consider. Connery had met plenty of professional muscle-men, and most fitted quite a different physical mould: they were squat, 5 foot-10-ish, bull-necked and thick-fisted. In contrast, he had a lithe sinewy frame which, in the words of a girlfriend, 'befitted a champion swimmer'. But Laurie's proposal was well-timed. Connery *was* seriously contemplating emigration – or at any rate some major redesign of lifestyle. Most of his friends on the *News* and elsewhere still lived at home, cherishing ambitions perhaps, but wistfully, immaturely. Connery considered it mildly shameful that, in their twenties, these clever young men were still dependent on a family roof.

He mulled over Laurie's suggestion for a few days, then agreed. Excited, Laurie revised the training schedules and set about making the arrangements for London.

Effie was unmoved. She saw the London venture as 'a bit of a joke', the natural extension of the boyish daftness of playing lifeguard at the baths or on Portobello beach. Jimmy Laurie anyway was sensible and reliable: he wouldn't lead Tommy into anything reckless. Neil scarcely turned a hair and Joe wasn't even present – he was away on a long-haul furniture run – when Tommy packed his single bag and left with Laurie for London. They planned to stay for a few weeks, taking a bedsit, for convenience, in Chelsea.

The Mr Universe contest at the rundown Scala Theatre in West London was a near-comic disappointment for Laurie and Connery. Laurie, according to friends, entered the competition too, but failed to win any placing. Connery was more fortunate. In his category he was third, winning a bronze. Laurie's disgust and embarrassment at the magnitude of their (relative) abject failure was mirrored by Connery. Years later he recalled bitterly, 'I did no good at all. The Americans always won those things. They were much bigger and everybody was impressed by the size of them. It was quite a disillusionment for me to meet them, because at the club I went to . . . we were all very health and strength conscious, and we used to run and swim and do many other things. But all the American and the London fellas seemed to be solely intent on acquiring inches and bulk. I was absolutely shattered to discover that somebody wouldn't run for a bus because he might lose some of his bulk. . . . Just to be a bulky physique would be boring to me. Not to run, not to play football, not to swim – a cul-de-sac.'

So Connery's gut response, the keenly honed sense of instinct that would serve him so well in his future career, had been right first time: he was not champion class in the unimaginatively standardised body-building stakes. Neither, he discovered, did he want to be. The fuss and 'glamour' of the occasion was fine, comfortably reminiscent of the Empire, even if the contenders left him cold. Since he had settled down after the Navy fling, Connery had developed and displayed a special fondness for a particular kind of casual acquaintance. He wasn't exactly your average star-struck stage-door Johnny but, Brady observes, 'he made no bones about the types he liked. Theatrical-type people, the nomads, the slightly way-out, if you like, appealed to him.' Another friend vividly recalls Connery raising eyebrows back home by strutting into a popular uptown young people's meeting place, the West End Café, with a coloured girl on his arm. 'Her name was Maxine Daniels and she was a top singer up north at the time. She'd been appearing at the Empire and was, we reckoned, right outside our league. I suppose you could say there were conventions about the kind of people one socialised with – but Tommy didn't bother about them. And it wasn't only Maxine. He kept other acquaintanceships going with theatre people – not, we thought, for any special purpose, mind. Among his mates the general feeling was that Tommy, or Tammy as we still knew him, had a power of attraction that enabled him to make a better 'class' of friend. Glamorous women especially were drawn to him, theatrical women. And of course he enjoyed their attention.'

By extraordinary chance, the theatre offered itself to Connery again just as he and Laurie were running out of cash and readying themselves for a home journey. They had kicked around London for a couple of weeks, drowning their disappointment in good brown ale, the landscape familiar. Never a slouch, he was attracted to blustery

46

Piccadilly and Charing Cross, the urgency of the crowds, the din of through-going important traffic. Nothing he had seen in the Navy compared with London at full charge, seen from the inside. Here was the true, fantastic metropolis, of which the stage was a vibrant microcosm. Part of him wanted to stay, but the impracticable aspect of merely lingering on affronted his basically responsible nature. Back in Edinburgh the *News* was waiting for him – a job he bragged to friends as his 'best yet', albeit one that partially stifled him. The press attention Laurie believed Connery might win had not happened but, at the very last minute, London yielded its real reward. Stanley Howlett, one of the Mr Universe entrants, detailed for Connery the side benefits of *his* weight-training: London's countless theatres were always looking for muscular, fair-looking fellows to heft svelte nymphs around or, at worst, shift props. Connery perked up immediately: he had experience on both sides of the theatrical backcloth. The men got talking, got friendly.

Howlett was currently one of the Navy back-boys chanting Rodgers and Hammerstein every night in the marathon classic *South Pacific*. 'Why not try it?' Howlett suggested. 'The show is winding down its West End run before going on tour, and they're looking for cast replacements. You have experience.'

'But I can't sing, or dance.'

'You've been in the Navy,' Howlett countered optimistically.

Connery and Laurie bulldozed into the auditions for chorus parts at the Theatre Royal, Drury Lane. If there was hesitation in Connery about the negative factors of a long engagement in a London-and-touring job it centred only on losing out with Bonnyrigg Rose football team. Otherwise, Connery auditioned because, quite passionately, he wanted the job. Jerome White was the producer who oversaw the auditions, assessing in an afternoon some twenty-five hopefuls. Connery impressed him with a slick combination of toughness, conversational circumspection and shining self-confidence. 'Are you an actor?' the casting director boomed. Connery nodded from the splendidly ornate stage. 'And you sing?' Again Connery nodded. 'I've done plenty of rep in Scotland,' he lied boldly. 'Singing, dancing, you name it.' When it came to reading a test line or two of dialogue, Neil says, Connery's nerviness got the better of him. He dropped the pages of his script and heard the director call him clumsy. Enraged, Connery flung the script aside. He pounded towards the wings but was stopped in his tracks by White recalling him politely. 'Read again, please.' Connery composed himself, remembered the Empire, relaxed and rendered a half-dozen American-accented lines. 'I did the best I could,' he says. 'I more or less mouthed one of the songs from the show and did a few fancy steps that were a hangover from my ballroom dancing. . . . Not bad, I concluded as I left the stage, but obviously not professional enough for their demands.' Before dismissing him, White asked Connery a few questions about his physique and background.

Most aspirant hoofers and singers retired in shaky-kneed deference after this final exchange but Connery stalked forward and called over the footlights, 'What's the wage?'

Not at all amused, White barked back, 'It doesn't concern me.'

Po-faced, Connery retorted, 'But it concerns me.'

A whisper of amused discussion ran through the production group in the stalls long after Connery's exit.

But the consensus weighed in favour of his ability to reverse the disaster. Two days after the audition a phone call came to the Chelsea bedsit, informing Connery, 'OK, you got the part. You're in.' £12 per week was offered, and accepted. Laurie, unfortunately, had failed, but they went out to celebrate anyway, then made a lightning trip back to Edinburgh to break the news.

'His phenomenal self-confidence was *the* quality,' a neighbour from 176 remembers. 'It was nothing ordinary. Maybe it stemmed from the girls who threw themselves at him, maybe that boosted him. But you got the impression he could choose or do *anything*.' Back at 176 Effie smiled to herself when Tommy expounded the significance of 'the break'. £12 a week for working a few hours nightly was money for jam! He would have his days off to do with as he pleased; he would read, educate himself, maybe get some useful part-time work. After London there would be a tour. There was even the possibility of further, better paid stage work. Howlett had stories. . . . In her heart Effie knew Tommy was merely trying to sugar the pill: the simple truth was he was done with Auld Reekie.

Neil vividly remembers Tommy's excitement on his return from London. Others shrug their shoulders: Big Tam liked money before anything, the chorus work was just rich light labour – sweetened by the ticket to a more permanent London. Connery himself surveys that first crucial toehold on an acting life with some self-mockery. Just before the triumphant Drury Lane run ended he joined the company but 'the whole idea of travelling round the country was what appealed to me. I didn't seriously consider myself as an actor . . . it all seemed like a giggle.'

If it started as a giggle, the humour died quickly. Jerry White was a man of great wit and generosity, but he was running in the shadow of fellow-countryman Joshua Logan who had hiked *South Pacific* to Broadway success, and he was determined to keep the quality comparison. For him the upcoming tour would be arduous and trying; there was no room for lazy amateurs or star-struck 'boys'. White needed to be surrounded by committed perfectionists.

After a short time Connery realised that *South Pacific* trundled forward by grace of its wonderfully conceived construction (a discovery, this: entertainments didn't just happen – they were lovingly sculpted) and authoritarian rule. The strict authority of the Navy had not suited young Connery. White's methods did.

Back at the machine room of the Edinburgh *Evening News* there were those who patiently believed Big Tam would get his picture in the paper, earn a bob or two, and be back begging off the personnel manager by Christmas next year.

5

Love in the Sticks

A conversation about Ibsen transformed Connery the odd-job man to Connery the actor. Robert Henderson, the American actor-director, remembered the occasion well: '*South Pacific* was a quarter-way through its long and extraordinarily successful tour. We'd just done Scotland and we were then in the middle of nine weeks at the Opera House in Manchester. Sean and I were in the same lodging house, a bit away from the theatre, and it just happened we walked home together one night. We were chatting and I mentioned Ibsen and Sean said, "Who's he?" So I told him – he's this famous modern dramatist, and all the rest. And I suggested he read a few of Ibsen's plays, thinking of course I'd hear nothing about it again. Those musclemen, you see, weren't employed for their brains. In the strict sense it wasn't chorus boys the show's management wanted, just capable big fellows for the "Dame's" routine.'

The plays Henderson loaned Connery were *The Wild Duck*, *When We Dead Awaken* and the classic *Hedda Gabler*. Connery read them, obviously with some difficulty here and there, but surprised Henderson by returning to discuss them intelligently. A voracious student of all theatre but (by his own admission) with no particular eye for new talent, Henderson was flattered and intrigued by the burst of avid interest displayed by the chatty 'muscleman'. Connery, in turn, was grateful for a sympathetic ear, most of all someone who was rooted in the milieu and knew his p's and q's. A considerable part of

Connery's problem in comfortably settling into the show was his accent. 'In the beginning very few of the cast would speak to me,' he said. 'For some reason they thought I was Polish!' The accent certainly jarred with Henderson – 'very awkward', Henderson described it. 'I urged him to get rid of it, and he did soften it down.' (Interestingly, some Edinburgh friends claim Connery has consciously preserved his rolling dialectal accent. 'There's a scene in *You Only Live Twice*,' an old neighbour says, 'where Sean and the girl [Mie Hama as Kissy] are about to climb the volcano slope. "We must get *up* there," Sean says. That small sentence, the stress on the demonstrative "up" – that's pure Fountainbridge. Get a Glasweigan, anyone, to say that and it'll be totally different. No doubt, Sean kept on being a Fountainbridger in that regard.' The director John Boorman recalls a dinner party where Connery was queried about his brogue – playing an Arab – in *The Wind and the Lion*. 'Sean's a wonderful mimic, but his response then was, "If I didn't play in my normal voice I wouldn't know who the fuck I was".')

Speaking with Henderson it is easy to imagine how Connery's enthusiasm was fired. When I interviewed the actor-director shortly before his death he was – proudly – 77 and still robustly passionate about theatre life. He came to London in '47 to direct, he told me, then graduated to musicals and won attention for fine performances in *Damn Yankees* and *West Side Story* in the late fifties and sixties. Marriage to the celebrated character actress Estelle Winwood (who starred with Connery in *Darby O'Gill and the Little People*), reinforced his devotion to all things theatrical, and his career was, as he described it, utterly rewarding. Of Connery, he had the fondest, most vivid memories: 'The chap had Romany blood in him, he must have. The features, the eyes – it's there all right.' But if Connery's matinée-idol features won over successive future talent scouts, it was his 'divine curiosity' that captured Henderson's special interest. 'It was quite remarkable. After Ibsen he wanted to know more and more, and he seemed deadly serious about it. So, with a twinkle in my

eye I listed for him just six books that were worth studying.'
There was Proust's *Remembrance of Things Past*; *War and Peace*; James Joyce's *Ulysses* and *Finnegans Wake*; the Bernard Shaw–Ellen Terry letters, and Thomas Wolfe's *Look Homeward, Angel*. Henderson considered the books 'a dry choice, but they led to endless channels that have been explored in the theatre. I wondered would he pursue them.'

Quite apart from Henderson's contribution, Connery was already showing signs of progress in his new job though, objectively, such progress probably had more to do with energy than ambition in career terms. On the tour's first visit to the King's Theatre in Edinburgh Connery was still hand-springing with 'the guys', blaring 'There is Nothing Like a Dame!', but he was understudying two reasonably important parts and his salary was up to £14 10s. When Neil saw him during the first tour visit he found him to be 'as happy as I'd ever known him', and eager to prove his worth to the show. A fellow actor on the tour comments, 'It was jokey at the start and then, very quickly, he wanted to do well. He had a bit of a chip on his shoulder to my thinking and figured he could do as well as anyone out front. Early on I knew he'd stick with it, and try for a proper part.'

Among the men his own age – those who did not mistake him for a Pole – Connery was popular, though considered 'bloody independent'. He was a star player at the weekend poker sessions in damp-scarred lodging houses, cherished centre-forward with the cast football team and hoarder of rare Scottish jokes. His allegiances, it seems, were confused. 'He loved Scotland, sure,' Robert Henderson said, 'but you get the impression he never wanted to live there again.' Most old Fountainbridge cronies lost touch around this time. 'He changed,' one recalls. 'In London there had been a blow-up with Jimmy Laurie. Something boyish and crazy. Let's say Tommy was a grafter and Jimmy got fed up with London work. So the flat they shared came unstuck, and Tommy hit the road. After that Tommy didn't want to look back, he just wanted to get himself on.'

Jerry White, Robert Henderson and the rest knew

Connery only as Sean. The origin of the name-change reaches back to childhood. Connery had a primary school friend nicknamed 'Shane' and it is likely that George Steven's Oscar-winning film starring Alan Ladd, released in 1953 – about the time Connery restyled himself for Drury Lane –influenced the final choice of a new name for a new career. Connery saw and admired the movie *Shane*, which, in the character of its lone-protector western hero, had much in common with Connery's eventual cowboy creation *Shalako*.

Meanwhile, Connery's mode of transport was by 3-horse-power motorcycle, a post-war relic that reliably took him from town to town in the tracks of the tour party. The bike gave him a charge of power and freedom he enjoyed, and the chance to go for country spins, where he could flee alone to the great outdoors beyond the Manchester Opera House and contemplate *War and Peace*. Henderson's speculation about young Connery's earnestness came to an abrupt stop just a week after the 'dry booklist' had been proposed. It came to general notice that Connery was devouring Tolstoy and Proust – 'on loan from the library of course,' said Henderson. 'He's Scottish, what else would you expect?'

Henderson's key snatch of advice came, coincidentally on the eve of a momentous occurrence in Connery's foot-ball life. 'He looked basically like a lorry driver to me,' Henderson said. 'So I told him, "Tolstoy will lead you on to Dostoevsky and Stanislavsky and so on. Now I don't know a lot about these things but I have a feeling you could be a big star. I don't know about Britain, but you could be something in the States. Now, if you can talk Dostoevsky and look like a truck driver you've got it made. Speak one thing, look another. That's the essence of an artist." And Sean said, "Yes, yes," like he meant it, as though he'd discovered *gold*.'

Next day Connery was on the football field, leading the *South Pacific* crew against a local junior team. Among the onlookers was Manchester United's manager and architect supreme, Matt Busby. The match was a raging, close-fought affair, with the *Pacific* team clutching victory in the last minutes. Busby was exhilarated, excited particularly by the aggressive style of forward Connery. In the changing shed after the game he took Connery aside and offered him a place at Old Trafford. Connery asked for time to consider: he was stunned by the unexpected breakthrough and fully aware of its value. Fellow actors enviously patted his shoulder, sure in their hearts he would drop from the tour. That night, back at the lodging house after the show, Connery knocked on Henderson's door and explained Busby's offer. 'Don't take it,' Henderson advised. 'Remember what we discussed. If you can take Tolstoy, and *take your time*, you'll make it in the movies.'

Connery slept on it, and decided to decline Old Trafford. He rang United with the news and proudly spread the word around the cast. When Jerry White heard he was appalled. Backstage at the Opera House he confronted Henderson, red-faced. 'Do you know what you've done?' he ranted. 'You've built up the kid's hopes with this talk about movie success. United was offering him something positive, the chance to earn bloody good money for a couple of years. In this business, he has no guarantees. He's a nobody, he might always be a nobody.'

Henderson was apologetic but showed no remorse. 'In the space of a few weeks,' he said, 'Sean proved his worth to me. Lots of young actors are dead keen to become a star. Lots of young actors are also dead lazy. Sean had a real insatiable desire to learn the business. Later, when people looked at the cool urbanity of Bond and the huge success, they said, Wow, that was easy for him. But, by God, it was sweat and tears all the way. I know. I saw it from the start.'

On stage Henderson, along with other major characters in the cast like Millicent Martin and Michael Medwin, were taken with Connery's calm aplomb. 'He had his qualms in daily life,' a fellow actor states, 'but once on stage, in Henderson's words, 'he hadn't a nerve in his body'. In many unscheduled incidents along the two-year run, Connery distinguished himself with sheer neck, often demonstrating that incompliant reluctance to accept the word 'failure'. Michael Medwin recalls the simulated night-time bomb attack sequence, where black-clad bit-part actors pranced on an unlit stage, invisible to the audience, but flashing flare lamps that burnt briefly bright, like ground gunfire, while in the background sound effects duplicated a noisy raid. On one occasion Connery, draped in black, leapt out to the wrong cue, slap in the middle of a tame, quiet scene. For a frantic second he hopped round, arms swirling with the flare torches, like some maniac on the loose. A gasp of shock came from the audience. In mid-stride Connery realised, in the sudden horrific silence, that his timing was wrong: he belonged backstage at the poker table, not here. He froze, dropped his torches by his side, grinned widely and ambled off. The audience breathed easy, and the show rumbled on.

About a year out on the tour, at the Brighton Hippo-drome, Connery at last got elected onto the printed pro-gramme, taking over the part of Lieutenant Buzz Adams, originally created on the West End stage by Larry Hagman, later JR of *Dallas*, the record-breaking television show. A small-time Australian actor had been holding the part and when he quit, Henderson led the group of principals in a deputation to demand Connery's promotion. Connery had been popular, now he had their respect: all the major actors in the production felt he had the strengths for a regular speaking part. Jerry White needed little persuasion. Connery became Lt Adams and assumed responsibility for his first true acting scene. 'It wasn't a very big slice,' Henderson said, 'but it was important. I was playing Captain Brackett and Adams was to come to my hut and tell me about the marine landing on the Japanese islands. It was quite intense, I suppose, and Sean delivered it beaut-ifully. From the first night he was flawless, not a bit scared by the onus of a speech.'

Connery's strength was Henderson's tutorage, most agree. The speak-one-thing-look-another trick became the staple of Connery's acting philosophy, utilised for the first time with Buzz Adams and never abandoned. Almost thirty years after *South Pacific* director Fred Zinnemann pinpointed for me the 'special qualification' that made

Connery right for the part of Douglas, the lovelorn mountaineer in *Five Days One Summer*, a movie the legendary film-maker had been planning for years: 'I wanted a man who could convey profound sensitivity, yet who could look capable of, and indeed partake in, the very physical feats required of him. He had to be two things at once – complementary strength and weakness.' There was no immediate comparison with Zinnemann's other favourite hero, Gary Cooper. 'Yet both easily achieved that magical aura of compassionate hero.'

'I was twenty-five years Sean's senior,' Henderson said, 'so I guess he regarded me as some sort of father figure on the road to a new life.' He hastened to add: 'But don't let anyone kid you. I didn't discover Sean. The gifts he had were already there. I just encouraged him to let them show.'

Two women figured large in Connery's touring life: one he loved; the other adored him and, like Henderson, was convinced he was a budding international talent.

Carol Sopel, a gorgeous, gentle-souled young actress joined the company in the middle of the tour to take over the part of the Polynesian girl whose jolly featured piece 'Happy Talk' was, from town to town, a show-stopper. Tsin Yu, the Eurasian actress, had held the role till then, but Carol's serene ingénue was imbued with near genius. A punctilious and serious actress, Carol was also 'great fun, and a favourite among the cast very quickly', said Henderson. Her experience wasn't wide, but she was eager to cultivate the flair she had and, in that, found a soulmate in Sean Connery. Connery fell in love with Carol in a matter of days and, though Robert Henderson stressed he involved himself hardly at all in Connery's private life, he was close enough to observe that 'Sean felt deeply, deeply for Carol. They were the closest of friends.' Naturally the relationship intensified as the tour progressed, and Connery spent more and more of his free time with Carol. By now, to Henderson and Carol at least, he had confided his certain resolve to apply himself to an actor's life, for better or worse. At night in his lodgings he read into the small hours. By day he studied with the aid of a portable tape-recorder, practising speeches from Ibsen and Shaw, working on his accent. Whenever the tour hit a big town Connery and Carol went to 'anything else that was playing at the matinées. All the local reps in whatever plays they were doing.' Connery assimilated material very fast, displaying, said Henderson, 'the quality of a sponge – as though the cultural desert of Fountainbridge had wrung him out and he needed to absorb nourishment quickly.' Carol kept the pace and though Connery was – and is, according to Honor Blackman and most others – 'first and foremost a man's man', for several months through 1954–55 the couple became almost inseparable.

Eventually the subject of home-making reared its head and Connery hinted to several members of the cast his intention to wed Carol. 'He wanted to marry her,' said Henderson. 'Of that there's no doubt. And as they grew closer eventual marriage became, we thought, inevitable. It was just a question of where and when.'

Temperamentally, careerwise, in every way, Carol and Connery suited each other – but the cloud that darkened their lives from the day they first met finally descended and took the shape of the dreaded insurmountable obstacle. Carol was Jewish, and her parents strongly orthodox. They might have liked their daughter's devoted inamorato, but tradition would not permit them even to consider allowing a marriage. Carol wrangled and begged but in the end conceded to her parents' wishes. Almost as suddenly as it had begun, the love affair with Carol was over. Connery was shattered, his closer male friends on the cast truly surprised. One actor says, 'They were compatible, they didn't ever argue, but when the break-up came it was blunt and final.' The conscience-searching agonies of the parents and Carol's withdrawal upset Connery greatly. When he visited Henderson to explain that Carol had broken it off he wept. 'You can't imagine it, I know,' said Henderson, 'but it was terribly sad to see this tough guy we've all come to see as ruthless James Bond so heartbroken.'

Consolation of a sort came from another girl Connery

became friendly with during *Pacific* – Julie Hamilton, step-daughter of Labour Party leader Michael Foot. Julie was a 'Fleet-streeter', a freelance photographer who often worked for the *Daily Mail* and whose favoured patch was theatreland. On a job assignment at the musical she met Connery and fell for him. 'Nice girl,' Ian Bannen says, 'but not a great photographer. She photographed me at the Old Vic in the *The Iceman Cometh* . . . but for some damned reason it was always out of focus. I began to wonder was her eyesight impaired.' (Julie became romantically involved with Bannen after her break-up with Connery.)

Julie found Connery's striving self-improvement obsession magnetic. She was young but well-educated and impressively versed in the history of theatre. Connery's quest for knowledge, intensified somewhat as a compensatory measure after the break-up with Carol, led him to anyone who was prepared to share expertise and experience. In character Julie was Carol's absolute opposite – she was witty, articulate, pushy – but Connery started to date her, and for a while they got on famously. 'It was quite simple,' said Henderson. 'Julie wanted to help Sean's career. That was the foundation of that affair.' Sean, for his part, wanted all the help he could get.

With *South Pacific* nearing the end of almost a two-year tour, Connery recognised the watershed he was approaching. He could look back on a bumpy period of his life which had marked him emotionally, given him a real education, real fun and, above all, unscrambled his needs. The joys of the childhood freedom he cherished in Fife were distilled and crystallised in an acting life.

On the second tour visit to Edinburgh Effie greeted a rowdy, happy bunch from the cast at 176: Tommy had brought them home to show them off, indifferent to whatever any thespian 'nob' thought of the rundown stair. Effie knew then that Tommy had chosen a definite career at last. Even Joe learnt to encourage what to him appeared a wayward and distinctly odd profession. Tommy was truly, consistently happy, that was all that mattered. The one wee doubt for Effie, as for Tommy of course, was the future.

South Pacific ended in Dublin at the Gaiety Theatre and Connery toasted his success in a Liffeyside pub. In all he had understudied five parts, succeeded well with Buzz Adams, and advanced further than any other 'muscleman'. He had a few pounds in the bank, and the loving support of Julie Hamilton. But the future, in work opportunity terms, was a colossal question mark. Henderson said goodbye to Connery to go on to *Damn Yankees* at the Coliseum. 'It looked like it was going to be lean for him, but he was decided to stay at it. We promised to keep in touch and I wished him luck.'

Back in London and out of work Connery moved into a one-room basement flat at 12 Shalcomb Street, off the King's Road – arranged by Henderson as a reward for upholding the acting commitment. He signed on at Westminster Labour Exchange (£6 per week unemployment benefit) and, with Julie's prompting, commenced elocution lessons. Neil reckons his weekly outgoings were about £10, so Connery was feeling the economic pinch within a matter of weeks. Various steps were taken to counter the crisis: his motorcycle was swapped for a lady's pedal-cycle, second-hand, costing £2; nightly entertainments – the odd booze-up, the cinema – were stopped; even daily food was rationed. Henderson remembered Connery keeping a pot on the stove 'day and night. It was a combination of porridge and stew . . . and I never touched it.'

Connery toured the major agents' offices, brashly proclaiming his talents – but achieved nothing. He tried the theatres, without luck, and came close to despairing when money ran dangerously low. Consolation came from other ex-*Pacific* out-of-workers and from Julie; the tireless voice of encouragement from phone calls to Henderson. 'He never let any of us know if anything was wrong,' Neil wrote later in the Scottish *Sunday Express*. 'Even when he was ill and in bed for something like three weeks with a soaring temperature we knew nothing about it until months afterwards. And only then because one of his friends happened to mention it.'

Just when the lowest ebb was reached and the situation

seemed untenable, Henderson came back to the rescue. Assigned as director to that 'exquisite Agatha Christie play' *Witness for the Prosecution*, at the Q Theatre, Henderson phoned Connery and offered him the very minor (non-speaking) court usher part. Connery jumped at the £6-weekly fee, and stayed on the dole. Any murmuring doubts that lingered in Henderson's head about Connery's maturity for 'major' stage playing were silenced by an incidental event which almost escaped the director's notice.

Rehearsals were fine, the unstarry cast competent. Connery's part involved nothing more than shifting documents of evidence from one side of the stage to the other. Then the first night came. 'Sean was your average usher,' Henderson recalled, 'wearing this full black cloak. My concentration was on the main players obviously but then it was brought to my attention that Sean's movement across the stage was, well, too eye-catching. He had this way of walking, a great, elaborate stride that swished the cloak all over the place . . . it looked absolutely great, he looked great – but after a performance or two I had to take the cloak off him. He was just diverting too much attention. It was all in that *walk*.' (Five years later Harry Saltzman claimed his main reason for allotting the Bond role to Connery was the actor's walk. Cubby Broccoli later said, 'Only one other actor moves like him, and that's Albert Finney.')

At the Q over a patchy period – 'I was out of work for seven months' – Connery found further parts in the popular plays *Point of Departure* and *A Witch in Time*. Elsewhere he was less lucky. At the Old Vic Michael Bentall rejected him on the basis of inadequate diction. Despite Connery's best homebred efforts, then, the fruits of elocution training seemed unsound. But no one who met Connery around this time denied the impact of what Henderson called 'his beautifully perfect figure'.

Scottish actor Ian Bannen's very first meeting with Connery was in the foyer of the Q Theatre. 'I was appearing in an Anouilh play and Sean was waiting to see the director, hoping to land a part. My memory of him is as a towering, huge fellow with hair everywhere – all over his cheeks, huge eyebrows like a squirrel's tail, the lot. He looked formidable, like some sort of gangster. I felt I wouldn't have liked to meet him down some alley.'

The director Lewis Gilbert, who directed Connery's wife-to-be Diane Cilento in *The Admirable Crichton* (1957) and was later to reshape the Bond series with *You Only Live Twice* (1967), recalls early meetings with the struggling actor: 'I can't say there was anything striking about him, no sense that he would one day be a superstar. But he was good-looking, and he had a build that made you look twice.' Michael Caine, who became friendly with Connery in the late fifties, puts a different perspective on Gilbert's comments: 'In my eyes, Sean had it from the word go. You must remember that Lewis was viewing him then from a different level. Lewis was working with established great stars, people like Kenny More and Virginia McKenna. He was very successful and operating on a different plane from most of us. It's significant that he took *any* note of Sean. Sean, to me, had charisma. He looked great, had a great line in chat and, well, look at the way he was built!'

An abhorrence of idleness and a sustained burst of job-hunting in the middle of 1956 broke the ice with decent, if secondary, speaking roles on stage – and paved the path for a first, lukewarm incursion into television. Part-time rep work at the Q led to offers to appear at Oxford as Pentheus opposite Yvonne Mitchell's Agave in *The Bacchae*, and with Jill Bennett in Eugene O'Neill's *Anna Christie*, a play which, in its revival on television some twelve months later, was to assume a special significance in Connery's life. Television parts were found in *The Condemned* and *Epitaph* at the BBC, and as a smalltime hood (serving Bannen's fantasy fears) in an episode of *Dixon of Dock Green*. A BBC floor assistant recalls Connery's 'awe' when rehearsing this early live TV but the pleasant surprise was a singular adroit gracefulness of movement that had him zipping round cluttered sets in no danger of toppling trickily balanced arc lights. No one 'discovered' Connery during this jerky run: critical reviews scarcely mentioned him and the only press coverage worth bragging about was a rather banal interview about the 'South Pacific star' in a home-town paper. Connery didn't mind, though Julie Hamilton probably did. For Connery, the actor Robert Hardy says, 'the joy was always the work'. During the Oxford run of The Bacchae Connery was pleased to boast about 'driving back to London late every night to rehearse The Square Ring for TV in the daytime, and then driving all through Saturday night to play football for the Showbusiness team on Sunday. I didn't feel I was being done out of free time. I was enjoying myself. I believe a lot of people would enjoy themselves going hard at it if they had the kind of work they like and created the kind of surroundings they could respond to.'

By the end of 1956 Connery was in no doubt that he had found exactly the kind of work he liked. But he was less sure of Julie who, in the words of Henderson, had learnt 'the knack of making a nuisance of herself' in Connery's company. The lean time at the beginning of the year taught Connery a lesson about showbiz that crowned the advice Henderson had given and created a very clear pattern for future survival: very little about showbusiness was 'a giggle'; one must study and graft, and one must scrimp and beg and push. Such effort required *all* one's energy. Connery had the advantages of the spiritual strength derived from fighting his way out of the swamp of Fountainbridge, and the physical stamina acquired on building sites. If he could merge his strengths and *push*, he might grow to live out Henderson's vision. But a wife, or a live-in lover, would be a distraction and present problems. Connery had great respect for Julie but, Henderson believed, she began to make demands he found difficult to cope with.

In the spring of '57 Connery was doing well enough in theatre and bit-part television to discharge himself from the dole queue. An agent had even been secured in the person of the zesty young Richard Hatton, then making a good name for himself with the television companies. Connery was building up a few pounds' savings again and signs were good for a new suit or two, maybe even a new motorbike, by summer.

At the BBC, Canadian producer Alvin Rakoff was in pre-production on an American play, Rod Serling's *Requiem for a Heavyweight*, scheduled for live transmission from Studio D of the new Wood Lane Television Centre at 8.30 p.m on 31 March. A variety of top name artistes had been considered for the lead part (boxer Freddie Mills was among those mentioned) before Rakoff settled on Jack Palance, the craggy American star who had featured in the American version on TV and had had a monster hit with the movie, *The Big Knife*, a year before. Ten days before transmission, three before rehearsals, Palance's agents cabled the BBC to cry off: a Hollywood engagement would delay the star, there was nothing they could do. Rakoff grabbed the casting directory and rushed into conference with his assistant Kay Fraser and Drama Chief Michael Barry. With rehearsals set for Monday, 25 March, Rakoff drew up a list of three major actors he thought would fit the bill. He saw each on the Friday, and had not decided on the Saturday morning when, on his way to the BBC, his girlfriend Jacqueline Hill (who starred in the play, and later became his wife) mentioned Connery's name.

Rakoff had used Connery already, engaging him for some three small parts in *The Condemned* the previous year. Connery had originally been assigned one bit-part, that of a soldier, but he was 'so full of ideas, so keen', Rakoff recalls, that his function was extended. On location at Dover Castle Rakoff had given him the part of a soldier who throws a grenade . . . and the bandit who receives it! Later, for studio taping in London, Connery played another small role. Rakoff saw Connery only as a background player and so asked Jacqueline why she thought he of all people might fit this demanding lead role. Jacqueline was to be the 'love interest' in *Requiem* and she replied chirpily that 'every woman would like to watch Connery'. Rakoff went to his office and pondered.

He tossed the idea about and received a generally positive response. People remembered the Scotsman who had been 'interesting' in *Dixon* and had just won himself a little part (with Richard Hatton's help) in a little movie called *No Road Back*.

Rakoff decided to interview Connery afresh.

6

Heavyweight Success

In the summer of 1956 Connery had earned his first few days on a film set, auditioned and employed by second-feature writer-director Montgomery Tully to play near-silent stooge to Alfie Bass's unfortunate villain in *No Road Back*. Korda's old assistant Steven Pallos's Gibraltar Pictures understood exactly the market they were feeding: rattish gangland thrillers facelifted by the appearance of a 'name' American star – in this case Skip Homeier – were always popular Bs no matter how improbable the story or incompetent the cast. In this case Tully's task was made immeasurably easier by a reasonably original storyline (even a credible sub-plot love story) and the crack performances of Margaret Rawlings and Canadian Paul Carpenter.

No Road Back went on circuit release belatedly and was guaranteed oblivion by its rigorous adherence to current convention in conception, style and promotion. Connery understood that fully, as did everyone else involved. For Alfie Bass, the movie was just another exercise in thriller playing; but for Connery it was a memorable first – the break into the rarefied acting life, the cinema, where everything was Big Screen, Big Stars, Big Glamour.* 'I doubt if Sean was paid much,' said Bass, 'because a system was popular then whereby studio chiefs giving breaks to

---

* Connery is known to have done some film extra work, appearing in crowd scenes on location. A crowd part in *Lilacs in the Spring* (1954) was his first screen role.

newcomers smartly drummed down fees. I'd suffered that myself a few years before when I was contracted to Sidney Box. It was very nice and above board, but by the time all sorts of considerations were out of the way one was coming out with pennies. The interesting thing about Sean, though, was his intelligence. We had a lot in common. My background was, in a roundabout way, in cabinet-making too, so we could talk shop easily. At Pinewood, where the film was shot in about six weeks, we shared a dressing-room. Sean liked to natter and it came clear nothing less than "making it" was on. He had great ambitions. And talent. He was competent, he never forgot a line.' Emphasising the impact the eager newcomer had on the movie-weary veteran, Bass elaborated: 'How able was Connery then? Let me say this. I'm known as the shrewdest git in the business. And I would have happily become his agent.'

Connery was relaxed and comfortable on the movie set and, instantly, he saw it as some sort of terminus. The stage, television – they were fine, bristling with challenge. But the movie world was the pinnacle. Stage stars belonged to the toffee-nosed of Edinburgh's West End; movie stars were for Fountainbridge, for everyone. Connery also liked to observe the fuss around Homeier and Carpenter, the big cars at the studio, the smell of wealth wafting from others' dressing-rooms. At the same time, he wasn't so success-obsessed as to be impervious to the side-show offerings. Bass remembered, 'One thing everyone knew about Sean very soon: he wasn't queer.' A couple of days after he started on the film he was befriending young starlets and production assistants. Inevitably, he was asking Bass to vacate the dressing-room at the convenient time. 'He wanted to entertain some bird,' said Bass. 'And a half-hour was all he needed.'

Toronto-born Alvin Rakoff, later to emerge as one of TV's pre-eminent directors of the sixties, had one major credit behind him in the National TV award-winning *Waiting for Gillian* (1955) when he set out to tackle *Requiem for a Heavyweight* in 1957. A thrusting, sure-footed young director, he had a reputation for taking chances, an attitude which did not exactly endear him to some BBC lords but which, whether they liked it or not, produced the results. He had not seen Connery's début in *No Road Back* when they met again at the BBC to discuss the possibilities of his upcoming play. Rakoff remembered Connery as a beefcake boyo. But very quickly he was struck by the actor's new confidence. Rakoff was left in no doubt of Connery's ambitions, nor of the basic intelligence which dressed itself in showy, half-educated patter. He warmed to Connery and cast him, after readings, as the main character in *Requiem*, Mountain McClintock.

The significance of Rakoff's risk in taking Connery, especially in the light of its repercussions for the actor, is easy to miss. In 1957 the BBC was warily pioneering refined TV drama with the newly-formed ITA shambling far behind. But 'format' drama, with its Punch-and-Judy pre-dictability was still dominant, and the focus of change during this era was more concentrated on experiments with film technology, as opposed to variations in casting or drama style. New writers with innovative ideas faced an uphill struggle as did daring directors like Rakoff who were boldly inclined to seek out iconoclastic scripts, even Ameri-can scripts. It often appeared to be a losing battle. In 1957 *The Times* reported that the BBC and ITA 'seeming to despair of obtaining new plays of any value, are relying on alternative sources. For their serious productions the independent networks tend to mount adaptations of estab-lished stage works. The BBC do this rather less often; they regularly present dramatised novels and, having dis-covered the Victorian idiom to be apt for television, return to it again and again.'

The best writers resisted the fail-sale traditionalism and soldiered along the edge of rejection. The groundbreakers in Britain were Elaine Morgan and Iain McCormick and in America (where things were not much better) Paddy Chayefsky and Rod Serling. These writers acknowledged Chayefsky's theory that 'television drama cannot expand in breadth, so it must expand in depth' and that TV writers should concentrate on intimate dramas – 'intimate meaning minutely detailed studies of small moments of life'. Morgan, Serling and the others kept their cherished ideal alive in their plays and passed the problems – technical and commercial – squarely over to the likes of Rakoff.

In undertaking Serling's *Requiem for a Heavyweight* Rakoff knew he had a challenge: a slow-paced tragedy about a fallen boxing star that made no concessions to glossy entertainment and could easily become maudlin if mishandled. There was nothing to be gained and everything to lose in livening up the production with slick camerawork and fast scene-changes, so Rakoff grew to believe success depended on the workings of a close-knit, true-to-life acting team. The weary old manager (George Margo) must have desperation in his face and manners, the thick-ear boxer, Connery, must move, look and think like a down-and-out with hopes. Rakoff made *Requiem* in his unconventional casting. His on-the-night direction was minimal, and brilliantly understated even at that.

At rehearsals on the Saturday afternoon and Sunday (from 11 a.m. onwards) everyone felt a quality production was on the cards. Warren Mitchell and Fred Johnson as trainer and ring doctor were powerfully good and Connery's relaxation was 'quite remarkable'. He was not intimidated by the centrality of his role, or the huge amount of lines, nor did he seem in any way conscious of his mistakes. He blundered and was corrected: it was as simply professional as that. Rakoff was more sure than ever he had talent. But others considered Connery a bit slow, too raw. Michael Barry, the much-liked Drama Chief, watched one rehearsal and was frankly disappointed; he didn't think Connery 'had it'. 'Far as I was concerned,' says Rakoff, 'what he didn't have could be fixed by clever camerawork, switching from one camera to the other at the right time and so on.'

There were no hitches or tantrums – then the big night came. Rakoff was in his control box, readying himself for transmission time, with the actors simmering on the floor. Just seconds before 8.30 p.m. a gaggle of grey-suited BBC men stormed in, led by Michael Barry. 'They looked like

Mafia,' Rakoff recounts, 'and I didn't know what the hell was going on. I asked Michael, but he hushed me and before we knew it we were rolling, the show was "on". Everything cruised smoothly: I missed only one shot, and that was where Fred Johnson was stitching some of Sean's facial cuts. I wanted a close-up, but Fred's hands were shaking so bad I couldn't do it. The pressures of live TV took their toll on everyone.' Half-way through the ninety-minute play Rakoff found a quiet time to whisper the question again to Michael Barry: what were the grim-faced BBC execs doing scattered round the studio? Barry explained tensely: studio electricians were threatening strike action and there were fears the plugs would be, literally, pulled. 'The junior executives had agreed to stand by to push the plugs back in. Half the nation was watching us. The show *had* to go on.'

At home in Fountainbridge Joe, Effie, Neil and a neighbour friend from down the hall, Mrs Pearson, watched on Joe's new 17-inch TV set. It was the first time any of the family had seen Tommy on screen. Neil, an impressionable eighteen-year-old, drank in every growling syllable of the drama and, he says, Effie was moved close to ears. When the play ended Joe seemed lost for words. The best he could manage was, 'By heavens, that was smashing.'

Viewers across the country and the critics, it soon emerged, unanimously agreed with Joe's assessment. BBC Drama received appreciative letters and the top journals afforded broad space to Connery's performance. As Mountain McClintock, Connery portrayed the unbeaten hero of 111 fights who, because of eye damage, is ordered out of boxing for good. A manager mercilessly hounded by creditors tries to trade on his name by urging him into show wrestling, finally humiliating the fallen fighter and losing his loyalty by asking him to appear as a clown wearing a coonskin cap. J.C. Trewin in the *Listener* slavishly, mockingly, recorded the dialogue's propensity towards repetition. 'At first I thought I might take the count ignominiously in the first minute,' he wrote. But those who, like him, hung in 'were grateful for . . . the oddly wistful performance of Sean Connery as the man who was once

69

almost heavyweight champion of the world . . . too modest, too bewildered, and too naturally kind to be a connoisseur of the cauliflower ear.' Trewin was less kind to Serling: 'This is neither a fragrant little play nor a tribute to the noble art. . . . But its producer, Alvin Rakoff, let it have every chance, and the dramatist ought to go down on his knees to Sean Connery.'

In the *Evening Standard* the Boulting brothers lavished praise on Rakoff, Connery, the concept. *The Times*, outrageously, thought Connery 'physically miscast as the fighter', but praised 'a shambling and inarticulate charm that almost made the love affair (with Jacqueline Hill) credible'. Six months later *The Times* was still warmly recalling *Requiem*. In a well-publicised article about the problems plaguing modern TV drama Iain McCormick had pointed a finger of blame at English acting. Stage actors, he claimed, lacked the capacity to underplay correctly for television. 'This,' *The Times* countered, 'is overstated; the recent BBC production of Mr Rod Serling's *Requiem for a Heavyweight*, to take only one example, displayed ensemble acting of precisely the type Mr McCormick recommends.'

Before leaving Television Centre on that wet Sunday night Connery knew he had pulled off a fine coup: he did not need Julie or any of his friends to tell him. Rakoff was pleased – 'but drained, as everyone was after such a complicated, multi-set live play' – and the small technical crew impressed enough to extend genuine congratulations. Usually the post-transmission knees-up took place in the nearby Black Prince pub but that night, because everyone was dizzy with excitement, a small party in one of the dressing-rooms sufficed. 'Then,' Rakoff says, 'everybody went off into the night and caught their bus. It was the norm to take a long lie-in the following morning, to recover. I remember I didn't come alive till midday, then I bussed back to the Beeb. I read the evening papers with the glowing tributes on the bus. Later on, Sean phoned me with a thanks.'

The Monday review in *The Times* highlighted for Rakoff

exactly what he believed was the real triumph of *Requiem*: the play differed from the usual Serling/Chayefsky in that the central character was 'intrinsically dramatic'. This was the power, Rakoff agreed, and his real achievement with the production lay in casting Connery who, in the ignorance of his inexperience, interpreted 'intrinsically dramatic' as classically heroic, mimicking every muscular dab he had seen at the Blue Halls, and overlaying the whole with a smattering of the intellectual whimsy Henderson had pushed on him. Arguably in *Requiem* Connery first struck the golden vein of hero portrayal that would eventually lead to his colossal success as James Bond.

At the one-room flat in Brondesbury Villas, Kilburn – probably arranged by Julie – where Connery was now living, celebrations after *Requiem* were no grander than a hot stew, Connery's favourite meal (with lots of tomato flavouring) and a glass of beer. The pay cheque for the play was £25, but that was to represent the tip of the iceberg in terms of material pay-off. The very day after transmission, according to Connery, the film companies started their pursuit of him. 'Not unusual,' says Rakoff. 'British films, though they didn't realise it then, were giving their dying gasps. Movie people watched TV and culled whatever of quality they could from it. I knew what the direction of Sean's career after *Requiem* would be. I told Richard [Hatton] so. Rank was the first on the phone to Hatton, suggesting a long-term contract.' Connery impulsively passed the message along that he would 'think it over': terms were vague and complex and by now, balancing what he had learnt from co-workers like Alfie Bass, he was wary of involved contracts. There were a few independent enquiries, up-and-coming producers with their own companies. And, best of all, the international major, Twentieth Century-Fox, then moving well enough, was making overtures. But Connery hedged. Already, as a result of *No Road Back*, he had engagements on two other movies at Pinewood and Beaconsfield, both bit-parts. So there was no urgent need to dash into any contractual trap. Connery suddenly wanted breathing space, time to meditate and orientate himself. At Brondesbury Villas the people he shared the house with recorded his cool and mature reaction to the exciting shock waves of *Requiem*. No one was surprised when he took time off to go home, with Julie, to Edinburgh.

At this key time in his career, when choosing the right avenue to take caused much suppressed concern, Julie's demands overreached. In Fountainbridge he introduced her happily, but the confrontation that others, like Henderson, foresaw developed quickly in what must have been, for Julie too, an unusually strained environment. The incident that ended the love affair concerned what Neil called the Scottish 'masculine prerogative' – a jar in the local pub. The family was gathered round the fire in the butt-and-ben, with Julie chatting to Effie, when Connery silently gestured to Neil his desire for a drink. Both brothers slipped quietly away, crossed to the Fountain Bar and ordered their pints. 'We had no sooner settled ourselves with a drink apiece,' Neil said, 'than Sean's girlfriend put in an appearance.' Julie was insulted at being left behind and let Connery know it. There was a row and 'that did it . . . that was another of Sean's romances that died the death'.

To most, it seems, Connery and Julie outgrew each other. Over the year and a half of their friendship, as they drew closer, so they recognised the facets of each other's lives that did not match their needs. If there was any anger or sense of failure at the break-up, it was no more than tepid emotion. They parted, and Julie went back to her thriving London life and Connery to his chances.

Connery's second movie role, in Cy Endfield's *Hell Drivers*, at Pinewood, gave him no chance to shine, though the film was above average in every way. The prolific and action-minded writer John Kruse, who later went on to inject such vitality into the television 'Saint' series – and feed Leslie Charteris some ideas – devised the simple story of a road haulage company whose crooked manager forces aggressive competition on its lorry-driving staff to the point where personality conflicts flare and murderous emotions grow. Connery played Johnny, one of a half-dozen loud-mouth blackguard drivers who race along death-trap roads. Connery had no more than ten lines, mostly thrown over Sidney James's (as another driver) shoulder, but he looked convincing in scenes where he could easily have half-tried – particularly his longest scene, where the truckers enjoy a boisterous night off at a dance-café and an all-out fist-fight, with Connery to the fore, breaks out.

Rank distributed *Hell Drivers* through the Gaumont chain of cinemas and, while it played to moderately good business, it failed to win the kind of recognition director Endfield had hoped for. Within the production business, the film was admired for its racy pace and good photography by Geoffrey Unsworth, a cinematographer bound for glory with classics like *2001: A Space Odyssey* (1969). Chastened but not deterred by his first major in Britain (he had directed second-features in America). Endfield went on to a few slicker and more generally successful films, notably *Zulu* (1963), considering *Hell Drivers* to have been an excellent market gauge that pointed him away from gritty thrillers.

Side-by-side with Endfield's film, Connery did a few hours on *Time Lock* for the Gerald Thomas–Peter Rogers director-producer team, then just months away from *Carry on Sergeant* and the beginning of the outstandingly popular comedy series which would, in its quiet way, be the only consistent rival to Bond during the sixties. Made at Beaconsfield Studios, *Time Lock* concerned the nail-biting attempts to rescue a six-year-old boy accidentally trapped in a Canadian bank vault with a time-device lock set to spring days hence, after the weekend holiday. Connery was last on the cast credits, appearing as '2nd Welder', his smallest film part to date, and his screen impact was negligible. But *Time Lock* was a good vehicle, and association with it helped.

Before *Hell Drivers* or *Time Lock* had made their appearance in the late summer of 1957 Connery had hammered out a contract deal, under Hatton's guidance, with Twentieth Century-Fox. The bind was long-term but

Connery had reason to be optimistic: Fox, above most, held a high profile in international production and had ambitious projects on the go in Britain and the States throughout '57. Connery had no reason to believe they would do anything other than use him – and promote him hard to get a return for their hefty investment. And the Fox investment was considerable. By 1958 Ian Bannen reckons, Connery was 'taking in £120 a week from that contract, but he was doing nothing . . . in today's terms you're talking about a contract actor sitting back and taking in, say, a thousand a week.' At Brondesbury Villas and among his small circle of not-too-intimate friends Connery's initial reaction to the Fox signing was described as 'silent delight'. His landlady recalled, 'Any other actor would have been delirious at the sudden upsurge in his fortunes, but not Sean. He took the whole thing very calmly. He did not even celebrate.'

The silent delight hinged on sudden wealth: Connery did not advertise it loudly but his professional friends were aware of the deep satisfaction triggered by real financial security at last. Counter to that, however, was a troubling awareness, which seemed to blossom very swiftly, that Fox, in spite of its outlay, in spite of *Requiem* and all that bit-part work, was not about to fling its neophyte 'star' into any star dressing-rooms. There were a few interviews, an audition or two with important directors, even talk of detailing Connery opposite Ingrid Bergman in *The Inn of the Sixth Happiness*, a part given eventually to Curt Jurgens. Connery was disgruntled. He wanted to work, he wanted to prove himself, even try himself. It was then, he complained, he suffered his 'too' period. 'For a while I was *too* big, or *too* square . . . whatever. I just couldn't fit the parts they wanted to fill.' One part he did fit: director Terence Young was casting *Action of the Tiger* for fledgling producer Kenneth Harper's company, to be released through MGM. Through contacts Connery offered himself for a role and was given the part of Mike, a dishevelled ship's mate whose most taxing pitch is a pass at sexy Martine Carol. Connery travelled to Spain for brief shooting in early summer.

The story was, at least, geographically ambitious. Van Johnson played Carson, a philanthropic mercenary, persuaded by Carol to help her sneak her political prisoner brother out of Communist Albania. Johnson fumbles through a tangled skein of misadventures before finally escaping to Greece with Tracy (Carol), the brother and a string of refugee children in tow. Young made a game effort at direction but the screenplay was never right and Johnson coasted as though wearily anticipating the kind of critical stick the humdrum aspects of the yarn would give rise to. The best parts of *Action of the Tiger* revolved around the displaced children and feckless bandits; indeed some of the very minor playing was exemplary. But, as so many reviewers were to note, the cinema had not quite got to grips with the Cold War and efforts like these to tell political parables usually foundered in caricature. In an important sense, though, *Action* is interesting as an extravagant, if not necessarily original, cinematic blueprint of anti-communist 'entertainment' propaganda. In the spirit of detente the later James Bond movies, from *You Only Live Twice* onwards, veered away from contentious East–West relations, but the early films, especially *From Russia With Love* and, more circumspectly, *Goldfinger*, based themselves on the Cold War tensions and fears. In this regard, *Action of the Tiger* is a distant cousin of Bond – a dry run, if you like, at spiked political thrillers.

To director Terence Young's thinking, he had personally botched the movie. Never a man to show his weaknesses on set, he kept a brave face while filming and was perhaps the most excitedly animate creature within a mile of the location. Privately he expressed his doubts and later, in many interviews, he confessed it had been 'a pretty awful film'.

Connery meanwhile, displayed his complete (and understandable) lack of discernment in movie matters by suggesting to friends and others his belief that he was onto something good. Alvin Rakoff, on reflection, is not at all surprised by this: Connery, in his eye, was 'rough-hewn, with little understanding of how the industry operates'. As the film neared completion Connery approached Young, speculating on the likely success of the movie. The role had been his biggest so far for cinema and he clearly had confused visions of another *Requiem*-like hit. 'Sean equated the foreign locations, big stars [Johnson was the highest-paid performer he had yet worked with], and the recognised director with success,' says Ian Bannen. 'He definitely considered this movie to be important.' Young was sympathetic towards the actor's naive expectations. 'He came to me and said in that very Scots accent of his, "Sir, am I going to be a success in this?"' Aware already that he had irredeemably 'mucked it up', Young was blunt: 'No,' he told Connery, 'but keep on swimming. Just keep at it and I'll make it up to you.'

7

Another Place Called Hollywood

The 'glamour' of success that interested Connery in a secondary sideline kind of way became a very palpable reality in the middle of 1957 when Lana Turner walked into his life. The Sweater Queen of MGM had just been fired after eighteen years with the studio and her career was nosediving. Paramount, never one to miss a bargain, picked her up cheaply and found the ideal vehicle for her, a fire-and-ice love drama that embraced both her sophisticated acting style and her reputation as a man-eater. Turner's love life was, to say the least, chequered. Her five marriages were incident-filled, her romances – with Fernando Lamas, Sinatra, Howard Hughes, gangster Mickey Cohen – legendary. Tyrone Power, everyone knew, was her truest love but Lana's thirst for varied male company was unquenchable. In the spring of '57, after the break-up of her marriage to 'Tarzan' Lex Barker, Johnny Stompanato, formerly Cohen's bodyguard, entered her life.

Stompanato, according to writer-director Kenneth Anger, had been in big demand from certain prominent film ladies on account of his own 'prominent endowment which had earned him the sobriquet "Oscar".' Stompanato was a harsh and arrogant lover but Turner, it was widely reported, craved excitement and wasn't averse to being knocked around a bit. She had been thrown downstairs by one husband, struck in public by another, drenched in champagne at Ciro's by another. Stompanato's violence satisfied her needs and when they separated for her trip to Britain to make the Paramount movie *Another Time, Another Place*, her love letters home made explicit her yearnings for his rough handling.

Though Fox was profiting nicely with films like *The King and I* and the seemingly endless Monroe moneyspinners, no one had yet come up with a suitable niche for their beefy new contract player, Connery. 'One of his main problems,' a Fox producer recalls, 'was that damned accent. Sometimes it seemed tolerable, but when he speeded up, like all Scotsmen, you couldn't interpret the babble.' Hatton and Connery kept the pressure up and finally Connery was auditioned for the Paramount picture. Turner had co-star approval and she watched Connery's test, and liked him. In build and looks, many noted, Connery and Stompanato were not a million miles apart. Fox made the formal settlement for the loan to Paramount and Connery had his first major Big Screen part, in an incredible stroke of luck, his friends thought, featuring opposite and making love to a Hollywood goddess.

Turner's initial personal response to Connery was favourable, though it was reported he had caused her some embarrassment by picking her up for an early social date on his motor-scooter, clad in T-shirt and slacks while she was in formal fur and jewels. It was, the tabloids reported, something of a fiasco . . . 'but they got into her car, or at least one she'd managed to commandeer, and things went along all right.' Rumours circulated very fast that romance was in the air. Unquestionably Connery did date Turner and told friends he liked her and that her professional advice was helpful. At that time there was no special woman in his life, but he certainly wasn't at a loose end and, according to Ian Bannen, most of his energies were absorbed by the small mews house in North London he had bought and was beginning to renovate, and by the nightmare atmosphere on the set at MGM's Borehamwood Studio. 'Sean was never anyone's fool,' said Alfie Bass. 'If he appreciated Turner's company it still didn't divert him from what that golden opportunity was all about. And it was not all plain sailing.'

'The script wasn't entirely satisfactory,' Connery said, 'and they were rewriting as they were shooting. So they started with the end first, and I was dead at the end . . . so by the time they led up to me I was a picture on the piano. The movie wasn't very good. It was beautifully lit by Jack Hildyard, but dreadfully directed by Lewis Allen.'

In fairness, Allen was working with a tricky story – a movie that divided neatly in two, the unbalanced halves seeming to belong to different genres. Connery had fourth billing, playing Mark, the dashing BBC war correspondent who seduces American newspaperwoman Sara Scott (Turner) in London in 1944. Their brief affair is passionate, then Mark is killed flying to Rome to cover the German surrender in Italy. Devastated by the news, Sara is hospitalised and on her release makes a pilgrimage to Mark's hometown in Cornwall. Pursued by her devoted boss (Barry Sullivan), she evades him and makes friends with a Cornish woman (Glynis Johns) whom she discovers to be Mark's wife. The shock of discovering that Mark was married and has a son, and Sara's attempts to share the wife's memories and grief make up the latter part of the movie – a turgid, at times exhausting 50-odd minutes. In contrast, the first half – where Connery hides behind sandbags reporting unexploded buzz-bombs and wriggles in and out of bed-like couches with Turner – is nimble and, with Sidney James's American-accented roguery pointing up the nonsense, fun to watch.

Taking into account the chronology of shooting, it seems Allen perked up as he went along. Then again, the chemistry between Turner and Connery (who vanishes entirely after the first half-hour) might be the secret. At any rate, taken as a whole, the film is neither *Peyton Place* (1958) nor *Imitation of Life* (1959) – both Turner hits-to-come – though it vacillates tantalisingly between the types.

As shooting advanced and Connery's friendship with Turner deepened, out of the blue Stompanato arrived in Britain. Turner fixed a house for him in west London but friction swiftly arose between them. More than once Stompanato arrived unannounced at MGM studios, frequently insisting on observing the love scenes between Connery and his co-star, to the obvious chagrin of Allen and Turner. 'It doesn't take imagination to understand Stompanato's rage,' Alfie Bass commented. 'He'd been in Hollywood and around film people long enough to know when make-believe is make-believe. But he knew Sean and Lana were getting too close for comfort.' Old friends of Connery's broadly hint that the friendship did eventually bloom into an impassioned affair. Tommy had Hollywood incarnate in his arms and he did with it what he did most effortlessly – he made love. His intention wasn't the cold calculation of a nepotistic leg-up, rather the idea of proving something to himself; rough-hewn and all, as he may still appear, he was capable of slotting sweetly into the star world. He could cope with the work hassles, and the intellectual demands – and he could cope with the capital egos too.

Kenneth Anger in his *Hollywood Babylon* suggests that Stompanato outranked Connery in giving Turner the kind of treatment she wanted. He pushed her hard, says Anger, warning her, 'When I say HOP, you'll hop! When I say JUMP, you'll jump! I'll mutilate you, I'll hurt you so you'll have to hide for ever.' Anger describes Stompanato's arrival on the set, brandishing a gun, ordering Connery to 'Stay away from Lana'. 'Connery decked him,' says Anger, and the studio, with a little help from Scotland Yard, had Stompanato put out of England.

Though Connery was fond of Turner – 'a lovely lady,' he remembered twenty years later – he was relieved when the film ended and she flew to Mexico for a reunion with the gangster boyfriend. The publicity he had gained while co-starring was welcome but he was personally depressed by the movie. His professional associates had told him this was the *key* film, the one that would get wide distribution in the US and could make his name overnight, but he knew before he saw the release print that everyone had, in the words of a technician, 'blown it'. 'Sean is not a patient man when it comes to incompetence or stupidity,' says director

Richard Lester – and in the case of *Another Time, Another Place* he was annoyed that rich potential had been crippled. The script, Turner, possibly Connery himself in his newness to star playing, were contributive factors, but Lewis Allen took the brunt of Connery's blame.

At Wavel Mews in north London where Connery had his new home – a spacious three-room affair above a huge garage that he later converted into a sitting-room – he defused his disappointments by embarking once again on a strenuous get-fit programme. It served a dual purpose: it helped work off the needling frustration and it reminded him of home, of adolescent pleasures from a life that seemed rosier from afar. Ian Bannen was as close as anyone to Connery during this period and, while he too was into weight-training, he saw himself as 'a total amateur' compared with Connery. 'He had all the equipment, the weights and expanders and bars, and he was deadly earnest about it. I spent quite a bit of time at the house; very ordered and pleasant it was – that was Sean's way, he liked things tidy – but sometimes it was like a gym!' Despite his sizeable weekly earnings from Fox and his admiration for the movie glamour-world, Connery still favoured a style of living that was not far from frugality. 'He went around on this motorbike,' says Bannen, 'which remains in my memory only because he was always falling off. Didn't seem he could go down a bloody road without hitting some tree or something.' He ate simply too, confining his lavish sprees – which in themselves were never extreme – to occasional weekend binges. Michael Caine, whom Connery had met for the first time on *Requiem* where Caine was a walk-on extra, was himself struggling at this time, with only tenth billing on the limp *How To Murder a Rich Uncle* (1957) to boast about. 'It was hard and worrying obviously,' Caine says, 'but Sean never showed any weakness. He had a star temperament, he knew what he was about.'

During the decidedly grim time of *Another Time, Another Place* Connery did not despair because, in his own simple explanation, 'I was eating regularly.' Others from cosier backgrounds might have expressed alarm at the failure, but Connery, outwardly anyway, kept his cool. He had had two big non-starter flops so, to rekindle his sense of purpose, he turned back to beavering at television.

His most exceptional part came in August 1957 in the ATV Playhouse production of the Pulitzer Prize-winning *Anna Christie*, the explosive O'Neill play that had fared so well at the Oxford Playhouse (and other venues) the year before. The role of the prostitute struggling for redemption, haunted by the sea, was given by producer Philip Saville to a Big Screen actress, relatively new to TV but very able, the ash-blonde Diane Cilento. Connery portrayed her lover. A taxing and wordy play, *Anna Christie* required extensive rehearsal to establish the proper rapport between the major characters. Since Connery had the upper hand of familiarity with the work, he suggested to Cilento they rehearse after hours, in their free time. Cilento was married to Italian writer Andre Volpe and had a baby daughter Giovanna, but the couple's living arrangements were loose; friends suggest they were on the point of separation even then. So Connery was invited to Cilento's flat, where work commenced.

Two more different people, socially and academically, it would be difficult to find – and yet temperamentally they had a lot in common. Cilento was from the top of the social ladder, a 24-year-old multi-linguist whose deep love was for writing. Her Italian-born father, Raphael Cilento, settled in Queensland, Australia, since long before Diane was born, had been honoured with a knighthood for his services to medicine; Phyllis, Lady Cilento, her mother, possessed a bright artistic flair and was herself by profession a physician. Diane's early life in Queensland was one of luxury, but at fifteen a gypsy spirit akin to Connery's led her to New York where she started drama studies. Later, studying at RADA in London, she rejected her parents' support allowances and earned her own way working in a wine shop and, for a spell, at a circus. Her first film part was in 1952. Four years later she was high on the billing working with director Lewis Gilbert, and by the time she met Connery she was being described in the popular press, rather mindlessly, as 'a high IQ sex kitten'.

Robert Henderson remembered her as 'a tough, independent little cookie'. Her crusty core, combined with fierce single-mindedness, appealed to Connery and he later admitted that, from the beginning, 'She swept me off my feet.'

Initially Cilento's reaction to Connery was unexciting. Quite apart from the shadows of her marital ties she found him a jagged-edged personality, too free with a lashing critical tongue and, beyond the passionate range of the character he was rehearsing, a shade heartless. 'My first opinion of him,' she said, 'was that he had a terrific chip on his shoulder. He'd come to my place and stretch out on the floor. I felt he was trying to see if he could make me angry, so I purposely didn't react. Finally I realised he had no ulterior motives, that he was just being himself.' An actor friend who knew both paints a different picture: 'Maybe he didn't admit it to himself – and he could be stubborn, so that wouldn't surprise me – but Sean was in awe of assured actors and actresses. Lana, Diane – he saw them as some sort of challenge to his ego as women. They were the best any man could get, so he wanted them for that reason. But, as well, there was this need to assert his talents against theirs. In those circumstances Diane considered him – probably rightly – to be overweening.'

But Cilento thawed, and a close friendship sprung out of *Anna Christie*. Artistically the play was a success, not exactly *Requiem* league but certainly, to Connery's mind, the best thing he had done in half a year. He was pepped up, not only by the quality of the results but also by the nature of this new relationship. Cilento, he told colleagues, was like no one he had yet met in the business. In effect, he was saying she treated him – as she did – with the kind of respect he believed was an artist's due. Raw and all as most considered him, she, the experienced movie actress, had relied heavily on his support during the play. He was flattered, but enthralled too by her obvious competence, her self-possesion, her iridescent intelligence. They dined together, and enjoyed many social evenings and she encouraged him to talk about his fears and ambitions within the business. 'Diane was his first real confidante in the industry,' Ian Bannen says. 'Up till then, with the exception of Hatton, he kept troubles to himself.'

Cilento pushed Connery towards formal dramatic training. He enrolled, alongside her, in Yat Malmgeren's 'Movement' school – an extraordinarly pointless exercise, Robert Henderson believed, because, 'even from *South Pacific* days Sean's grace in movement was amazingly good.' Malmgeren, a Swede, was not an actor but a former dancer in the Kurt Jooss Ballet Company. 'He taught the study of action – attitudes and drives,' Connery said. 'It was based on the concepts of time and motion evolved by the Hungarian dancer Rudolf von Laban . . . I used to go there three times a week, doing theory. We learnt a cohesive terminology that applied to the whole group, so that there was no problem of communication as there so often is with expressions that mean one thing to one person and another to somebody else. It was a remarkable period for me. It proved that with the proper exercises you can reshape your physical structure. Nothing like the weight-lifting exercises I'd done, but attacking yourself from within, from the head through to the base of the spine – to awaken yourself physically, completely, so that you become a much better tuned instrument.'

Under Cilento's influence he read more widely, extending himself to the fullest with Stanislavsky and the Shakespeare he hadn't covered during the last touring months of *South Pacific*. For a time, with friends, the tone of his conversations changed: he became 'heavyweight' and seemed to disdain the philistinism that attended commercial movie-making. There was nothing pretentious about this 'new Sean'. On the contrary, having suffered disillusionment in his first run of movies, he was sensibly reassessing the requirements of theatre and arty TV, the media he was, conceivably, best suited for.

Early in 1958 he concentrated his energies on renovating

his home and resumed small theatre work, but the bitterness of cramped opportunity returned. Fox's cash was nice, but there seemed something indecent about earning ten times what Joe was pulling back home for doing no more than sitting by a phone. Then, out of the gloom, there was sudden opportunity. A casting crew from Walt Disney studios in Hollywood touring the British Isles in preparation for a major feature saw his Paramount movie, auditioned him and, with Fox's agreement, offered a contract for *Darby O'Gill and the Little People*, to commence shooting at the Burbank Disney Studios in May.

Connery was ecstatic. Stanislavsky wasn't forgotten, but for the moment he was pushed aside. Robert Henderson recalled: 'I was appearing at the Coliseum in *Damn Yankees* and I wanted to see *Madame Butterfly*, a new production of the opera, which was opening at Covent Garden. I couldn't get along at night, so I was given permission to attend dress rehearsal in the afternoon. I'd just arrived when a phone call came through to the box office and it was Sean saying, "Robert, I've got to see you right away. I've been offered the chance to go to Hollywood for a Disney and I want to know I'm doing the right thing." I told him a Disney movie was good for anyone, and I suggested he come right over to the theatre if he wanted a chat so desperately. About a half-hour later he arrived and I came out to the lobby just as the marvellous first act climax was on . . . We had our talk and he decided himself happily on taking the Disney offer.' Even in his heady glee, Henderson reflects, Connery showed that 'specialness, the divine curiosity that distinguished him from the bunch'. Overhearing the strains of *Madame Butterfly* as they discussed Hollywood, Connery suddenly asked, 'What's that?' 'Well, that's the next step to becoming a powerful actor,' Henderson replied. 'That's grand opera, Sean. You're earning a little money now. So why don't you buy a ticket and go see some, learn about it?' Connery did, to Henderson's eternal joy. 'Soon,' Henderson said, 'he was able to tell me about Maria Callas and the whole business. That encapsulated Sean's attitude. He didn't just want to make it big in Hollywood or wherever – he wanted to learn too, he wanted to be big and good.'

While Connery was packing his bags for Hollywood and preparing to hand over his house to Ian Bannen for the duration, *Another Time, Another Place* opened, inevitably, to terrible notices. British papers revelled in the fiercest criticism, tagging it melodramatic, confected, unreal rubbish played 'without style or enthusiasm' (*Monthly Film Bulletin*). By the time it opened in America Turner was in trouble. On 4 April 1958 Cheryl, fourteen-year-old daughter of Lana and in-between husband Steve Crane, fatally stabbed Stompanato, having eavesdropped on a furious row in which the gangster seriously threatened to 'cut up' Turner.

Cheryl was charged and brought to trial, with Turner as a defence witness. As it turned out, a jury which retired for only twenty minutes pardoned Cheryl by finding her guilty only of justifiable homicide. But for the months the case held public interest Turner was pilloried, her scarlet past raked over and over. The moral majority in the States saw to it that none of this new-found notoriety helped *Another Time, Another Place*. Box-office takings were bad and reviews across the country unsympathetic. Connery's first big chance to win American attention, which he reckoned would fail anyway, was largely buried under an avalanche of dirty linen. The esteemed Bosley Crowther in the *New York Times* tore the picture to shreds, stating it was 'a long way from making any contact with interests that might serve to entertain . . . This one was made in England . . . evidently as a part of the current Go-Home-Yank plan.' A few critics did notice Connery. One New York writer observed, 'The BBC commentator is played by a newcomer to films called Sean Connery who will not, I guess, grow old in the industry.'

For all the wounding flak, Connery arrived in Hollywood in a mood of optimism – not quite childishly wide-eyed but, in the words of Henderson, 'zinging with drive'. 'Disney was a benevolent despot,' says Michael O'Herlihy, technical adviser and dialogue coach on *Darby O'Gill and the*

Little People, 'but he was a fine boss and many people, like myself, were fortunate in getting a break from him. Once he took to you, you were his for life. He took a fatherly interest in everything his employees did. After *Darby* I did a spell with Warner Brothers. I did a long run on *77 Sunset Strip*, and broke into directing. In '66 Walt gave me my first chance at a feature – *The Fighting Prince of Donegal* – and I was quite amazed that he'd seen *everything* I'd done in the intervening years. He was a very caring, charming man, and I think he quite liked Sean . . . but in an average kind of way.'

The working atmosphere at Disney Burbank studios cheered Connery immensely. The 'ensemble' spirit of the acting team – Janet Munro, Kieron Moore, Albert Sharpe, Estelle Winwood – relaxed him, recalling rep and *Requiem* and all the successful things he had done; the weather was superb; the Californian girls a revelation. Everything was shot within the studios, the Irish backgrounds matted in. Disney visited the set every day, chatted with Connery about his Scottish life and theatre experience, even gave him a tip or two. For a first exposure to the Hollywood system, Connery had fallen on his feet. 'I suppose he, like so many, had a vision of a licentious, crazy holiday camp governed by demigods,' says co-star Kieron Moore, 'but in fact Hollywood was a duty-conscious business town. People went to bed early and rose early. There was work to be done and the standards were high. It was a town of professionals; Disney was the most professional, and Sean admired that.' The problems of a rather dull, conventional director were leavened by Disney's charm, and the professionalism and jollity of the group sharing lodgings at the Burbank motel actor Jimmy O'Dea had christened 'Fatima Mansions', after a slum estate in Dublin. Robert Stevenson was an Englishman with an all-American outlook, directing a bog-Irish fairy story (the 'little people' were, of course leprechauns), largely from story-board, picture sketches of scenes as opposed to written script. 'He wasn't, let's say, bursting with imagination,' Kieron Moore skirts deftly. O'Herlihy is more to the point: 'Stevenson didn't talk to actors, that was his trouble.'

Connery, however, bore up well. From his experience with Lewis Allen he had learnt the trick of conserving energies while bumbling directors wrestled with themselves. Privately he felt the story was good and his third billing part afforded him the chance to drift through a variety of light but interesting emotions. In the film he plays Michael McBride, prospective lover of Katie (Munro), daughter of the deposed caretaker of a massive estate, Darby O'Gill (Sharpe). Fearful of his daughter's standing in the community because he has lost the estate job, Darby connives with the King of the Little People (Jimmy O'Dea) whom he has captured to ensure that McBride, who will take over as caretaker, falls in love with and marries Katie. Pony Sugrue (Moore) contests McBride's job and love for Katie, but is eventually outdone in a spectacular fight scene. As children's entertainment it was Disney at his near-best and what script did exist (written by Lawrence Edward Watkins) was, Connery thought, beautifully judged. He even had an opportunity to sing – the first time since *South Pacific* – and though Stevenson contemplated dubbing him, his rendition of 'Pretty Irish Girl' was left on the soundtrack.*

Ironically, the aspect of the film's shoot which vexed most of the leading actors didn't perturb Connery at all. Stevenson's most aggravating habit was a penchant for 'the buckshot theory' whereby eighteen to twenty takes were called before a selection of the best one or two for printing was made. In the heat of the Californian sun Irish tempers grew distressingly short. 'It was tiring for the actors,' O'Herlihy says. 'There were make-up problems and continuity and some of the actors were floored by the time a scene was declared in the can.'

---

* Connery's only singing record, *Pretty Irish Girl* (Top Rank JAR163) was released in Britain in April 1959. On the disc he duets with Janet Munro. The flip of the disc is 'The Bally McQuilty Band'. Connery described the experience: 'Janet went out and got a bottle of vodka, came back and we had two very large vodkas, and they gave us the [music] sheet . . .'
    Ruby Murray and Brendan O'Dowda cut a cover version on Columbia records that was more successful.

In the evenings the tradition of rueful Irish revelry was maintained in 'wakes' at Albert Sharpe's favourite pub, the Skid Lid. 'Sean was brave all day,' says O'Herlihy, 'then he sank a few at night – like myself. I won't say I ever saw him flattened, but he had fun.'

Well aware of the rumpus surrounding former flame Lana Turner, Connery, without advice, made no effort to contact her. With a similar prudence she avoided him, but a fair amount of muffled gossip circulated on the set during June and July. 'Sean never spoke of Lana,' O'Herlihy says, 'and as far as I was concerned he was just another contented bachelor in the best town on earth for bachelors to live in.' With a few white lies and his British motorcycle licence, Connery managed to rent a flashy American car. He learnt to drive around Burbank and took his casual dates for nerve-shredding spins. Once, on a wall on Sunset Boulevard, he was shown the scars of what was patently gunfire. He asked about them and was told that someone had tried to assassinate Mickey Cohen, firing from a passing car. Knowing Cohen to be a former lover of Turner's and cognisant of the spread of rumours about his London affair with her and the row at Borehamwood with Stompanato, ex-guard of Cohen's, Connery was shocked. 'He didn't have the sense to be alarmed,' an actor friend says, 'until somebody who knew Turner and understood the shady subterranean life of Hollywood phoned him up and spelt out the dangers.' In his calm indifference to locale, the caller suggested, Connery was offering himself as a sacrificial sitting duck. Mickey Cohen, still faithful to Stompanato's memory, wanted to see blood spilled. Connery saw the light: 'He was out for revenge. Apparently he didn't believe that Cheryl had killed Stompanato. He thought the killing had been engineered in some other way. My pal warned me: "You don't know how these boys work out here. They play for real. Anyone who had any association with Lana Turner and Stompanato in London would be wise to get out of the way."'

Towards the end of the fifteen weeks of Disney, Connery moved out to lodgings in San Fernando Valley, several miles safe from Hollywood. 'Disney himself must have known about the rumours,' Michael O'Herlihy says. 'I'm not saying Sean had any charges of misconduct to answer, but Walt Disney had an image to preserve. Let's put it this way: Disney would no more have employed Lana than Mickey Cohen – right?' Whatever troublesome gossip persisted, Connery evidently managed to quash it discreetly and to maintain Disney's approval.

Complicated effects and process work remained. 'A helluva job,' O'Herlihy says, 'superimposing the "little people" and faking the magic. At one stage we overloaded every circuit and blew every dynamo in Burbank.' But the big people had given their best and discharged themselves with honour. Connery found first-time Hollywood a great experience. And the compliment, it appears, was returned in kind. Forgiven for *Another Time, Another Place*, he had been given another Big Movie chance, and had, Kieron Moore was in no doubt, 'pulled it off creditably'.

8

Faltering Fox and the Classic Anchor

As befitting the nature of the project and the conscience of a man who claimed to be a descendant of a General Disney who fought on the 'right' side at the Battle of the Boyne, Walt Disney premiered *Darby O'Gill* in Dublin in June 1959. The film was Connery's first hit and though he later parried attempts to analyse his work on it he told the journalist, Freda Bruce Lockhart, 'I wish I'd had a share in the profits.' Probably because of the surfeit of family-orientated and fantasy films on the market at the time Disney, whose praises had been deafeningly sung through the early fifties, was now, a publicist says, on the critics' hit list. Despite the huge business the movie did all over the world very few journals reviewed it favourably. For *The Times*, the whole thing was 'fatally lacking in lightness and charm' – an evaluation that suggested to a heartier reviewer that the *Times* man was facing the wrong way in the theatre. Connery's notices, along with those of the leprechaun king Jimmy O'Dea, were good, though the almost inevitably dissenting voice of the *New York Times*, in the person of A.H. Weiler, branded him 'merely tall, dark and handsome'.

Disney's magic spell worked, as Robert Henderson had anticipated, very quickly for Connery. Within weeks of completion of the movie Paramount was seeking to borrow him again, this time for another heroic-fantasy epic, a

Tarzan feature. 'He was a rich man then,' Bannen says. 'The tables had turned since I'd met him in the foyer at the Q. There was I, still on the boards, and Sean hopping from feature to feature. We all envied him madly.'

Bannen vacated the mews house and Connery began converting the garage into a 35-foot sitting room. Diane was still around – 'in the background constantly,' Bannen says – as were Yat Malmgreen's dramatic movement studies. Connery still seemed very intellectually earnest, yet he was equally keen to ride this new-found popular success. The Paramount picture, *Tarzan's Greatest Adventure*, was conveyor-belt stuff, made at frantic pace by the formidable John Guillermin. Connery was pleased with the calibre of his co-stars – Anthony Quayle and Gordon Scott – and, though he had no illusions about the class of material, he was appeased by the respect that his association with Disney had engendered. After the invaluable baptismal experience of Disney's perfectionist Hollywood he was, Michael O'Herlihy says, 'brilliant in the junk' of *Tarzan*.

'His sense of proportion was precocious,' says an actor friend. 'Even at this early stage – and let's face it, he was still *new* – he could divine good from bad and assess the amount of effort individual projects were worthy of. His delight at being accepted in the business goes without saying but he always showed an uncustomary fussiness. It might or might not have been *Tarzan*, but I remember him brooding over an early script, learning lines I think, then tossing it into an armchair, "What's it like?" I asked, suspecting he was less than blissful. "Lots of lines," he grinned sardonically, "just lots of lines".'

The same friend recalls the books littered round Connery's rooms: 'It was funny, really. You had this great mountain of a fellow lifting body weights and checking out his muscles in the mirror . . . and on the shelf, in a chair, you'd see something heavy, some Russian writer, or Balzac . . . and it wasn't just effect, he read them, I swear.' Yet, the friend adds, 'Often you felt he was embarrassed about his aspirations. You'd say, "What's this, Sean? O'Casey?"

and he'd give you a twitchy look and say, "Let's have a pint."'

Curiously, however deep the artistic conflict ran, Connery in the immediate aftermath of Disney was at peace with himself. Through 1958 he had had little or no time for television (he did no BBC work: he was hotly fond of the BBC and liked their standards), but as soon as a decent part came up, coinciding with a free period, he leapt at it. *Riders to the Sea*, a widely successful play in mid-'59 was his first 'respectable' achievement since *Anna Christie*. 'He enjoyed that TV work,' Robert Hardy says. 'I'm sure it had nothing to do with his relative lack of success in cinema till then. I think he just liked the austerity, the technical restrictions that invited a disciplined man to do his best.'

In 1959 too he returned to the Oxford Playhouse stage where his champion, the gifted producer Frank Hauser, carved parts for him in the classics. 'He wasn't always good,' says director Lewis Gilbert about those early sallies, 'but he was always interesting.' Joan Littlewood, whose trend-setting Theatre Workshop was consolidating, quietly prided herself on the discovery and coaching of half-formed talents like Michael Caine and Richard Harris, whose celebrated break was in Littlewood's production of *The Quare Fellow* in 1956. She saw Connery on stage and, like Gilbert, found him interesting. She was planning for her Workshop *Macbeth* tour of Russia and Eastern Europe and, seeing Connery's potential, considered him ideal for a principal role. Through friends she approached Connery – and to the same friends' surprise, he turned her down. 'He spoke to me about it, giving no hint of his reasons,' Robert Henderson said. 'It was a wonderful offer, but maybe he'd committed himself secretly to the cinema solely by then.' It is equally possible that Connery's growing love for Diane Cilento obstructed Littlewood's *Macbeth*. In 1959 Cilento became ill and tuberculosis was diagnosed, a harrowing shock that triggered what she later called 'a two-year rethink about my life'. For a while she was gravely ill and Connery was never far from the telephone. Producer Samuel Bronston (*King of Kings*, etc.) and director

Anthony Mann, in the throes of planning the eleventh-century Spanish epic, *El Cid*, a vehicle intended to project Sophia Loren to a wider international audience, favoured Connery for one of the four lead roles – probably that of Count Ordonez, later given to Raf Vallone. Again Connery rejected. 'In that case,' Ian Bannen says, 'he wanted to do Pirandello's *Naked* [directed by Minos Volanakis] at Oxford. Yes, he understood the high designs of *El Cid* – but Diane was well then and she wanted to do [the play], so he had to be by her side.'

While Cilento was fighting TB, with Connery always close by, *Tarzan's Greatest Adventure* opened with a decidedly gaspy whimper. The sanctity of such matinée 'junk' was so entrenched in the tenets of light cinema criticism that just about no one dared to call it bad. The *Observer* and *The Times* circumspectly *described* the movie, and even the *Monthly Film Bulletin* hedged with 'the production values are above average and the various villains suitably larger than life; Jane is non-existent, the natives and the chimpanzee comedy element are restricted to one short scene, and a literate and grammatical Tarzan gives vent to his famous war cry only at the finish . . . If the same team comes up with a better story the next Tarzan might be more worthy of the tradition.'

The story, in fact, was the problem. It was a too-many-crooks effort, overbaked by Berne Giler, Guillermin and Les Crutchfield with a modicum of a Burroughs's sub-plot thrown in. Tarzan (Gordon Smith) played manhunter, trekking up-river to find and bring to book the villainous Slade (Anthony Quayle) and co-killers like O'Bannion (Connery). Slade is hell bent on scooping a hoard of diamonds from a hidden mine known only to him, and has killed ruthlessly to advance his aim. Encumbered with Angie (Sara Shane), an action-woman plane-crash-survivor-of-convenience, Tarzan plods through unexceptional fracas, is rescued from ineptitude by the much-suffering Angie and finally corners Slade. The humdrum showdown has treachery in Slade's camp – Slade naturally kills the traitor – and a clifftop struggle between Tarzan and

Slade, with Slade plummeting to his death. Predictability kills almost all tension in the story, though Gordon Scott manages to articulate his Tarzan nicely while conforming to the usual square-chin mould. In about thirty minutes of screen time Connery relates no more to his audience than the cub philosophy that makes O'Bannion a killer, though occasionally his grace in the action sequences holds the eye. Measured against its class, *Tarzan's Greatest Adventure* could score no better than six out of ten and it inspired some discussion in the summer of 1959 about Connery's future with Twentieth Century-Fox. *Picturegoer* journal speculated whether Fox would drop him, and a few close friends reciprocated by passing round the word that Connery's patience had run out. The game was uneven, Connery suddenly felt. He had 'pulled off' Hollywood and was consistently proving his talents in a vast range of disparate parts in theatre and television, yet Fox was only sporadically tossing him scraps of hints of projects that might be coming or auditions elsewhere he should try. In 1960, on loan again, now to Anglo-Amalgamated, he was returned to the gangland thriller, this time accepting *The Frightened City* only because of an unquestionably able cast and a good script by Leigh Vance (later more popular as a TV writer with *The Saint*) and others. The film's publicist, Brian Doyle, says, 'Sean gave the impression of being pleased with that movie, and he was terribly professional – that's what I recall more than anything. All told, working relationships were good. Our goal was a better-than-average thriller entertainment. Sean went along with that fully, and I think we reached our objective.'

The Frightened City, directed by John Lemont, was the peak of Connery's pre-Bond cinema effort though, very strangely, it failed to gain anything like the recognition that most involved with it felt was its due. Connery was thirty when it was made, amply experienced and splendidly aggrieved by Fox's mishandling: the new profound bitterness about Fox's lassitude brought a tight-lipped ferocity to his part as the protection-racketeer enforcer that made the entire business strikingly credible once he sidled onto screen. He was Paddy Damion, a soft-hearted, hard-headed crook employed by Harry Foulcher (Alfred Marks) to collect 'security' money from London clubs and cafés in a protection scheme devised by the ostensibly respectable accountant Waldo Zhernikov (Herbert Lom). Damion is a complex, tragic figure worthy of a latter-day Shakespeare: he is scrupulous in his loyalties but confused by the blurred borders of right and wrong; he works out in a rundown gym organised by 'gentle' villain Alf Peters (David Davies) – a member of Foulcher's racketeer team, whom he devotedly respects – but accepts the immorality of forced collections only because he needs an income to look after his crippled pal (Kenneth Griffiths) and to court Sadie (Olive McFarland). When Foulcher murders Peters, Damion quits his commitment to close dependants and revokes his former principles. He kills Foulcher – but in self-defence – and is on the point of executing Waldo when the police (led by John Gregson) steps in. In the penultimate scene Damion is led away in custody, his gestures and monosyllabic grunts underpinning the perfectly struck image of a senseless, faithful beast lost to understanding in the concrete jungle.

Everything Connery had filched, stumbled upon and been taught in six years of acting was piled in ideally concentrated measure into *The Frightened City*. The much-commented-upon 'rawness' that was the inevitable legacy of Fountainbridge, the movement techniques of his studies (particularly noticeable in his hand gestures), his laconically witty speech deliveries learnt from long-time film performers like Diane, all blended to create a powerfully memorable character who, as Henderson hoped, looked one thing – indomitably tough; but was another – humane. Those who worked with Connery on the movie reckoned he deserved good notices. Brian Doyle believes he 'just about dominated the picture' – but the rewards didn't come. On the circuits *The Frightened City* did very average business and though the popular dailies flagged it 'the toughest crime exposé ever made', just such a commendation assured box-office disaster. Dosed to drunkenness with the annals of Scotland Yard at work round London's docks, moviegoers were refreshing themselves with the sour medicine of middle-class life-as-it-is in kitchen-sink dramas like *Saturday Night and Sunday Morning* (1960) and *A Taste of Honey* (1961).

After *The Frightened City* Connery's relations with Fox were reportedly very strained. David Shipman in his encyclopaedic *The Great Movie Stars* states that the facts about the termination of the long-term contract are 'muddy', but it does seem that the bond of mutual interest had come unstuck by the time Connery took his first leading role, that of the gormless gag-feeder to a rather gormless Alfred Lynch in another loan-out, Cyril Frankel's *On the Fiddle*, based on a novel by R.F. Delderfield, a laughless comedy that could have ended a lesser actor's career. Ben Fisz, producer of *Hell Drivers*, and Anglo-Amalgamated, had confidence enough in Connery and the property, to pair them with an investment of a few hundred thousand pounds. The movie flopped, but it did serve to win Connery his first prominent notices – if not all good – and bring him to the attention of people like Dennis Selinger, the agent who, under the aegis of the influential International Creative Management, would direct Connery towards the great successes of the post-Bond years like *The Man Who Would Be King* (1975). For Selinger, Connery was 'quite fun' and 'allowing for the bumpiness of the vehicle, undeniably in possession of something one could only term star quality'. Close associates attest to the fact that Connery has always liked the notion of working in comedy, but the role of the dumb foil was, most felt, misjudged. The director Guy Hamilton, who was soon to direct *Goldfinger*, summed up the flaws in concept and acting in *On the Fiddle* when he said, apropos of Connery's talent: 'His power as an actor is built on strength: it can be shaded down to suit the circumstances of a scene – but Sean is greatest as a strong character.'

The plot of *On the Fiddle* is wafer-thin. Horace Pope (Alfred Lynch), tricked into joining the RAF during the war, joins forces with gypsy recruit Pascoe (Connery) and, for laughs and cash, starts up a lucrative conning racket among his colleagues. The no-gooders eventually show

97

their bravery when they make accidental contact with the enemy in France, and end up as much-decorated heroes. Paradoxically the divergence of opinion about the movie and Connery's effectiveness yielded fruit. By the summer of 1961 magazines and dailies all over the British Isles had commenced a rowdy 'Will he/Won't he succeed in movies?' debate, which Connery tactfully participated in. 'It is a real mystery to me why no film company has built Sean into a great international star,' wrote Freda Bruce Lockhart in *Woman*. '[In a recent TV play] Sean reminded me of Clark Gable. He has the same rare mixture of handsome virility, sweetness and warmth. His attractive speech . . . has the vigour which many find lacking in the pinched vowels of London-trained actors. Above all, Sean has size. I don't just mean . . . height. I mean, too, the breadth and all-embracing effect of his personality.' Connery co-operatively agreed: 'They'll offer me anything on TV, as opposed to stage or films.'

In her feature on Connery in the doldrums, Lockhart concluded with word of his newest TV venture. BBC producer Rudolph Cartier had chosen Connery to play Vronsky opposite Clair Bloom in *Anna Karenina*, a prestige production scheduled for November 1961. Before that there would be a West End play, Anouilh's *Judith*, at her Majesty's Theatre. 'I hope Cartier's production brings him luck,' Lockhart enthused, 'for it is my conviction that he is one of the biggest hopes among promising present-day actors.'

Diane Cilento was in full agreement, but Fox was quietly preparing to close his file and wave him goodbye. In its eyes budding talents galore peopled the pubs and billiard halls of Shaftesbury Avenue, all awaiting dotted lines to scrawl upon; most would be more compliant and less tetchily ambitious. Sean Connery proved himself – sure. But in the words of one Fox man, where in God's name could one fit him? Who wanted a Scottish giant in kitchen-sink drama? As for Hollywood? Well, Disney had not asked him back and Mickey Cohen was still alive. Sean Connery might never make Hollywood again.

'When I directed Sean in Shakespeare's *Henry IV* in the

spring of 1960, eighteen months before James Bond, he was already a star,' says Michael Hayes. 'You knew that by his behaviour – instantly. He wasn't loud or showy but compared to the other fine people we were using – Esmond Knight, Julian Glover, Patrick Garland – he was gold-plated. With the exception of Esmond, of course, who had vast experience, we were all new young bucks trying to make our way. Sean was different. He had a car . . . in fact several over the time I knew him. I remember once he'd bought a little Fiat, around the time of *Henry IV*. I asked him, just in passing, what had become of the other model, which had been very respectable. "The ashtrays were full," he retorted. Sounds like a cliché star story – but it's true.'

Everyone close to Connery rejoiced in his success as Hotspur opposite Robert Hardy's Prince Hal in *Henry IV*, one of the fifteen hour-long live Shakespeare plays that ran under the banner title 'An Age of Kings', produced by Peter Dewes and described by *The Times* as 'an astonishing achievement'. Among those round to kiss him congratulations was Julie Hamilton. A worker on the series recollects meeting Julie at a Wavel Mews party after the play. While stressing that there was no lady-in-residence, he elaborates that, with Julie, 'there was some up-and-downing, that's for sure. I know their close relationship was ended, but there were reverberations right into '60, perhaps even later.'

Recovering well from her illness, Cilento was work-active again but discreet about the extent of her relationship with Connery. 'Of course I knew about Diane,' says Michael Hayes, 'but I didn't know her. Sean brought only one face to the studios: that of the consummate pro. One was left in no doubt about his priorities then.' Did he display angst about his jerky movie career? 'It would have appeared churlish. I mean, he was more renowned than the rest of the cast. He was a star with a star's outlook – what more could he have wanted? Hayes was pleasantly surprised by Connery's ease with live Shakespeare. 'Hotspur's speech is not versified in the way others' are, so Sean had the advantage there, but he carried it off with such dash. His *relaxation* – that's what I remember; that's the gift he brought to us from films. Technical proficiency that allowed him to bawl.' Robert Hardy had a wider knowledge of Shakespeare, stretching back to the Histories at Stratford in 1951, where he had understudied Richard Burton's Prince Hal. With Connery, Hardy felt he was 'in the presence of a man who had the capacity to be truly great; he had charisma. Hotspur is a difficult character temperamentally, many people express their doubts about him. And indeed, after 'Age of Kings', many people complained about Sean, saying they found his accent hard to swallow. But I think it lent something to Hotspur which *was* Hotspur. We were lucky to have Sean.'

And then came *Anna Karenina*, the giant production that journalistic bright lights like Lockhart had uttered predictive hopes about. 'Sean was anxious and excited about it more than anything he'd recently done,' a BBC technician says. 'A lot of it probably concerned Claire Bloom, who had come to pictures via the Old Vic, done all the classics where Sean had done just a handful, and had big screen triumphs like *Look Back in Anger* behind her. Sean was racing then. He was keen to get more classic roles under his belt. We'd had him in a Terence Rattigan (as Alexander the Great in *Adventure Story*) and he was regularly at Oxford – but *Anna Karenina* was a milestone.'

'Discontinuous recording' (in the BBC's phrase) of the play by Marcelle-Maurette, adapted by Donald Bull, started on Friday 23 June 1961 at Television Centre Studio 3, and went on till Sunday night. Cartier, who had previously directed Connery in *Adventure Story*, struck a cracking passionate atmosphere that forced the best from the leads, Bloom, Jack Watling, June Thorburn, Connery. 'Sean had a childlike regard for Cartier,' a technician explains, 'and was almost over-anxious to please. But Bloom counterpointed beautifully. There were many retakes, but the whole thing was so *intense* it had to be good.'

While awaiting transmission of the Tolstoy classic, scheduled for 3 November Connery did a short run in the

West End biblical play *Judith*. 'He was the one who, in the Bible, slays Judith,' Robert Henderson said. 'He hadn't got much to say but he attracted attention because he was almost naked on stage, wearing only a loincloth. Never before on the legitimate stage had he the chance to show off that remarkably beautiful physique. It was mildly sensational but it didn't necessarily help the production.'

Judith was panned by many critics and its run was cut short, but the chance afforded Connery to exhibit his near-nude body paid dividends. One admirer in the audience at Her Majesty's was director Terence Young, already in discussion with two ambitious foreign producers about a strategy to emulate the success of Ian Fleming's James Bond books in movies. The first name mooted as a possible screen Bond was David Niven, Fleming's favourite actor, but in months of negotiation the idea had cooled. Fleming, who had the power of veto by virtue of his supreme literary standing, now fancied the notion of a newcomer – someone with charm, grit and intelligence who might, in some way, perhaps mirror himself, Bond's true alter ego. Young watched Connery from a half-full theatre and mused. He remembered his promise to the Scotsman on *Action of the Tiger*, that he would 'make it up to him' for the inadequacies of that movie.

After a spate of angry wrangling that marked the end of their contractual marriage, Fox at last mustered a jumbled project, *The Longest Day*, that allowed Connery a minute 'star part' – virtually hidden in a forest of 43 stars of current cinema. No fewer than four directors vied to leave their imprint on this well-reconstructed (but dry as old toast) account of Operation Overload, the Allied invasion of Europe on 6 June 1944. Ken Annaking directed the Juno Beach British sequence in which Connery plays Private Flanagan, 'the seasoned veteran [said Fox publicity] whose Irish temperament saw him through the landings'.

Connery was passable, but the strain of mounting this gargantuan production – two years in the making, nine months and seventeen days in principal photography, 31 locales, almost a hundred main actors – showed in almost every foot of every reel. Bosley Crowther, the respected American reviewer, liked it but added the telling remark that 'no character stands out particularly as more significant or heroic than anyone else'.

To friends Connery dismissed his contribution. The film belonged to John Wayne, Mitchum, the megastars. Fox and its wayward production navigator Darryl F. Zanuck, returning after many years' absence as executive president, never saw it any other way. It was no compliment to his talent, no gesture of appeasement from the company.

All hopes pinned to *Anna Karenina* were fulfilled. Audience response was, according to the BBC, 'very satisfactory' and most of the dailies greeted it boisterously. The *Listener* thought it deserved, if not prizewinning status as the year's best, then at least 'a distant salute'. *The Times* was unequivocal in its estimation of the winning factors. The players involved, the review said, achieved 'variable success'; but 'most successful was Mr Sean Connery, a headlong, passionate Vronsky'.

Harry Saltzman and Albert R. Broccoli, the producers who had acquired the rights to film James Bond, watched *Anna Karenina* on the advice of Terence Young. But, while they were intrigued by the old-trouper tricks this new boy employed to knock Claire Bloom right off the screen, the exercise was academic. Connery was already top of their poll.

By the middle of November it was decided: Sean Connery, in contravention of what financial backers United Artists thought best, would be James Bond.

If, in Michael Hayes's eyes, Connery was already a star, the glowing pride of achievement one might assume to be his was not as complete as most judged. Away from film journalists, away from the production offices, he revealed his weary side. At the out-of-work actors' gathering places he loved to frequent – the Buxton Club in the Haymarket, the Arts Theatre, the Salisbury in St Martin's Lane – he was, says Michael Caine, 'still the struggling young fella, unknown outside his profession, looking for the right break'. Ian Bannen was aware of the frustration of faltering movies too: 'Sean was slaving at theatre and the classics, using them as a kind of anchor in the storm.'

With the Bond break the storms of uncertainty were about to abate, to be replaced by a tempest of frenetic adulation and unstoppable fame.

9

Enter the Walking Aphrodisiac

The first attempts to put James Bond into movies failed. Under the intended sponsorship of millionaire businessman Ivar Bryce and his one-cylinder Xanadu production company (their sole venture had been Kevin McClory's financial failure *The Boy and the Bridge*), Ian Fleming, McClory and top British screenwriter Jack Whittingham developed a plot – which later became *Thunderball*, book and film – but abandoned it when Bryce and Fleming got cold feet. It had been Fleming's hope that established producer-directors like Anthony Asquith or Alfred Hitchcock would take up the rights of the *Thunderball* treatment, but when Hitchcock flatly rejected it Fleming decided to withdraw. Jack Whittingham's fee for the final script was £5000 and the project was shelved indefinitely. Fleming wrote to Bryce: 'Showbiz is a ghastly biz and the last thing I want is for you to lose your pin-stripe trousers in its grisly maw . . . nor, of course, do I want the first James Bond film to be botched.' A literary perfectionist with a penchant for collecting rare classics but reading trash, Fleming had more in common with Sean Connery, the man who was to breathe life into his dream-hero, than many recognise. Compared with Connery's upbringing, Fleming's childhood was crème de la crème – country seats, town houses, Eton, Sandhurst – but both men shared an ambition which, to some, was almost ugly in its intensity. Both enjoyed risk-taking, both acquired sophisticated tastes. 'Don't be misled by Sean's lorry-driver press,' says Honor Blackman. 'The man exuded high-living refinement when I got to know him.'

Within a few months of Fleming's postponement of screen Bond, the Canadian producer Harry Saltzman, acting on the advice of his and Fleming's lawyer, Brian Lewis, optioned the existing Bond novels. Saltzman's option covered seven books in print. One Bond title, *Casino Royale*, was unavailable, having been sold to Gregory Ratoff for $6,000 in 1955. Another title *Moonraker*, had been purchased by Rank, but Fleming's agents, Music Corporation of America, retrieved the rights in 1960. Saltzman's track record was superb – he had been the driving force behind Woodfall, the production company partnership with John Osborne and director Tony Richardson – and had been partly responsible for the success of new-wave ciné-realism, hawking such projects as *Saturday Night and Sunday Morning* and *The Entertainer*. He was also, Honor Blackman recalls, 'a hard man, a dedicated deal-maker'. With Bond, however, his deal-making prowess initially faltered. Having paid Fleming $55,000 for a six-month option, 28 days before expiry he was at sea, no nearer a financing deal than he had been at the start. It was then his writer friend Wolf Mankowitz introduced him to Broccoli, the 50-year-old New Yorker who was himself a longtime Bond admirer, and whose contacts in financing circles were impressive. Broccoli's experience was every bit as colourfully wide as Saltzman's, though he was irritated by the relative lack of success of some recent endeavours. A good scholar and avid reader, he had a degree in agriculture and a spell as assistant to Howard Hawks behind him when, after the war, he transferred operations from Hollywood to London and started a series of adventure films in partnership with Irving Allen, earning the distinction of producing the first ever Anglo-American features. Saltzman's proposal for a partnership arrangement to launch Bond was based on his belief that, after kitchen-sink, people wanted 'something different, strong plots with excitement, fast cars, bizarre situations, drink and women' – the antidote to a post-fifties malaise which resounded with the memories of the leanness and suffering of the Second World War's aftermath. Broccoli needed little persuasion. In 1959 he had been tentatively negotiating for Bond: he wanted in.

A fifty-fifty deal was eventually struck, though Saltzman would have preferred terms more favourable to himself. All that then remained was choosing the book to film, drafting the screenplay and casting the essentials – Bond and his bedmate.

Richard Maibaum, who had written Broccoli's *The Red Beret*, went to work, initially on *Thunderball*, while Broccoli commenced talks with film backers in May 1961. Columbia Pictures considered the Bond offer, then turned it down. Maibaum switched to *Dr No*, having received word that the High Court action taken by McClory against Fleming's rights in *Thunderball* complicated its ready availability, and Broccoli approached United Artists.

On 20 June 1961 in a brief boardroom meeting at UA headquarters in New York, backing was at last agreed upon. David Picker, later to run United Artists but then London chief, was the Bond fan in the UA camp who swayed company president Arthur Krim. Broccoli and Saltzman asked for a million dollars to put *Dr No* on screen, but were offered $800,000. It would be enough. Excitedly the producers winged back to London and started scouting for their director and crew. Disappointment marked the beginning of their work. First-choice directors Guy Green and Bryan Forbes refused the project. Guy Hamilton, later to take the challenge with *Goldfinger*, also rejected it 'because of intrusive private affairs'. Finally, Terence Young was approached, a little uncertainly, because his recent films had been, in the vernacular, 'uneven' – specifically, financial flops. United Artists agreed to accept Young provided the movie's budget was guaranteed with a completion bond: that is, if the film took longer to shoot than anticipated, the producers would foot the bill for the additional costs incurred.

Saltzman and Broccoli did not hesitate on the bond, reassured by what they perceived as Young's able and economical work on *The Red Beret* (1953) for Broccoli.

Casting for *Dr No* was well in progress when Young was officially assigned to the movie. Indeed, Sean Connery was already the front runner – ahead of Patrick McGoohan, Roger Moore and Richard Johnson. Fleming, who was quite happy with the professionalism and generosity of Broccoli and Saltzman, still promoted the idea of an established name lead. He mentioned Michael Redgrave and Trevor Howard but, after the fiasco of *Thunderball*, was very content to stay away from 'all this side of the business and all those lunches and dinners at the Mirabelle and the Ambassadeurs which seem to be the offices for all this huckstering'. By the time the search for Bond was at full throttle, according to Connery, Fleming was keen on the idea of an unknown, someone who would not overshadow James Bond.*

Saltzman and Broccoli had first met Connery at a party, and liked his looks. Broccoli enjoyed his thick accent in particular and had further food for thought when, in Hollywood, he had viewed *Darby O'Gill and the Little People* and observed his wife's enthusiastic response: like Jacqueline Hill on *Requiem*, Dana Broccoli found Connery's macho aura inescapably attractive. By coincidence, in London, film editor Peter Hunt, who was to edit almost all the Bond movies, was recommending *On the Fiddle* to Saltzman. According to Broccoli, Terence Young was not consulted in the final casting of Bond.

Saltzman phoned Richard Hatton, and Connery was called in for interview. He approached Saltzman's South Audley Street office casually, expecting nothing. He had been through the casting maze too many times to believe

---

* Fleming did reasonably well by the film deal. He was guaranteed a minimum of $100,000 per movie, with 5 per cent of the producers' profits. By the time he died in August 1964 he had probably banked about a quarter of a million dollars from the movies. He left a half million dollars in his will.

that cheerful grins won any prizes. Instead he stepped out of his small car as though heading for the grey offices and familiar foursquare grilling of the BBC. He wore a brown shirt, brown suede shoes and no tie – garb befitting the Buxton on a Friday night, hardly a million-dollar movie audition. In their first-floor office Broccoli and Saltzman greeted him coolly and Saltzman, ever the inquisitor, fired the questions. Connery's answers came pat, in the perfect animal burr Broccoli found riveting. Yes, he had read Fleming – *Live and Let Die*, some years back. Yes, he thought the concept of a Bond series viable. No, he didn't regard himself exclusively as a classics actor, or a stage performer or whatever – he had yet to find his niche. The warm and candid tone of the chat altered only when Broccoli queried Connery's style and dress sense. At one juncture he told the producers, 'You either take me as I am or not at all.' Saltzman may have had reservations – according to one associate he 'liked his subordinates to know their place' – but Broccoli found Connery's authority a 'definite plus'. 'He pounded the desk and told us what he wanted . . . we agreed, he walked out of the office and we watched him bounce across the street like he was Superman. We knew we had got our James Bond.'

Others had yet to be persuaded.

Connery started rehearsing at Pinewood, opposite an unending queue of aspiring female leads. When some of this test footage was sent to New York, UA glanced over Connery and cabled back: SEE IF YOU CAN DO BETTER.

Broccoli and Saltzman ignored the cable because they had already committed themselves to Connery, signing him in November for a multi-picture deal that would engage him till 1967, allowing one non-Bond picture a year. His up-front fee for *Dr No* was £25,000 – 'a fortune' to Robert Hardy and other friends.

Connery had not undertaken *Dr No* and the long-term deal lightly. When the offer was made he took time to consider it, consulting Hatton and Cilento. After Disney, he had been offered another long-term contract, to join either the *Maverick* or the *Wyatt Earp* TV series being

108

churned out, supermarket-style in Hollywood. That proposed deal wasn't exactly bounteous in rewards, but it would have granted him the permanent access to Hollywood which he hungered for. He had turned it down, firstly because he thought he would be short-selling himself to run-of-the-mill TV and secondly because he wanted to be near Diane. Now, with Bond, Diane took a hand, giving forceful advice. Fleming's books were immensely popular, with yearly sales nearing the million mark. It was significant too that they attracted praise from all sections of the community, and had been likened to Buchan, Sapper – the best of twentieth-century popular fiction. Raymond Chandler had written glowingly about Bond. The poet William Plomer had been instrumental in seeing him through to publication, advising both Fleming and publishers Jonathan Cape. Even Somerset Maugham was an admirer. . . .

Agonising over submitting himself to another long contract, Connery confessed his greatest fear, that of signing his services away for the crucial period of most actors' lives – his thirties. Looking back on Fox he explained the frustrations of his misuse as feeling like 'a man walking through a swamp in a bad dream'. He knew if he was to make it internationally it must be soon. He saw himself primarily as a romantic lead, not a character actor. He wanted success while he was still fit and young enough to exploit it.

Cilento urged him to take Bond. 'If it were not for me,' she told an American magazine writer in 1964, 'Sean might never have become James Bond.'

Reflecting on his casting interview with Saltzman and Broccoli, Connery later admitted he had 'put on a bit of an act'. Intuition carried the game: though he hadn't worked out the pros and cons, he had sensed the importance of Bond just as, seven years before, he sensed *South Pacific* was right for him. Intuition and Cilento clinched Bond.

With shooting scheduled for January 1962, Terence Young and his assistant Joanna Harwood entered a preproduction run that gave every indication of disaster looming.

There were five different scripts, all scrappy, and Broccoli, who had been largely absorbed with casting, was at war with Saltzman, in charge of the writing. Young recalls that, in the end, Broccoli's nerve went. Flinging the mountain of wildly derivative scripts aside he shouted to Saltzman: 'Look, we've paid all this fucking money for this James Bond book and we're not using a word of it. Now, Terence is a writer, he's the quickest writer I know. He's got ten days to put it back. He can take all the scripts we have . . . and whatever he writes we're going to be stuck with and, Harry, if it's bad it's your fault.'

Young and Harwood took a room at the Dorchester Hotel and began rewriting, going day and night. Meanwhile, Saltzman had equal reason to lose patience with Broccoli. 'Cubby was the tit 'n' bum man,' Guy Hamilton says. 'He had fixed ideas about the type of girl he wanted in Bond's bed. And one thing he wanted was good tits.' Julie Christie, among a score of others, failed the tit test. Broccoli had seen her on TV and summoned her. No one doubted her talent, least of all the discerning Cubby, but, close up, her bust just didn't reckon. Finally, in a stack of new-star photographs, Broccoli came across Swiss-born Ursula Andress. In the cheesecake publicity shot she was wearing a wet T-shirt that moulded her hard-nippled breasts. Glancing over her curriculum vitae, Broccoli was encouraged: she was the right age (25) and height (5 foot-7), had made films in Rome – which stood for nothing in talent terms – but had been briefly on contract to Paramount. Without meeting her, Broccoli wired a Hollywood friend for testimonials and received exactly the affirmative response he wanted. Interviewed later, Saltzman unwittingly mocked the casting process that had cost so much concern and cash: 'We chose Ursula because she was beautiful and because she was cheap. We didn't have the money to spend on anyone else.' Andress received £300 per week for the scheduled six weeks. (The film overran: she claimed she was not paid dues for extra work.)

Among Connery's friends at the West End actors' clubs word was out that Fleming's 'Establishment hero' superspy was his. 'I was amazed,' Michael Caine states candidly. 'I was sure they'd give it to Rex [Harrison], because he was your living image of upper-crust good-living.' Robert Hardy thought it 'oddball casting, but a tremendous compliment to Sean . . . everyone banked on something contrived and Englishy, but Sean presented one with an entirely fresh perspective on British cult heroes.' Around the Buxton in particular surprise – and sour grapes – was hugely evident. The *Saturday Evening Post* quoted a movie director who knew Connery saying, 'He was on the garbage heap of acting until Bond'. Connery himself experienced what might best be termed polar affections once news circulated. 'Actually it was a bit of a joke around town,' he conceded. 'There were those in the Buxton club who thought Bond a backward step, B movie stuff, and those who imagined Sean Connery clad in anything other than Levis and beatniky suede shoes a travesty.' But Diane Cilento, who was closer than anyone to unrolling events, understood that *Dr No* was to be no Monogram or Republic conventional B, but rather a force-fed pop-epic. All of Connery's artistry would be called into play and the end result would be the most stringent acid test of his skill.

Young hurried Connery into a crash course in social grace that made cynics snigger. 'Terence *was* James Bond,' says Zena Marshall, who starred as the murderous sextigress Miss Taro in the film. 'When he cast me, all he said, the way he behaved, told me he was projecting himself as Bond. He had incredible style and complementary gentleness and strength.' For sure, Young's background was closer to Fleming's outline for the superspy than Connery's. The son of Shanghai's Commissioner of Police, he was educated at Harrow and Cambridge and served in the war with the Guard's Armoured Division. His tastes were for the good things of life. 'Terence loved to be surrounded by pretty furnishings, champagne, attractive people,' says Molly Peters, whom he cast in *Thunderball* three years later. Young had also worked, for a short time, as a helper to Hitchcock, as, significantly, did screenwriter Richard

Maibaum. (Though Young and Harwood rewrote much of *Dr No*, with Berkely Mather, Richard Maibaum received the main screen credit. He went on to write most of the Bond films.) Elements of Hitchcock infested all the early Bond movies, by way of tribute rather than accident. 'I sent Sean to my shirtmaker,' says Young. 'I sent him to my tailor. I used to make him go out in these clothes, because Sean's idea of a good evening out would be to go off in a lumber jacket . . .'

Feeling much out of his depth by the curious workings of this curious film world, this same domain that had defeated him two years before, Fleming's reaction to progress was confused. At first he wasn't happy with Connery, though he kept up a brave face when he cabled Bryce about Saltzman's conviction in the 'absolute corker, a 30-year-old Shakespearian actor, ex-navy boxing champion, etc, etc'. With Young, whom he knew through mutual acquaintanceship with Noël Coward, he was more cruelly honest. At a UA London function he squared up to the realities of an untested director guiding a half-known ex-labourer star into James Bond's elegant world. 'So they've decided on you to fuck up my work,' he charged Young. Young was not shaken. 'Let me put it this way, Ian. I don't think anything you've written is immortal as yet, whereas the last picture I made won a Grand Prix at Venice. Now let's start even.'

Dr No, 'started even' with location shooting in Jamaica on Tuesday 16 January 1962, and Andress joined the team ten days later to film her Crab Key sequences on the north shore. Her husband John Derek (later self-styled 'creator' of third-wife star Bo) accompanied her. She fitted in well, though Young found her strangely built: 'She had the shoulders, stomach and legs of a boy, but with this great face and breasts.' Shooting her to advantage was not as easy as it might have been, though by Connery's side her bulky proportions looked about right. Connery liked the Dereks, and laughed a lot with Ursula. She had a waspish, rebellious side to her that brightened the mood of relentless time-is-running-short tension and though her squeaky accent caused trouble from day one, her discipline impressed him. Later he called her his favourite Bond co-star – and indeed she proved an invaluable asset to the yearly rethreading of the Bond mythology: for a million Bond fans Andress, white-bikinied with hip knife on a Carribean beach, became the symbol of luxurious, sexy, inviting adventure.

Pleased with Connery's work in Jamaica, Young brought the team back to Stage D at Pinewood in the middle of February, where Ken Adam, a long-time associate of Broccoli's, had been labouring on some imaginative set designs with a budget of only £4,000. Here the interiors would be shot, and the famous introductory scene, where a suntanned Connery announces himself as James Bond to Eunice Gayson's Sylvia across a gaming table, went in the can on the second day. A few days later the seduction of busty, dangerous Miss Taro was filmed. Zena Marshall recalls: 'I spent the entire day in bed with Sean, so you could say it was fun! But it was hard work too. Ian Fleming came on the set and had several words with me. He seemed to think my role important, this enemy agent making love with Bond, each tacitly knowing the other is out to kill them. There were a few retakes, because Terence wanted us to relax into the mood of love-making, and we did some sections twice for the different markets. In Ireland, for example, they couldn't see my tits, so more covered-up [publicity] shots were taken . . . Sean was very rough and raw, but his charm was exceptional.'

Day by day Young preached etiquette. Once he checked Connery for eating with his mouth open (during dinner with *Dr No*), on another occasion Connery's accent thickened in the excitement of a scene. One or two errors of class slipped through: Bondphiles blast the sartorial blunder of Connery at Strangway's house, buttoning down the last of his suit coat buttons, spoiling the cut of a finely figured outfit.

The film story of *Dr No*, Fleming was relieved to see, differed only in small detail from his novel. Young considered the yarn ordinary, Connery thought it good. John Russell Taylor, the film historian, isolated the formula shrewdly: Bond spends one half of the movie getting into the villain's clutches – and laying the girls on the way – and one half fighting his way free. In *Dr No* the journey into trouble begins when Strangways (Tim Moxon), our man in Jamaica, is murdered while investigating the 'toppling' of American rockets from nearby Cape Canaveral. MI6 agent Bond is yanked away from his current flame (Eunice Gayson) and ordered into the inquiry. Following Strangway's trail, he meets the treacherous duo, Professor Dent (Anthony Dawson) and Government House secretary Miss Taro, and, after their conspiracy to kill him fails, he executes Dent and has Taro arrested. Dent's plot leads Bond to Crab Key, the island fortress of *Dr No* (Joseph Wiseman) where, after incarceration and a bold breakout, Bond thwarts Dr No's latest attempt to topple an American rocket and kills the villain. His accomplice, from the middle of the second act, is the lovely Honey Rider (Andress), a shell-collecting island-drifter.

The completion of the film in March marked an occasion for muted celebration. Small problems rankled: Andress, it was decided, would have to be dubbed throughout. Monty Norman's music score was inadequate. Fresh thematic music was needed. Connery was good, but. . . .

UA officials flew from New York to watch a preview in a private cinema in Mayfair in Connery's absence. Saltzman liked the picture well enough, 'but then I liked *Look Back in Anger* . . . and that died the death of a dog.' The distribution money-men silently watched ninety minutes of Sean Connery then, in unison, grimaced. He was 'all right', average detective hunk, self-conscious in the close-ups. One top-ranking executive reportedly said, 'I can't show a picture with a limey truck driver playing the lead.' Somebody else took consolation from the fact that Broccoli and Saltzman had only overspent by $110,000: 'We can't lose too much, anyway . . .'

Thus decided, UA would splash nothing on promoting *Dr No* in America. The film would, no doubt, get some rentals and earn a few bucks, but the likelihood of financing for a follow-up was a little less than slight.

Connery, on the other hand, was resolutely optimistic. He told friends the film was 'bloody good' and, no matter what UA felt, he was prepared to 'sit tight and wait'. Sue Lloyd, the actress, had become friendly with him, having met him at the Buxton, and shared a few loving evenings with him at her flat – 'never his: I never saw the inside of his place, and only had the vaguest notion he lived somewhere in the NW region'. She found him 'quietly optimistic'. A few weeks after completion she met Andress at Shepperton Studios where both were vying for an upcoming part in a minor movie. 'Ursula had no idea what the repercussions of *Dr No* would be. We were chatting and she said, "I've just been in Jamaica enjoying the sun, doing this thriller with Sean Connery" – and it might have been any thriller, with any actor. It meant nothing to her beyond another job. She held no hopes for it.' But James Bond remained at least a literary institution and Connery was intent on doing his share of pre-promotion. He gave several interviews, stressing his pedigree (the whistle-stop *Macbeth* he had done for Canadian TV the previous autumn, just before he signed for Bond, figured large), and promulgated a James Bond philosophy. He told the *Daily Express*: 'I see Bond as a complete sensualist – his senses are highly tuned and he's awake to everything. He likes his wine, his food and his women. He's quite amoral. I particularly like him because he thrives on conflict – a quality lacking in present-day society.' With wary respect for UA he added, 'I've been asked if I'm worried about getting tagged as Bond . . . Bond is a "bracket" for me. It's a one-million-dollar production and the people who set up and cast the film have a healthy respect for a pound and dollar tag.'

While professionally Connery sat tight during the summer of 1962, in his private life tumultuous changes were under way. The desultory love affairs that filled the vacuum of an actor's 'resting' days – brief flings with model Joyce Webster, Sue Lloyd and others – were suddenly stout-heartedly replaced by a new and vigorous relationship with Cilento. 'As far as I was concerned,' an actor friend says, 'Andre Volpe no longer existed. Diane's marriage had been over quite a time, but now divorce proceedings were going and she and Sean were settling down together. They spent several nights a week with each other and we waited for the knot to be tied . . . we waited for a move from Sean anyway, Diane was another kettle of fish. You see, Sean, under it all, was a one-woman man. Diane, well, she had a career to be catching up with.'

At home in Fountainbridge, in the same stair, Effie and Joe were told of Sean's new love in a phone call. Later, briefly, Sean brought Diane home and the family reunion was serene. Effie read between the lines and guessed the seriousness of the affair. She smiled when, in the autumn, she read a national newspaper interview where Sean extolled the bachelor life: 'No one to tell you what to do . . . I can leave my socks on the floor, play poker all night, come and go as I please . . . I couldn't ask any woman to put up with that.'

By the time the interview was published Diane Cilento was several months pregnant, expecting Connery's child, and he was about to apply himself to the difficult task of persuading her to marry him.

United Artists was stunned. Having sidestepped the option of a fanfare première in Chicago or New York, it opened *Dr No* in the Midwest where, if destined, it could die a quiet death. By the time of the American opening the movie was a massive European success. Premiered at the London Pavilion on 6 October 1962, with Paul Getty in attendance, by the clever news-conscious design of Saltzman and Fleming, gross receipts amounted to almost £1 million within a few months. Unstinting superlative reviews sung paeans of hope for a British cinema with American values (at last!) and reversed anything ever breathed in blasphemy about Connery's talent. Awed by the trendsetting zest of the escapade, the MGM-at-its-peak-style décor, the Fritz Lang echoes, *Films and Filming* could only pant, 'There hasn't been a film like *Dr No* since . . . when? There's never been a *British* film like *Dr No* since . . . what?' 'Carefully, expertly made,' said *The Times*. 'Magnificent mayhem' agreed the *News of the World*.

Connery's personal reviews were no less enthusiastic. Peter Green in *John O'London's* believed there was 'no doubt that Sean Connery with his Irish good looks, splendidly hairy chest, and tough but elegant charm, embodies this modern male compensation factor [James Bond] better than most actors could.'

At the première, where Zena Marshall took Connery's arm and Saltzman for once sat back to allow his movie to speak for itself, audience response was electrifying. Zena Marshall, viewing the whole assemblage for the first time could not but be impressed. 'The theatre was deadly silent at the beginning, but as it went on they were shouting for Bond. Sean's performance was so smooth he riveted the eye. I remember Anita Ekberg was there, sitting just along our row from Sean. Throughout the movie she couldn't keep her eyes off him – not on screen, in *person*. Later at the reception at the Ambassadeurs it was the same. Whatever effect he'd had on women up till then was doubled. James Bond made him a walking aphrodisiac.'

The clutter of media attention that surrounded the New York opening at the Astor, the Murray Hill and other theatres in the 'première showcase' group in May firmly and irrevocably stamped approval on Connery, the Star. Bosley Crowther recommended the film as 'lively and amusing' though 'not to be taken seriously as realistic fiction or even art, any more than the works of Mr Fleming are to be taken as long-hair literature'. A *Variety* reviewer predicted, 'As a screen hero James Bond is clearly here to stay. He will win no oscars, but a lot of enthusiastic followers.' Tongue crushed in cheek, *Time* magazine gave an unprecedented leader to the British import: 'Agent Bond, in short, is just a great big hairy marshmallow, but he sure does titillate the popular taste . . . at last the varlet pimpernel can be seen on screen. He looks pretty good. As portrayed by Scotland's Sean Connery, he moves with a tensile grace that excitingly suggests the violence bottled in Bond.'

There were quibbles of course, most, like the Queequeg article in the *Spectator*, beefing about script departures from Fleming's original. But, overall, throughout the world, *Dr No* succeeded.

By the time the New York journals were card-indexing 'Connery, Sean', the 'new' actor, *From Russia with Love* was already filming at Pinewood, backed by $2 million from a humbled UA. On the home front Connery was decorating his new property, a three-storey mansion overlooking Acton Park, and worming into married life with Cilento and a ready-made family – step-daughter Gigi and five-month-old son Jason.

Fame had taken its time. But in some regards some matters were moving too fast.

10

Hitch, Effortlessly

'I don't think I'm meant to be married,' Diane Cilento told an interviewer in March 1961, propounding tersely the reasons for the failure of her union with Volpe. Two years later, six months after marrying Connery, she was reminded of that conclusion. Asked to comment she replied tartly, 'I got married.'

The beginnings of the new marriage were not auspicious, though the affection and regard Connery and Cilento held for each other is beyond question. By her own admission, Connery had to talk her into tying the knot. Beneath the dedication to his craft and his pugnacity of purpose, Connery in his thirties was surprised to find 'the old John Knoxian influence' working away – a realisation that struck him whenever, after long absences, he came back to Fountainbridge. On discovering Cilento was pregnant in the summer of 1962, shortly after just such a refresher trip to Edinburgh, he promptly set a course for marriage. Time and circumstances were right for him: with his Bond contract he was assured good money for a few years; his existing savings were considerable; he was past thirty, and tired of philandering; most important, Diane was a supreme career navigator, blessed with a conscience that divided good from bad irrefutably. He proposed, but she refused. 'I didn't want to get married,' she said later. 'Having made a bodge of it already I didn't rate marriage. I thought it was too stifling.' Discussions about alternative lifestyles stretched into September, but Connery was adamant in his reluctance to settle for separate lives, with the new child farmed on loan every other week. 'Sean was never enamoured of the idea of children,' a friend says, 'but he was anxious about the baby once he knew the die had been cast. And he loved Diane, remember. He told people she reminded him of his mother – bright, strong, firm.'

In the dazzling afterglow of the *Dr No* première, over dinner, Connery finally persuaded Cilento to agree to his proposal. He had already made a major gesture of resolve: he had purchased for £9,000 a twelve-room house in Centre Avenue, Acton, formerly the home of twenty-five nuns of the Order of Adoratrices. He had drafted in an interior designer and decorators, and he was building a nursery. Cilento was flattered, but she laid down conditions. She told the *Sunday People* later: '[Sean] was so sure we could make a go of it . . . I wanted us both to retain a fair amount of freedom. I don't like ownership in marriage. I don't like too many promises either. There is no way of being sure you can keep them.'

Days after Cilento had accepted Connery the wedding ceremony took place in Gibraltar. Gibraltar was simplest for many reasons: in Britain the couple would have had to wait three weeks after the posting of banns, and the bush telegraph that operates through registrars' offices would have meant unwanted press coverage. As it was, certain jaundiced circles were still abuzz with the scandal of a scarlet lady, just one month divorced, seven months' pregnant and hopping in and out of love with Connery. 'She jilted him a few times,' one acquaintance claims. 'He was never too sure of her.'

At first in Gibraltar Connery thought he'd got the ultimate jilt. Cilento was in Spain, staying with friends, and arrangements had been made by telephone for her to meet up with Connery at the appointed registry. Connery, travelling on his British passport, had no trouble entering the colony but Cilento, with her Australian documents, was delayed at the frontier. The ceremony was postponed for a few hours, new witnesses had to be roped in – two taxi-drivers, for convenience – and, at last, vows were exchanged. Connery's mood was foul, but Cilento thought the whole affair 'like a funny TV show. He was all feet, all thumbs, frustrated.'

Nerves were not given long to settle. It was suggested a trip up the Rock might be appropriate – a chance to watch evening falling on the Mediterranean, bask in the sun sliding down over Africa, romantically tip a glass to the future. But they stayed up too long, and strayed into a military preserve on their way down. Locked in, with night descending, they were lucky to find a sentry with a sympathetic ear after an hour. According to Cilento, they repaired to their honeymoon base, the Rock Hotel, exhausted, facing a night of anti-climax after the dramas of the day. Subsequently they stayed at a villa rented from the Marqués de las Torres nearby on the Costa del Sol.

Six weeks later in London, on 11 January Jason was born, by which time the family – with Gigi looking ever more on Connery as Dad – had moved into Acacia House in rough 'n' ready Acton. Connery personally supervised the several thousand pounds' worth of reconstruction, frequently haggling with the builders and challenging costings. 'I'd been on building sites,' he said. 'I knew how corners could be cut, what was feasible and what wasn't.'

Space and colour were the main considerations. For the 37-foot living-room Connery insisted on 'bright red carpet, white paint, lots of very bright cushions . . . colour is necessary.' A year later he was watching Jason 'reaching for the lights and the brightest colours, laughing . . . he will grow up to memories and experiences that will be . . . inescapable.' The simple sentiment revealed the naive but idealistic urge to displace Fountainbridge once and for all. 'Sean was never ashamed of Edinburgh,' says Ian Bannen, 'but he acquired a liking for good material things. I suppose he tried to impose it [on Fountainbridge] in some ways. For instance, I remember he took me home there and he'd bought this very modern gigantic fridge for his parents. Huge thing, it was crammed into this tiny room where everyone had to squeeze round it. It was quite ridiculous.' With the upfront money for *From Russia with Love* he was now trying to lure Effie and Joe away from the stair. He offered them a flat in London but Effie pointed out that she needed to be near Helen and Neil, her parents, then living in Corstorphine and very dependent on family help. The fact that the McEwans Brewery was beginning to annex nearby properties did not deter Joe. 'This is so handy,' he told the *Sunday Express*, fending off his son's offer. 'London is such an enormous place, and there's always so much bustling and hustling.'

But now, with Cilento's guiding influence stronger than ever, bustling London was the place to be – a thoroughly manageable empire falling, street by street, cinema by cinema, to Sean Connery's advance. *Dr No* ran virtually non-stop, somewhere or other, during 1963. Back in Fountainbridge, old friend John Brady saw it and thought, 'That's it – Tommy's made it for life.'

United Artists was a little less sure, but it was certainly investing more executive interest, as well as cash, in *From Russia with Love*. Terence Young was now flavour of the month, and UA executives waited patiently while, over many laborious months, he chewed over casting, determinedly seeking the perfect villains for Fleming's enigmatic Red Grant and Rosa Klebb. Finally he chose Robert Shaw, who had to put on weight and muscle, and Lotte Lenya. He also wanted a heroine to outstrip – in every sense – Ursula Andress. Young commuted sleeplessly between European capitals, according to press reports, interviewing some two hundred girls for the role of Tatiana, the turncoat Russian. Among those in the running were Austria's Elga Anderssen (dropped by UA decree when she spurned an executive's advances), Roman Lucia Modogno, English roses Margaret Lee and Sally Douglas, Pole Magda Konopka, Yugoslav Sylvia Koscina and a Miss Universe 1960 runner-up, Italian Daniela Bianchi. In March Bianchi was told she had the job and on 1 April filming began, again at Pinewood's Stage D, utilising most of the proven technical talents from *Dr No*.

Over sixteen weeks Young took his team from Pinewood

to Turkey, Scotland and Madrid, shooting more extravagantly than he had on the first Bond, and running weeks over in Turkey where there were union troubles and minor cast illnesses. Connery was exhausted but he perked up when director Basil Dearden approached him, offering a lead role in the upcoming *Woman of Straw*, co-starring with Ralph Richardson, an actor he had admired since he was a child. Connery agreed without seeing the script, and revived for Bond.

As a consolidating choice, the one to secure the Bond series, *From Russia with Love* was evidence of Broccoli and Saltzman's brilliant market sense. Undeniably Fleming's most ambitious and strangely structured book, he himself had reservations about its worth. Before the book was in proof in 1956 he wrote to his publishers about his fear of staleness and the contrivances used 'to fill the vacuum created by my waning enthusiasm for this cardboard booby'. As it turned out the public, and President John Kennedy to boot, loved the novel and turned it into a perennial best-seller. Dick Maibaum, the screenwriter, wisely chose to retain as much as possible of Fleming in his script, a punch-heavy story of a plot by an international crime organisation, SPECTRE, to kill Bond, steal a decoding machine and confound both British and Soviet spy services. Tatiana (Bianchi) is the bait, duped by Russian Rosa Klebb into believing she is serving the Motherland by luring Bond to Istanbul to hand over the prized decoder. Tatiana is ready to defect for the love of Bond and double-cross Klebb but psychopathic Grant is despatched to stop them as they travel westwards across Europe on the Orient Express. In a brutal clash aboard the train, Bond kills Grant and later eliminates Klebb in like fashion.

Superb photography by Ted Moore, adventurous editing by Peter Hunt, Bianchi oozing sensuality with every timid arch of a brow and the coincidence of the assassination of President Kennedy six weeks after the London opening all joined to elevate *From Russia* into the realms of stellar immortals. Effie and Joe came to London to join Diane and Connery for the première and were floored by the extent of unanticipated success. Effie maintained that deadpan aloofness that had kept her through the bleak days of the Depression, but Joe was fully at a loss. The crowds, the glaring manifestations of a wealth he could only have dreamed about in drunkenness, the autograph hunters screaming for Tommy – it was all too much to digest. At the reception after screening he told a film journalist he believed his son would 'get quite popular' in the immediate future. Already at work on *Woman of Straw*, Connery seemed almost unaware that film history was in the making: *Dr No* could easily have been a fluke, but with the triumphant première of *From Russia With Love* a heavily backed series was guaranteed. Pressed to give an account of his personal recipe for Bond, Connery himself gave way to a hyperbole he soon grew to detest. He spoke of the lack of humour in Fleming's novels (a gross unfairness in the eyes of Fleming and those familiar with the undertones of black humour in the books), and of his and Terence Young's attempts to lighten the material with one-line gags and some self-mockery. Hyperbole was the order of the day. Fleming, who had privately expressed doubts about 'the labourer playing Bond', was now reported as saying Connery was much as he had imagined Bond. Were he writing the books all over again, he stated, Connery would be his clothes-horse.

Champagne had, literally, flowed day and night during the making of *From Russia with Love*. Now it seemed justified. In the wake of the October première floodgates opened. It seemed as if the worldwide media gave 007 an ovation. The write-ups were dramatically good. As a feat of technical virtuosity – the American production values – the movie defied any negative criticism. But there was much more than just appreciation for a stylish modern thriller. Wry political elements teased the super-highbrow critics prone to analysing cinema as a mirror of life. There were, of course, some dissenters. Philip Oakes in the *Sunday Telegraph* catalogued the voyeurism, sadism and lesbianism stacked in the film and suggested: 'It is a movie made entirely for kicks. Guns go off; girls get undressed; people have sex;

people die. Happening succeeds happening, but nothing and no one is of real significance.' What Oakes was circumspectly describing was the social fall-out of the new, liberal era. It was the era of Bond and the Beatles. An era of icon-replacement and irony. The youth culture. Bond was perceived by some as an establishment figure, but the kids knew better: Bond was for them, for kicks.

Duly, America fell. After the assassination of President Kennedy on 22 November, the Cold War intensified and the cartoon relevance of Bond versus the Beast was sealed. *Playboy* magazine, sub-literary voicebox of all America – young liberal and, in its own way, conservative – adopted Bond as its standard-bearer instantly, and in so doing assured colossal popularity through all strata of society during the confused sixties. (*Playboy* earned the distinction of serialising Fleming's last few novels prior to book publication. It also specialised in features on Bond movie girls, running nude or topless shots of Ursula Andress, Martine Beswick, Margaret Nolan, Molly Peters, Mie Hama and Lana Wood. Incisive superior articles and interviews with Fleming, Connery, Dick Maibaum and Roald Dahl, who wrote the script of *You Only Live Twice*, also frustrated lesser journals keen to cash in on the Bond boom.)

Connery's notices for *From Russia* jousted for pride of place with those of the lovable Pedro Armendariz as Kerim Bey, villain Robert Shaw and Daniela Bianchi. Bianchi particularly did well and many enjoyed her endearingly waiflike performance which, in spite of her newness, was consistent (though she was dubbed by British actress Barbara Jefford). In America, where the film opened in April 1964, the acid pen of hard-to-please critic Manny Farber decided the winner, though backhanding equal honours to the runner-up. In an article in *Cavalier* magazine he waxed eloquent on 'Robert Shaw's scene stealing . . . which is done alongside Sean Connery, who is a master in his own right in the art of sifting into a scene, covertly inflicting a soft dramatic quality inside the external toughness.' Bosley Crowther, meanwhile, in the *New York Times* was hollering, 'Don't miss it! . . . Just go and see it and have yourself a good time.'

'About half-way through *Woman of Straw*,' a film colleague relates, 'Sean's attitude to acting and stardom changed – overnight. Diane was behind him, so was Harry Saltzman maybe – though he lived to regret it – but suddenly Sean was *it*.' Strengthened by financial security and the gradual realisation of his greatest ambitions, Connery did appear to alter tack during the winter of 1963–4. One magazine article of the period quoted a press agent ranting: 'Sean Connery? You want my honest opinion? Sean Connery is a great, big, conceited, untalented, wooden-headed ninny.' Whispering tales were already circulating about his greed and big-headedness ('You couldn't drag him to a party unless there was something in it for him'). At Pinewood Studios, filming with the short-tempered Gina Lollobrigida, Connery was apparently asserting his equal-star-billing status. The on-set mood was reputedly horrendous and technicians reported daily conferences, where director Dearden cast oil on troubled waters. Connery was constantly suggesting script rewrites, though his friend Stanley Mann, whom he later grew close to, had co-drafted the original. Friends suggest Cilento had much to do with proposed alterations. 'Her stock was high,' says Ian Bannen. 'She'd just finished Tony Richardson's *Tom Jones* and gotten herself an Academy Award Nomination. She was still full of energy, and full of ideas for making Sean an "artist".' On location in Majorca cast relationships deteriorated alarmingly. Connery was allegedly 'sick and tired' of Lollobrigida's lapses. (Connery later denied any rift: he liked working with La Lolla, he said.) One scene called for him to roughen her up with a shake and a face slap. Furious after an earlier argument, Connery hit Lollobrigida too hard, sending her reeling. He later apologised, claiming accidental force, but expanded in an interview, 'Acting is a job, like carpentry or building roads. There are a hundred people involving in putting you up there on screen. The trouble with a lot of stars is that they develop heads as big as their close-ups.' His own head, he made clear, was unchanged in good fortune. 'If I wore hats,' he snapped, 'I think you'd find I still take the same size.'

Very intimate friends bear up Connery's declaration. His home life was simple. He kept one secretary whose function was to answer fan mail. He drove a Volkswagen (later a second-hand Jaguar) while Cilento had a small Austin Healy. His only notable indulgence was good eating. ('Sean loves his grub before everything,' says John Boorman.) The only appreciable change concerned his attitude to the work on offer. 'It must have been after the first or second Bond that he decided to quit the stage,' says Ian Bannen. 'He suddenly said he never wanted to do it again . . . that all that shouting hurt his throat. Simply, he wanted to do first-class films – and only films.'

Michael Caine says, 'He'd brought to Bond the gift every star actor has: he'd made Bond his own – doesn't matter what Ian Fleming originally visualised. Sean was Bond. But he knew his talents were bigger than that. Of course there was lots more he wanted to do while the going was good. He was smart about his breakthrough.'

In December 1963, just after *Woman of Straw* concluded, and distressingly early in the day for Harry Saltzman, Connery was telling *Photoplay* the extent of his unease at the prospect of typecasting. 'I remember once going to see a casting director for a role in a picture,' Connery said. 'When she asked me, "And what type of actor are you, Mr Connery?" I just got up and walked out. . . . An actor hates to be typecast . . . I don't want to be Bond all the time. It riles me when people call me Bond off the set. . . . That's why I'm making pictures like *Woman of Straw*, in the hope audiences will accept me in other parts.' But there was caution in such soul-baring too. Around the same time he was deriding the 'socially conscious plays and scripts [that treat] working men as noble savages'. He told the *Daily Mail*, 'There's so much bull about written by armchair socialists.' In that regard, by current cinema standards, he was lucky to be playing Bond, a cleverly concocted, subtly humorous, intelligent role.

Woman of Straw, as it turned out, did nothing to enhance Connery's reputation beyond Bond, though its critical assessment and damnation was unfairly based on comparison with the lavish production values of the Broccoli–Saltzman pictures. Predictably, Ralph Richardson earned all the praise, managing, by *The Times*'s reckoning, 'to extract slight fun from the glum proceedings'. The film was phrased, it is true, as pseudo-Hitchcock, and had a stagey feel (the later stage version by Catherine Arley and Ian Cullen worked better, capitalising on an easier evocation of claustrophobia). In the story, nurse Maria (Lollobrigida) is persuaded by Anthony Richmond (Connery) to marry his unsympathetic invalid uncle (Richardson) and so, in due course, inherit and share out the uncle's fortune, estimated at many millions. Maria grows to care for the old man, but when he dies prematurely she is convicted of murder. The dénouement is straightforward: Anthony has set her up, murdered the old man and, as next of kin, plans to net all the money for himself. The final scene has a rather predictable showdown with the police, unexpected evidence from the black butler who has come to like Maria, and the tables turned on Anthony. The *Monthly Film Bulletin* approved of Connery, but wished greater inventiveness with the material – the names of Welles, Losey and Hitchcock were invoked – but the *New York Times* blamed everything on Lollobrigida. 'Try as the script and camera may to convince us that Miss Lollobrigida is the most irresistible of females, she stubbornly remains her placid, matronly self – hardly the type to draw a passing snort from an old lion like Sir Ralph. No wonder Mr Connery double-crosses her in the end.' William Peper in the *New York World Telegram and Sun* complained that Connery cut 'a handsome but rather colourless figure' . . . and, inevitably, that he was 'much more fun as James Bond'.

Connery's immediate response to the poor reception of his first major role since Bond was submerged in the pre-production of the third Bond, *Goldfinger*, and, more excitingly, the frenzy of work on yet another in-between feature, though this was a somewhat special one, called

128

Marnie. 'I wasn't all that thrilled with *Woman of Straw*,' he said afterwards, 'although the problems were my own. I'd been working nonstop since goodness knows how long and [was] trying to suggest rewrites while making another film (*From Russia with Love*) . . . It was an experience, but I won't make that mistake again.'

Both Connery and the press were unfair to *Woman of Straw*, which stands staunch in retrospect, removed from Bond comparisons. As in *The Frightened City*, the seething aggression that Connery displays in his dark character counterpoints all other players beautifully. Richardson is subtly superb and, no matter what the *New York Times* says, La Lollo is a treat in slinky black underwear. Several years after its release, *Woman of Straw* was still ringing on the tills for producer Michael Relph and distributors and backers UA, bearing up well in its own right.

It could not, of course, keep pace with Bond. According to reports in *Variety*, within twelve months *From Russia with Love*, which had cost exactly $2 million, had grossed $12.5 million, overshadowing everything else at the British box office for 1963–4, and *Dr No* was already $5 million in the black. Sean Connery was in demand across the world and, understanding very well now the peak he was arriving at, he reached for the masters.

Almost precisely two years after hoofing out of his little Fiat and signing on for *Dr No* at £25,000, Connery and agent Richard Hatton were writing a thank you to Alfred Hitchcock and Universal for $400,000, the negotiated lead fee for a pet project of Hitch's, *Marnie*. *Marnie* began life as a novel by *Poldark* author Winston Graham, was purchased by Hitchcock in 1961 as the ideal property to reintroduce Grace Kelly, Princess of Monaco, into films, and had Universal's backing from the start. Joseph Stefano, who had so brilliantly adapted Robert Bloch's *Psycho*, wrote the treatment and Grace Kelly accepted Hitch's velvety persuasion. But at the last minute word of the project broke in Monaco, the princess's subjects were enraged and the movie ground to a halt. Hitch shelved *Marnie* and rushed into *The Birds*, testing the lead-playing potential of a new discovery, 26-year-old New Yorker 'Tippi' Hedren (Hitch always insisted on the quotes round 'Tippi'). *The Birds* did well enough to encourage Hitch to try Hedren in a stronger character role and, very abruptly, in 1963 he reactivated *Marnie*, engaging a woman writer, Jay Preston Allan, to develop the female title role for his new star. Connery had come to Hitch's attention in *Dr No*, which he is known to have watched with interest, having rejected Bond two years before. Cubby Broccoli also claims that he was responsible, at least in part, for Connery's casting in *Marnie*. At Connery's request, says Broccoli, he rang Hitchcock, and informed him of the star's interest in working with 'the master'. At any rate, once decided on his young male lead, Hitchcock was prepared to pay whatever asking price. $400,000 was a lot for a relatively new star, but Universal could swallow that. Less digestible was Connery's second stipulation: Hatton conveyed the word timorously – Connery wanted to read the script before committing himself. Hitchcock thought twice, concerned at the possibility of being hampered by the condition he despised above all, the star ego. But, as Michael Caine points out, 'no matter how it was for Sean, he never was one who had time for the accoutrements of ego: in that sense he was always an actor's actor.' Hitch clearly caught wind of this and ignored the prevailing gossip from certain quarters that hinted that Bond–Connery was becoming a monster. He told associates Connery had the perfect combination of youthful sexiness and relative inexperience which he always sought. He could mould Connery, which was what he wanted.

In London the pop press paraded the story of Connery's 'gruff individualism' with glee. Hitchcock's London agent had allegedly told Connery, 'Even Cary Grant doesn't ask to read a Hitchcock script.' To which Connery was supposed to have replied, 'Well, I'm not Cary Grant.' The Bondian devil-may-care tone was played to the hilt, much to the satisfaction of Saltzman and Broccoli. Even *Time* magazine in the States took up the *Marnie* propaganda line, eulogising a new breed of movie man: 'Connery's individualism is just right for Bond, who makes steely love, is a wine snob, and likes to rub people out without leaving blood on the carpet.' Privately Connery dismissed the fuss over his asking for the script. For a start he was exhausted, having worked without a break for more than a year, first promoting *Dr No* throughout Europe on personal tour, then dashing through *From Russia with Love* and *Woman of Straw*. Asking to read a script was no big deal because, much as he honestly revered Hitchcock, he wanted to be sure *Marnie* was not some sub-Bond potboiler possibly forced on Hitchcock by Universal, who were reportedly less than delighted with *The Birds*. Protesting about the to-do over what one newspaper described as his 'failure to conform to the established patterns of the film business' Connery explained, 'Look, for the first time in my life I can ask to read a script, and if you had been in some of the tripe I have, you'd know why.' In the end, he got the script, glanced through it and saw immediately that Hitchcock knew what he was about. *Marnie* was, simply, the finest thing he had been offered since *Dr No*. And – best lure of all – Hitchcock was giving him Hollywood again.

Before Christmas 1963 Connery flew to Los Angeles alone and was picked up by two Universal VIPs at the airport. He refused the chauffeured limousine placed at his disposal and asked for a small runaround 'like my Volks back home'. Taken to the fashionable Chateau Marmont, according to the *People*, he seemed horrified. 'Nice place,' he grunted, 'but what's wrong with the motel I stayed at in Burbank six years ago? Easy to get in and out of and very inexpensive.' And so he was taken to Jimmy O'Dea's beloved 'Fatima Mansions', the flat-roofed shack originally laid on by Disney. 'It was the same little game about restaurants,' an American magazine reported. Asked how he felt about Chasen's or LaScala, Connery bluntly stated his preference for American hamburgers. His idea of entertainments too caused surprise. No, he didn't want to take in local strip shows or star parties or touring musicals. He wanted to swim a bit, knock a golf ball round (he had just been introduced to golf by Terence Young), maybe collect a suntan more in fitting with the swanky American businessman he was to play.

Whatever lingering fears Hitchcock and Universal had about star temperaments must have dissipated within hours. Connery was not likely to shirk the discipline of the job. He had come back to Hollywood to work.

From their first meeting Connery and Hitchcock got on well. Hitchcock was a little unsure of Connery's blatant lack of social grace in some areas, but he enjoyed the Scotsman's appetite for work – monumentally more important in his eyes – and his speed with lines. Connery, for his part, liked the respect afforded him, not just by the master himself, but by the serious film press. There was talk of Bond, but intelligent questioning too. Later he guessed the reasons for his smooth professional acceptance was that 'Most of the younger British actors today, like Finney and O'Toole and me, are more organic, down-to-earth actors than previous generations. In America there is much more feel for realism than in Europe, where there is still a conception of an actor as being somewhat divorced from real life, and in Britain, where acting is still often associated more with being statuesque and striking poses and declaiming with lyrical voices.'

But Bond was taking America by storm while Connery was making his declaration of independence and, because a minimum of three Saltzman–Broccoli pictures lay ahead of him, he was forced to make some concessions to the pop press. Between takes at Universal Studios and on brief location in Maryland he was photographed with busty aspiring actress-models, and an informal chat with Hitchcock about the relative merits of British and foreign women received massive, nonsense cover. Hands contemplatively clasped around his paunch, Hitchcock restated his devotion to chilly English women: 'They are three-dimensional . . . the other type of beauty, the Italian, big voluptuous figures may look 3-D but, believe me, they are just cut-out dolls.' Connery retorted, 'You've just described my type.'

132

Marnie progressed well. A rift between Hedren and Hitchcock half-way through slowed proceedings for a day or so, but Hitchcock had been through the mill so many times he could, in the words of a technician, 'direct with his eyes shut and his cigar stone cold'. The plot had been doctored to accommodate a young lead. In the book the Connery character was an elderly man. Connery plays Mark Rutland, a rich company executive, who discovers that a junior in his employ, Marnie (Hedren) is a kleptomaniac. When he discovers her criminality he covers for her and cajoles her into marriage, believing loving attention will change her. But he finds her frigid and incapable of love. Challenged, he explores her behaviour and background, eventually discovering her to be the daughter of a prostitute whose lover attacked her and whom Marnie, in defence of her mother, killed. The neuroses explained, Mark leads Marnie off to a better life.

Hitchcock outlined for François Truffaut the attraction of the storyline. He wanted to make the movie, he said, because of 'the fetish idea. A man wants to go to bed with a thief because she is a thief, just like other men have a yen for Chinese or coloured women.' Mark was, to Hitchcock, mildly neurotic too – though none of this was relayed on set or in script to Connery. 'I had a great time with Hitchcock,' Connery said. 'He tells you on the set what moves he wants. The only major direction he gave to me . . . was when I was listening to what somebody else was saying in a scene, and he pointed out that I was listening with my mouth open – as I often do – and he thought it would look better shut.' But of the neurotic slant to Mark: 'He never got into anything like that. He used to tell me funny stories before a take quite often, but he never dwelt upon the psychology of the character. . . . His humour is pretty schoolboyish.' At one stage Hitchcock told Connery, 'If I'm paying you as much as I am and you don't know what you're doing, then I deserve what I get in the way of performance.'

For the latter part of the picture Cilento flew out to Hollywood with the children, and the family rented a lavish $1,000-a-month Bel Air bungalow complete with swimming pool where Cilento bathed naked daily. From there Connery made provisional arrangements with John Ford's agents to take the star part in the planned film biography of playwright Sean O'Casey, to start rolling in Dublin, towards the end of 1964 when, it was hoped, *Goldfinger* would be comfortably in the can. Cilento liked the ring of class to the project and backed up her man, as she did when he refused to don a Bondish Savile Row suit and set the cornerstone of MCA's new skyscraper, opting for a golf round with her with instead.

'The atmosphere was heavy with integrity and sophistication,' says a publicist, a shade sardonically. 'Here was Diane carrying round her Academy nomination and Sean working for Hitchcock and chatting to John Ford. There was a bit of hypocrisy, though – because Sean was already pretending that Bond was just the sideline, the money-taker, when in fact Bond was his *success*.'

Marnie, in its final cut, displeased Hitchcock to some degree. He felt the neurotic conundrums had not been delineated sharply enough and, though Connery had sailed through complex emotional variations quite effortlessly, aspects of the character which seemed to work on set did not carry over to celluloid. In his published conversations with Hitchcock, Truffaut suggested that the role of Mark had been miscast: Laurence Olivier might have reached the subtler heights. Hitchcock was inclined to agree: 'I wasn't convinced that Sean Connery was a Philadelphia gentleman. You know, if you want to reduce *Marnie* to its lowest common denominator, it is the story of the prince and the beggar girl. In a story of this kind you need a real gentleman, a more elegant man than we had.'

The comment was not intended to insult Connery personally. As a capable pro, Hitchcock had admired Connery more than many of his leading men, rating him somewhere below Cary Grant or Jimmy Stewart, but above Rod Taylor and Paul Newman. The technicians on *Marnie* shared the maestro's admiration. When the picture wrapped they presented Connery with a memento of the good times – a gold watch valued at $1,000. Connery found the sentiment 'rather touching', though he was less than touched by the postscript. On re-entering Britain in March, en route to start *Goldfinger*, Customs demanded a £25 duty on the 'luxury goods' import.

Marnie opened in the summer of 1964 to mixed reviews and reasonable business, helped, like *Woman of Straw* by the oblique Bond link. For Eugene Archer in the *New York Times* it was, regrettably, 'a clear miss . . . the master's most disappointing film in years'. Connery worked, he judged, 'commendably and well . . . but inexperience shows'. *The Times* was kinder; its critic believed the film 'manages remarkably well . . . it is easy to see why the plot outline should have taken Mr Hitchcock's fancy: it is essentially *Spellbound* turned inside-out . . . moreover, the film has plenty of material for the nuttier French Hitchcock enthusiasts: a dash of *amour fou* in the hero's obsessive devotion to a beloved he knows to be from the outset almost impossible; lots and lots about the crucial word which can set free (shades of *Upper Capricorn*) and the exchange of culpability.' Mr Sean Connery, for *The Times*, 'escapes quite effectively from the James Bond stereotype.' Almost all reviewers – and early audiences – joked about unusually bad process work, back-projection and obvious painted backdrops, the final set of the street where Marnie's mother lives earning derision everywhere – 'like something Trauner might have cooked up for Carne in the good old days,' *The Times* jeered.

In later years the very factors that damned *Marnie* were to be instrumental in securing its position among the cult élite. It was, historians reckoned, a picture that resided outside time, a compendium of all Hitchcock films, 'an illuminating portrayal of the delicate balance between sickness and health in everyone'. (Dr Donald Spoto, in *The Art of Alfred Hitchcock*, 1977.)

Connery, however, suffered the grey realities of the present. He had revelled in the optimism of the Californian winter, and disliked returning to the damp drudgery of another Bond at Pinewood. Hollywood was twice as attractive the second time round, because now there was the deep cushion of cash and recognition, and Lana Turner was small fry in the deep and misty past. But, for Connery, contractually bound to Bond, Hollywood was as far away as ever.

The frustrations and disappointments piled up. Despite high hopes, Cilento did not win the Academy Award in her nominated category of Best Supporting Actress: the award went instead to Margaret Rutherford for *The VIPs*. On top of that, Connery's professional momentum seemed once more inhibited by the Bond boom. Apart from John Ford's proffered *Young Cassidy* – which was destined to fall through anyway – the hoped-for deluge of Hitchcock-quality offers never came. Instead there were offers for tacky, clichéd sub-Bond trash, a multitude of scripts that insulted his intelligence.

Back at Acton the fans huddled round the high walls of Acacia House, as they had done intermittently for months, anxious to catch a glimpse of the neo-establishment super-stud hero who was cheekily outpacing the Beatles in the rapid-growth-phenomenon stakes. They saw instead a balding, angry man in a heavy overcoat, glowering, ready to do battle with Harry Saltzman and Cubby Broccoli.

11

Agony and Ecstasy and . . .

'James Bond came of age with *Goldfinger*,' says new Bond director Guy Hamilton, 'but in so doing stirred up a bit of a hornet's nest.' Greed, ruthless ambition, pomposity and a pervasive fear of failure almost strangled the Bond series at this bountiful time. The spring of 1964 was not a peaceful spring for anyone associated with Bond or the Broccoli–Saltzman company, Eon. Terence Young, who had been preparing the new script with Dick Maibaum, fell out with the producers because he demanded a cut of *Goldfinger*'s profits, and was replaced by ace action director Hamilton whose credits included *The Colditz Story*. A new screenwriter, the esteemed Paul Dehn, was summoned, and Hamilton began daily work at Dehn's Chelsea flat, rebuilding Maibaum's loose script. Saltzman, always the gadget man, was at war with Broccoli, ever the tit-and-action man, though both felt, in line with Hamilton's thinking, that the best and worst of the first two movies must be sifted and analysed in order to consolidate. Hamilton was keen from the start not to fall into the trap of 'doing the obvious in merely following what had gone before'.

Amidst this tumult, this measured strategy to make hay while the sun shone, Connery sauntered in with his gripe. 'Sean had risen to stardom very fast by most standards,' Hamilton says. 'Only five or six years before I had had nodding acquaintance with him at Gerry's Drinking Club, opposite the stage door of Her Majesty's. I didn't think he had too much going for him, but by *Dr No* he was proving his salt. He matured rapidly then, and the difference in performance between *Dr No* and *Russia* is vast. And so with the Bond success he was picking up offers here, there and everywhere. But the big problem, the cause of his disillusion before *Goldfinger*, was that the offers he could consider were restricted by the contractual commitments of doing Bond. Those Bond pictures took a hell of a time to do, and Cubby and Harry weren't naturally prepared to allow Sean to go after other jobs as they arose. *Woman of Straw* gave Sean no particular satisfaction because it wasn't the kind of film he wanted to be doing. He was concerned about his craft. He came back from Hollywood wondering what he was . . . he wanted to test himself and see if he was more than just Mickey Mouse as James Bond.'

Connery also wanted greater compensation for cramped opportunity. He had grown to dislike Saltzman intensely – 'mistrust him', in the words of Lewis Gilbert – and was suspicious of placatory suggestions made by Eon. Finally, reluctantly, he accepted $50,000 plus a percentage for *Goldfinger*, stemming his annoyance by putting out word, via Hatton and other close business friends, that he was seeking radical, typesmashing parts. The 'integrity' some associates snigger at seemed quite real. Despite the eagerness for change and challenge, Connery rejected the first draft script of *Young Cassidy* submitted by Ford, at which time Rod Taylor was marched in to plug the gap.

'After this one [*Goldfinger*],' Connery told an actress friend over dinner, 'it's got to be something away from the sauve gentleman. It's got to be a classy part.'

Physically, making Bond was tougher than ever, though Hamilton was a more ordered director than Young, the kind who plans every move, allows little improvisation and believes 'sorting out the locations is the hardest part'. Shooting began in March at Pinewood in an atmosphere co-lead Honor Blackman describes as 'furiously professional'. A director of vision and sound commercial instincts, Hamilton more than anybody was responsible for

138

the huge success of *Goldfinger*, the movie that rechan-
nelled Bond from the edge of earnest amorality to untouchable U-certificates. 'The difficulty was often the
divergence of opinion between Saltzman and Broccoli,'
Hamilton says. 'It became a case of why-is-your-idea-
better-than-mine? One had to sit around for hours
awaiting decisions. But once that obstacle was overcome,
it was fine. I had my say in casting. I believed Bond must
play opposite someone strong, someone to draw out his
strengths. That's why I wanted Gert Frobe, the German
actor who was very accomplished, and Honor. With
Honor, who is a powerful actress, there was a certain "Oh
my God, she's the *Avengers* girl and how do we overcome
that?" . . . and they said she looked like a raddled bag
compared with some of the young frillies they'd used. But
I said, don't worry, she's a fine actress, that's what is
important – and we can shoot her with filters to make her
look whatever way you like.'

Blackman herself was in no doubt that she had been
assigned because of her wide experience – plus the personal
following she had won with her kinky, leather-costumed
Cathy Gale in TV's *The Avengers*. 'I'm sure the appeal of
macho Bond versus kinky me was at the back of the producers' minds,' says Blackman. 'It obviously worked on
screen, this strong female persona – it substituted for the
lesbian aspect of the heroine Pussy [which was in the book].
It was decided this [lesbianism] would be understated in the
movie.'

Pussy Galore is Bond's first unfriendly lover, a lesbian
gangleader who assists megalomanic Auric Goldfinger
(Frobe) in his ambitious attempt to penetrate the gold
depository at Fort Knox, Kentucky, and contaminate the
contents by exploding a nuclear device, thereby incalcul-
ably increasing the value of his own gold reserves. Bond,
against the odds (indeed, against character credibility),
seduces Pussy Galore when all else has failed and wins the
day. Simple fare – but with the strong and imaginative hand
of Hamilton, some spiky Dehn dialogue and the creation of
prototype sub-villains (Oddjob, played by Harold Sakata)

and outrageous diversions introduced mostly by Saltzman (the gadget-laden Aston Martin DB5), the movie took on an extra dimension hitherto unreached in the series.

'I was helped, naturally, by what had gone before,' says Hamilton. 'But I wasn't, for instance, prepared to shoot miles of film and leave half of it on the floor, as had been the case. In *Goldfinger* Bond was sweetened, I suppose by the perfection of formula. There were only about twenty shots that never appeared on screen. Myself, Sean – we all knew what we were aiming for from day one.'

To Honor Blackman, Connery cut an impressive figure in two ways. 'Firstly he was downright perfectionist, as I am. I liked that. He would never expect one to buy a bad take. If he fluffed, he was the first to call a halt. But he wasn't a directorial voice. Guy had full command – so much so that he didn't balk at putting me in my place! There were elements of the lesbian character I would have liked to try out, but he said no. An in-joke or two was fine – like me calling my co-pilot girl Harry or Joe – but that was enough for Guy.' Blackman also admired Connery's scepticism of 'the publicity machine', a wariness made acute by what she saw was essential shyness. 'He was a reserved man,' she says, 'confident but private. As the film went on, obviously we got to know each other better. Privately. I found him attractive, sexy . . .' She laughs mysteriously. 'I think he's got a pair of the best eyes that have ever been seen on screen, apart from anything else he might have that's good – and let's say there's plenty of *that*.'

Shyness alone was not the root of Connery's troubles with publicity. Hamilton is quick to emphasise that, regardless of threatened rifts with the producers, Connery was keen to outdo *From Russia with Love*. He was willing to do whatever had to be done, but his patience was frequently tried by the constant interruptions at Pinewood, where publicists brought casual journalists onto the set. In one incident, during a key scene a French writer was landed abruptly on Connery. The lady writer began to shoot questions. 'First she asked what the film was called,' says Connery. 'I told her. Then what part I was playing. I told her . . .' The back-breaking straw came when the journalist jotted Gert Frobe's name on her pad as chief villain. 'I've never heard of *her*,' she mumbled. Connery exploded. 'I just blew up and walked off the set,' he recalls. 'So I suppose I'm considered rude by that person. Well I consider *her* disrespectful and incompetent, and both are definite sins. If someone treats me rudely or dishonestly, you see, I repay them an eye for an eye.'

As she had done with *From Russia* and the later films, Cilento coached her husband through *Goldfinger*, helping him learn his lines in his study at Acton by sitting in as Pussy or Jill (Shirley Eaton in the film). She confessed she enjoyed the Bond girl parts, but thought them fundamentally too facile and scant: she herself would never wish to star in a Bond. As it was, her own recently rocky career was stabilising. With Jason growing spirited and independent she had room to breathe again – and chase good parts. *Rattle of a Simple Man*, a minor movie that attracted good notices, was her first worthwhile occupation since *Tom Jones*, and now Carol Reed was offering a prestigious role in *The Agony and the Ecstasy*. Cilento was delighted with the new script and keen to have her husband star opposite her, but the movie was already fully cast, and he was stuck on Bond anyway. An alternative, for the future, was sought.

With perfect timing Terence Young came back into the picture. He was preparing his own movie version of the Defoe classic *Moll Flanders*, and was agreeable to the notion of pairing husband and wife in the leads. No sooner was Connery's appetite for challenge whetted than the idea was dashed. Reed's film was booked to start in Italy in June, but no definite finish date could be given. Young had to start rolling in the autumn. For a few days it was heart-rending stalemate, then Young moved on with other actors and the Connerys lost their chance. Cilento flew to Rome with her mother and children, *Goldfinger* duly wrapped in July and an atmosphere of gloom descended on the Eon camp. 'We knew Sean was pissed off with Bond,' a publicist says. 'We knew the series was threatening what he regarded as his actor status. I think probably he wanted out there and then but, like Harry and Cubby, he was kind of mesmerised by the potential. He was thinking, 'All right, it's a bore, a madhouse, but how much bigger can it get? Will *Goldfinger* earn – what? – $5 million? How much could I earn if I stuck with it? He was divided between what he was at heart, an old-fashioned, learn-up-your lines actor, and a businessman with his hands in a honeypot.'

United Artists pushed out the red carpet for *Goldfinger*, promoting it massively and planning close major premières in London and New York (September and December respectively). Connery, meanwhile, began his first holiday in nearly two years, flying to Rome to join Cilento with a script in his briefcase that he had first turned down when *Moll Flanders* was in the air, but which now interested him more than a little. The script was an adaptation of Ray Rigby's stage play, *The Hill*, about a North African detention camp for would-be deserters in the Second War. It had been given to him by Pinewood-based producer Kenneth Hyman, and was immediately attractive for the subtlety of its plotline and depth of its characters, factors Connery hungered for. Sidney Lumet, the celebrated American director of notorious films like *The Pawnbroker*, was to take the reins – another definite plus. In Rome Connery made his positive decision to do *The Hill*, and overnight the post-Hollywood, post-Bond depression lifted. There was other good news. Telephone negotiations were afoot with producer Doc Merman to co-star husband and wife in a movie version of the best-selling novel *Call Me When the Cross Turns Over* in Sydney, Australia, early in 1965.

The paparazzi and scandal-thirsty Italian journalists inevitably fastened onto Cilento, Connery, Cinecitta and the shortest distance between those points while 'James Bond' was in residence in their capital city, but excitement was hard to find. Cilento was a dutiful and admired actress, liked by co-stars Charlton Heston and Rex Harrison and almost too obedient to the camera call. Connery stayed in the pretty pink villa in the hills, reading, idling, going shoeless day and night, growing a moustache for *The Hill*, tending Jason, chit-chatting with the cook and Lady Cilento. A French journalist who spent an idle lunchtime with the happy family reported them 'ideally suited, as content as any young family could hope to be'.

Connery found preparation for *The Hill* more satisfying than any movie experience in his life so far. He ascribed his profound pleasure to 'the time to prepare, to get all the ins and outs of what I was going to do worked out with the director and producer in advance, to find out if we were all on the same track.' There were minor rewrites, but Rigby's script was so good and Lumet's envisaged treatment so assured that Connery felt that insistence on small alterations would be churlish.

Just before he departed for the Spanish location, news came through that Ian Fleming had died in Canterbury after a heart attack. Connery had liked Fleming – 'a dreadful snob, but a marvellous companion . . . we shared many fascinating conversations and his knowledge was vast'. Word of the death came while Connery was playing golf with Rex Harrison at Rome's Olgiata championship course. In apt tribute, the two stars played an extra eighteen holes, Connery teeing off with a Penfold Hearts Ball, the type Fleming dictated for James Bond in his match against Goldfinger in the novel. 'It seemed appropriate,' Connery said. 'I think Ian would have liked that.'

Fleming missed the triumph of the *Goldfinger* opening by just five weeks. For the first time mob-style crowds crammed Leicester Square for the grand Odeon première, attended by Honor Blackman 'wearing a solid gold finger-cast, quite stupid actually, and flanked by big security men'. Autograph hunters stalked everywhere. Fans ripped down poster hoardings and chanted for Connery. TV news picked up the opening night story. Bond was of age, all right – bigger in stature than Eon could ever have hoped for, even on the strength of previous successes. The financial rewards were astounding, in terms of immediate box-office takings. The *Evening News* reported that 'nothing like *Goldfinger* has happened in films since they discovered the word "stupendous".' For the last week in September the Leicester Square Odeon took £17,327 and the Hammersmith Odeon, which averaged £2,000 on its biggest Hollywood attractions, totted £10,000. In New York, weeks later, the phenomenon was repeated and embellished. *Goldfinger* cost $2,000,000, inclusive of artists' fees. *Variety* reported it had become the fastest money-maker in the history of motion pictures, grossing $10,374,807 in fourteen weeks in the United States and Canada. United Artists took the unprecedented step of announcing its expectations: by the time the movie ended its engagements in the US, about $20 million in receipts was expected, and this a conservative estimate.

On the critical front, response was neatly divided between the perspicacious and the snobbishly begrudging. *Punch* was open-handed in praise: 'The whole thing is glossy, entertaining, often funny nonsense.' In the *Spectator* Isabel Quigly was worried about the movie being 'the most overtly fascist of this insanitary series', but had to admit the audience approved, clapped, laughed, cheered its head off – and 'not just a hooligan patch of it'. *Saturday Review* admired Hamilton ('who has paced the action . . . faster'), Fleming, and Connery ('who has the role down pat by now'). Penelope Houston devoted a huge chunk of *Sight and Sound* to in-depth analysis, concluding that *Goldfinger* was 'rather a symbolic film' which, as Penelope Gilliatt had suggested of the Bond boom, encapsulated 'the brassy, swinging, ungallant taste of the sixties'. The *Daily Worker*'s comment that the entire business was 'one vast, gigantic confidence trick to blind the audience to what is going on underneath' was given short shrift. Leonard Mosley, always to the point, gasped, 'Even for eggheads, I swear this film is worth a visit. Honor bright. My word is my Bond.' *The Times* dryly observed: 'Superb hokum . . . Ian Fleming would have enjoyed it,' and Alexander Walker thought it, and Honor Blackman especially, the best thing since spliced film. In America, *Newsweek*'s lofty commentators noted Freudian undertones and wagged a heavy finger with the deduction that Connery-Bond was 'the only guy in the world who has satisfactorily resolved his Oedipus complex. It is an odd entertainment when the hero's strength is as the strength of ten because his gender is pure.'

Connery – the purity of whose gender had never been in doubt – was unmoved by all the tub-thumping. He was glad to repair to Almeria in southern Spain, away from prying flashbulbs and rubbish questioners, to join Lumet and his cast for what was to be his most physically gruelling film to date. Leaving the family again so soon might have presented problems, but Cilento was still contentedly dug into *The Agony and the Ecstasy* and Lady Cilento was there to be surrogate parent.

Ken Hyman, the producer, had expressly made clear the likely strenuous demands of *The Hill*. With his construction crew, headed by art director Bert Smith and manager Dick Frith, he had been in and out of Almeria for three months preparing the ground. The exigencies of film-making made it more feasible to base the production in Spain rather than North Africa, where writer Rigby – on whose personal experience *The Hill* was based – had been a prisoner of war during the Second World War. But Almeria was no easy alternative. The entire action of the picture takes place within a wired stockade under blazing sun, but the ideal site was hard to find. Smith and Frith finally found a sandy wasteland at Gabo de Gata where, over ten weeks, an area of 500 yards by 200 was cleared (one sand dune, 200 feet square and 15 feet high was bulldozed away), and the punishment hill of the title was built, using 10,000 feet of imported tubular steel, and more than 60 tons of timber and stone. From midsummer the sun was fierce – temperatures never fell below 115 degrees – and conditions improved not at all when the cast arrived.

'We were in the bloody desert,' says Ian Bannen, who was starring on screen for the first time with his old pal, 'and the water and food were ghastly. It'd be hard to find words to describe the location. Tough, that's all I can say. Real tough.'

Two thousand gallons of pure water were shipped in to keep crew and cast alive, but that didn't stave off dysentery. In the beginning, after the rest in Rome and buoyed with the enthusiasm of breaking from type, Connery bore up while others fell to sickness. The actors' working day was long – ten hours or more, six days a week – and fitness was the prime requisite. 'If Sean was uptight about Bond, Sidney [Lumet] kept him smiling,' Bannen says. 'I think *Time* magazine summed it up when it said Sidney makes love to his cast and crew; he's a great sweetener. Sean was fine at the start – despite the fact the location was as smelly as Aberdeen on a hot day. Fishy, that's what it was like, fish-smelling. Awful.'

Eventually Connery did fall ill, flattened by a combination of the heat, the rigours of running round and 'Spanish tummy', but he was on his feet in a day or two and not much shooting time was lost. 'It was the one picture I was on where there was no yellow, pink and blue [script amendments pages],' says Bannen, 'and that pleased Sean a lot.'

Connery in fact rated Lumet, the picture and the passion of purpose very highly. Despite the privations of Almeria, he loved every minute of the seven-week shoot – five in Spain, and two for interiors at Metro Studios in Borehamwood. Later he saw it as 'an example of a film which wasn't a success by the public's standard but eventually became, in terms of acceptance, a supposed classic. . . . The idea was to make an ensemble movie, and we made it. The writer, the director, the cast and myself all agreed we'd succeeded in making the movie we wanted to make.'

The Hill, Bannen observed accurately, was a man's film in many ways. The cast was all male, the story uncompromisingly brutal. In a British military stockade errant prisoners are repeatedly forced to climb an almost sheer man-made hill, weighed down with full kits, tongue-lashed by vicious sadists like Staff Sergeant Williams (Ian Hendry). Joe Roberts (Connery), court-martialled for striking an officer, is one such prisoner, pushed beyond endurance, but fighting 'the system' to the end. Bannen, who played righteous Sergeant Harris, thought the film a winner as soon as he saw the rushes at Borehamwood. 'But you can never tell from the bits and pieces. As it happened, it didn't take in the money and we were all, I'll

146

confess, disappointed. Sean more than most, I'd say. There were things that maybe were misjudged. The black and white photography was aesthetically fine but the American drive-ins don't like it. On the other hand, the movie was a big hit in Europe. I saw it, as a paying customer, in France and Italy. I was doing a Tony Richardson film, cruising the Mediterranean on a schooner, going from port to port. I remember seeing *The Hill* in Greece. It was incredible. I've never witnessed cheering and applause like it in a cinema before. The Europeans really appreciated it. For America, I think the director should have dubbed it and got out some of that background "left-right, left-right" . . . but it stands, I think, as a sound, good film.'

The release of the picture early in 1965, overlapping early production on yet another Bond, *Thunderball*, gave Connery his best serious personal reviews since TV. The *Sunday Express* recognised 'a masterpiece . . . Sean Connery reminding us what a really splendid actor he is'. The *Sunday Citizen* observed 'tremendous performances by Ian Hendry and Sean Connery'. The *Sun* considered Connery 'startlingly good', and the *Daily Express* capped the lot with a 'devastating film . . . Sean Connery gives one of the most disturbingly effective performances of the year. A more powerful film has not come out of a British studio for many a year . . . a superb all-male cast.'

To Connery's intense annoyance, once back in London, publicity surrounding *The Hill* focused more on the fact that he had cast aside the toupee he had worn since *Marnie* and allowed the bushy eyebrows that had been cropped for *From Russia with Love* and later films to flourish again. The fan magazines splashed 'Bond in *The Hill*' over double-page spreads that bullheadedly resisted distinction of character, and the tabloids published the Spanish location shots as 'James Bond at Play', interpreting the drawn features and scraggy moustache of *The Hill* as evidence of a jaded Connery at war with Eon. The game seemed endless. When Connery won a few thousand on roulette at an Italian casino, the papers screamed, 'Bond Breaks Casino Bank'. At the launching of Israel's branch of Variety Club

International, where Connery agreed to present the major cash donation, the *Daily Mail* ran the headline: 'Bond hands over £103,000 for Israel'.

Trouble, intimate friends believed, was coming. 'Sean makes a point of controlling his temper,' Cilento said. 'Only twice since we've been married have I seen his wrath.' At the time the media whisper that the marriage itself was likely to be the first casualty of the pressures had begun. Cilento stayed silent but then suddenly, in the run-up to *Thunderball* in the spring of 1965, everybody was talking about an imminent split. 'I don't know how it started,' says a friend off *The Hill*, 'but I will say Sean was a fairly faithful type. Diane, though, was a tough egg. When it began to look like their differences were going to open up into a real split, I guessed Diane was the one who wanted to end it.' Another actor says, 'Diane was jealous of the Bond success and she didn't hide it. Sean was jealous of the high-brow society Diane attracted. She was a real actor, he was hammy. Of course there was more than that. From the beginning she'd said she wanted freedom in marriage. I don't know if any husband could have given her enough. But certainly Bond gave her none. She was Mrs Bond and she would have none of it.'

Thunderball compounded the marital difficulties of Connery and Cilento in more ways than one. Worst of all, here were two people obsessed by the need for privacy attempting to resolve their problems in the eye of a showbiz publicity rave that was growing month by month. Legal hitches temporarily hindered *Thunderball* but by February the new script was ready, all production grievances settled and Connery, once again, financially seduced. His fee for *The Hill*, a relatively small-budget feature, had been an astronomical £150,000. For *Thunderball* it was reputedly upped by £50,000, with a percentage thrown in. Filming started in France in late February, by which time Connery had already met his female co-lead, another pneumatic sex-siren called Claudine Auger, at a London press party. Auger was neither the producer's nor director Terence Young's first choice. Saltzman had wanted Raquel Welch, having seen her overspilling a bikini top in the October '64 edition of *Life* magazine, and tentative arrangements had been made. But a phone request from Richard Zanuck, a friend of Broccoli's and production head of Fox in Hollywood, to release her for the forthcoming *Fantastic Voyage* had been complied with. From Christmas 1964 through to February 1965 a long line of glamorous half-known or unknown actresses was tested – by Eon's estimate, as many as six hundred. From them, after close misses by Yvonne Monlaur and dusky Gloria Paul, the former Miss France Auger was chosen for the lead part of Domino.

Married to the French director Pierre Gaspard-Huit, 25 years her senior, Auger 'always felt I would become Domino. I had read the book about seven times and knew her inside out. I am very much a Domino sort of girl myself, a fun-loving extrovert. Whatever I am doing I enjoy doing it – loving, driving, riding . . .'

Auger and Connery were photographed together at cocktail functions where she gushed fawningly about Connery's style and talent. Back at Pinewood in March rumours of romance started and on the second Friday of the month Connery quit Acton to move into a flat alone. The *Daily Express* conveyed a close friend's non-surprise: 'It is a great shame. They've tried to patch up their troubles, but it has not worked out.' The same article also reported that Twentieth Century-Fox had just disclosed the postponement of the planned Cilento-Connery co-starring movie. 'It isn't true to say Sean's mood after *The Hill*, or passing fancies on *Thunderball* or whatever else were responsible for the separation,' Ian Bannen insists. 'Anyone who understood their marital arrangement would know the process by which they broke up then. They were just two extremely independent types who had two very different-shaped careers. And Sean put his career before his home, and Diane did the same.'

A week after the trial separation had been announced Connery was back at their Acton home, sleeping overnight. The press pounced. Since his arrival from Spain he had been shadowed everywhere by reporters looking for a slice of Bondian wit or wisdom. Cilento brushed away the hysteria. Were husband and wife to be permanently reconciled? Was there another woman in Connery's life? Did he intend to stay at Acton now? 'You must simply draw your own conclusions from what you know,' Cilento hedged. 'All I can say is that Sean spent last night at the house and will spend tonight here too. A reconciliation? If that is your interpretation, yes, I leave it to you.'

But it was not a reconciliation. Connery moved out again and, as the antidote to encroaching depression, flung himself inventively into *Thunderball*. 'He was lovely to work with,' says Molly Peters, whom Young had plucked from the crowd scenes of his earlier movie *Moll Flanders*, to star as Patricia, the sexy health clinic masseuse who 'works over' James Bond. 'Very brotherly to me, because it was my first big part and I was desperately nervous – not only of the lines, but because there were these sexy bed and shower scenes I'd to do, one (the shower) where I was nude with him. He encouraged, and never showed impatience – unless it was with outsiders who intruded, publicity people and the like.'

Unlike Hamilton on *Goldfinger*, Young changed the script day by day. Molly Peters's dialogue was altered and, in very un-Hamilton fashion, some eight takes of the nude shower scene were run. 'But Terence made it easy, he kept the atmosphere humorous and he so obviously got on with Sean that we were, in spite of all that was going on beyond Pinewood's lot, like a little happy family. For the shower scene the make-up people wanted to use sticking-plaster on my pubic area and nipples, which I thought more obscene, if anything. In the end, they just covered my front, and my bottom of course was bare for the scene where Connery presses me against the glass and you see the outline. I remember, after all the takes, Sean joked it up. We went into the steam for take number eight or so and when it was over Sean came out on all fours, gaga, with a bowler hat on. He could laugh. And he could make one feel important, that was nice. Once, after a spot of private life bother, I broke into tears just before a take. Sean came up and put his arm round me and said, "Who's upset you? Tell me: who here upset you?" He was vexed for me, and I'd no doubt he would have sorted out whoever it was if I'd said a name.'

Molly Peters among others, observed Connery's attraction to 'glamorous women who came to the set, especially one fabulous Hungarian', but kept apart from his social encounters. A Bond girl says, 'Sean's attention was absorbed by Claudine. He went for continental types, and she suited him ideally.'

Late in March crew and cast flew to the Bahamas to resume filming and Cilento stayed behind with Jason and Gigi. The tiny archipelago was, in *Playboy*'s words, 'in a state of siege, occupied by an invading army of newspaper reporters, magazine writers and photographers from every major publication in America, England, Europe, Canada, Australia and Japan; TV crews from ABC, NBC and the BBC, silk-suited press agents and swim-suited starlets.' Auger kept Connery company discreetly, though they were pictured together daily, embracing, languishing in the warm Gulf waters, ambling along Love Beach. Perhaps the mandatory overt romance of Bond-and-bird was the most fortuitous natural cover. Then again perhaps it was, as a film colleague says, 'a nuisance. Claudine was a good friend to Sean and they liked each other's company. But Sean wanted Diane to come out to Nassau, he wanted her back.'

Scheduled to fly to Nassau after long telephone negotiations, Cilento cancelled when Acacia House was burgled and items of favoured jewellery taken. Days later, however, she did catch a plane, accompanied by Gigi and Jason. Connery met her at Nassau airport, suntanned, uptight, alone.

Asked about reconciliation he played dumb. Pressed with queries as to whether he was pleased to see his wife he answered smartly, 'Yes, of course.' Then the reunited group skipped into a Cadillac and motored to a bungalow specially rented for them on Love Beach. *Thunderball* kept rolling through Easter and Connery made love, for the cameras, to slinky, sad-eyed Auger. The word 'reconciliation' fell from the reporters' barrage. The couple were together again, the radical marriage resumed. Cilento told journalist David Lewin: 'I am through the other side now of being called Mrs Bond and although it still happens it cannot upset me any longer. Sean and I have our own lives to lead in our own way.' Ominously she warned, 'This industry can take hold of you and wrap you up like a piece of meat . . . neither of us will allow ourselves to become that involved. We are not going to let ourselves be merchandised.'

Connery, unfortunately, was already bought, packaged and sold. Succeeding with Bond he had, for the moment, lost himself.

12

You Only Live . . . Twice?

A kind of insanity overtook Sean Connery's life from 1965 to '67, the period during which the basis of his fortune was amassed. In 1965, thanks to *Goldfinger* mostly, he was number one box-office attraction in America, an unparalleled achievement in recent times for a British-based cinema star. In 1966 he still topped the polls, and his fame had well and truly conquered eastern and western audiences. In Japan he was idolised, ranking high above the Beatles in cultist status. In Germany, Scandinavia and France his celebrity had injected new vitality into cinema-going.

'The French were the first to recognise the Bond films,' he told Tony Crawley, and other journalists. 'In some ways the French are insular because of their chauvinism towards film, but they have always been very respectful of effort in new directions.'

'I suppose many actors envied him for the breadth of his popularity,' his friend Robert Hardy says, 'but the burdens must have been too extraordinary. You look at that period in his career and you simply nod in admiration. Others might have gone over the edge. He held himself with a lot of dignity and integrity.'

Connery's fee per film touched a plateau of around $500,000 during the heady mid-sixties, but overwork marred some of his performances. *Thunderball* was one. This new Bond had him tracking down a stolen Vulcan bomber, equipped with atomic charges, to its sunken hideout in the Bahamas. Largo (Adolfo Celi), was the chief

SPECTRE villain behind the enterprise and Domino (Auger) Largo's unhappy mistress. As in *Goldfinger*, Bond beats the villain by the skin of his teeth, abetted by the disaffected girl. The ambience of holiday brochure sea and sand and haute cuisine came over well, and the main trio of girls, Auger, Peters and Luciana Paluzzi, radiated a cruder sexuality which, in its gender-purity, probably shocked *Newsweek*. But structural faults, the tendency of the action to jerk as Bond hops from the tranquillity of a health clinic to gumshoeing in Nassau, to frenetic underwater escapades, are distracting. Connery too seems uneven in his performance – sometimes concentrated and effective; oftener a touch lifeless – despite the rigours of non-stop action.

Reviews were mixed. Bosley Crowther's love-hate affair with Bond in the pages of the *New York Times* went on: 'Mr Connery is at his peak of coolness and nonchalance . . . even the violence is funny. That's the best I can say for a Bond film.' The cautious Dilys Powell, ever eager to dispense with the blindfold of hype, wondered whether mechanical ingenuity wasn't undermining human interests, and the *Sunday Telegraph* stomped a heavy step further with the bold (and flawed) assault: 'There's no *story* in *Thunderball*.'

Later in this same review Robert Robinson opined, 'Bond is the magus to whom all things are possible, a sickly condition with a very poor prognosis, for once it is diagnosed by an audience it robs a character of individuality, and, at last, of interest. Where there are no limits, there is no story, and novelty is offered as a substitute.'

Substitution was the order of the day in other areas of Connery's hectic life now. With Cilento invited to Hollywood to make *Hombre* opposite Paul Newman, Connery and his agent, Richard Hatton, plugged for any American deal that would allow reconciled husband and wife a modicum of professional harmony. Since the Australian picture was off, the next best must be something near *Hombre*. Hatton tied down *A Fine Madness*, to be filmed on location in New York for Warners by Irvin Kershner. By coincidence Newman's wife, Joanne Woodward, had already been signed for the film. Although *Hombre*'s principal location shooting would be in Phoenix, Arizona, Connery and Cilento agreed to commute the considerable distance whenever possible to be together. The children, meanwhile, would stay with Cilento. 'Sean was too jaded by Bond,' Ian Bannen believes, 'to feel any jubilation at coming back to America for such a big picture.' Michael Hayes, the 'Age of Kings' director, considers it 'quite astounding that, amid all that Bond uproar, he could trim himself to the finesse of *A Fine Madness*. It spoke volumes for his self-discipline.'

Of the four or five movies that followed *Thunderball* in rapid succession, *A Fine Madness* is undeniably Connery's best, possibly because the character he portrays, Samson Shillitoe, the arrogant rebel poet, is an exaggeration of Tommy the Fountainbridge rebel. Samson is a wild beast, haunted by the epic poem he can't write and hounded by a wife he loves yet wants to leave but can't quite. Sacked from his job for blaring rudeness, he is chased all over New York for back alimony and falls into the clutches of a sophisticated Manhattan psychiatrist (Patrick O'Neal) and his wife (Jean Seberg) who try to help him. Corrupted to his hair-raising way of life, the sophisticates finally agree to release the untameable Samson and let him search for raucous peace with wife Rhoda (Woodward).

Hombre and *A Fine Madness* achieved more or less all their goals and that parallel success probably helped Cilento and Connery restrike the link of mutual confidence and commitment. Both movies were critically well received and Connery utilised his time in New York and the comfort of his ten per cent in *A Fine Madness* to steel himself for what was now announced to be his last Bond, the Japanese-set *You Only Live Twice*, scheduled to start shooting in May 1966. (*On Her Majesty's Secret Service* was originally to have been Connery's fifth Bond, and Guy Hamilton hoped to direct it, starring Brigitte Bardot as heroine Tracy.) The problems of co-ordinating production in time to use the spring snows of Switzerland, essential to the plot, stopped the project.)

A year earlier, reflecting on his gutsy role in *The Hill*, Connery had said, 'Some people thought I couldn't make a go of a movie without romantic interest.' That he obviously had was proved not only by the favourable notices, but by the genuine new attention paid to him by lofty 'names' in New York. A producer who knew him at the time says, 'Sean made a go of fitting into the Greenwich Village, arty swing of New York. He saw plays on Broadway, chatted with the moguls . . . even lived out something of his [*Fine Madness*] character. A certain clique took to him as artist, not James Bond, and he liked that. He was friendly with people like Sir Tyrone Guthrie, the stage director.'

After the productive few months in America Connery settled back with Cilento, Gigi and Jason in Acton in high spirits. Revelling in the New York reviews for *Madness* ('Give it A for effort and B for impudence and originality . . . Connery plays well,' said the *New York Times*), he was bursting with fresh, Bond-busting, ideas. With a side-jab at Eon he was telling the press, 'One should be paid what one is worth. Money gives you freedom and power. . . . I want to use that power I now have as a producer. In Hollywood I asked Sir Tyrone Guthrie why he had never made a film. "Because no one asked me," he said. Well, I want to ask him. In the same way that Burton asked Zeffirelli to direct the *Shrew* when Zeffirelli had never made a film before.' Connery added, with the fresh perspective of time in New York, that what he was really tired of was 'a lot of fat slob producers living off the backs of lean actors'. He wanted to wriggle free of the slob producers who had him in their grisly grip and he wanted to go back to purist roots. He would, he said, direct a play on Broadway next year. 'Of course a lot of people say that's madness – when thirty-eight new productions out of forty-four have flopped on Broadway in the past season this is hardly the time for an untried English director to be welcomed. But I'm going because I like the play and I want to do it.' The determination was admirable but ill-founded and the play, London-based Ted Allan Herman's *The Secret of the World*, announced to star Shelley Winters, never materialised.

156

Before embarking on the last exhausting Bond, Connery and Cilento took advantage of the lull to put their house in order. They analysed and confronted the conflicting aspects of their lives together. It seemed clear that they could not be an effective family unit while both pursued movie careers. Consequently Cilento decided to retard her film career for a while and concentrate on novel writing. (Her novel *The Manipulator* published in 1967, with the dedication 'For Sean', and the jacket designed by Connery, was a moderate success.) The continuing violation of privacy at Acton, especially after a spate of burglaries – five in all after the incident during *Thunderball* – was deemed unacceptable. And so it was decided to move. The house went on the market in April 1966, advertised openly under a rambling newspaper notice headed 'Sean Connery, the motion picture actor, offers . . . the self-styled queen of the suburbs'. The going price was £17,950, freehold. Connery explained his reasons for wanting out with typical frankness: 'People knew the house – after all, there aren't many actors in Acton – and would come and sit and stare at Diane and me in the main room. If it had gone on I'd have been found guilty of assault.' Renewed efforts were made to persuade Effie and Joe to quit Fountainbridge but the best Sean could do was nudge Joe into early retirement.

Property in Spain – a few farm acres with a nondescript house – was secured and, to the couple's initial great pleasure, an attractive Victorian house on Putney Heath, slap in the middle of actor-land. Cilento worked on making it home while Connery grimly taxied to Pinewood for script talks on *You Only Live Twice*. 'After this,' he swore to reporters, 'I will only do the things that passionately interest me for the remaining thirty-five years of my life.'

Lewis Gilbert, fresh from the award-winning *Alfie* with Michael Caine – a movie destined to give Bond a run for his money at the box office throughout late '66 – approached his first commission on a Bond with reservations. 'In the beginning I turned it down,' he says, 'because four had already been done and the natural reaction was to say, well, what can I contribute, it's all been done. But then Cubby rang me again and said, you can't turn this down because you have the biggest audience in the world sitting out there waiting for you. And that *was* interesting. I mean, you can do the greatest picture ever and it will still not find an audience, but with Bond you are guaranteed. Then of course there was the investment. This picture would cost seven or eight million dollars, and, like a general in the field with his tanks and resources, that kind of back-up for a director is pretty alluring. So I decided I'd do this Bond, and try and contribute my own little something to making the saga different.'

With their fingers on the market pulse Broccoli and Saltzman saw the need to freshen Bond too, but their individual ambitions were dogged by personal unease. 'There was a dreadful divide,' Guy Hamilton says. 'Harry had wandered off into projects he whimsically wanted to do, like those Len Deighton spy films (Michael Caine as unglamorous agent Harry Palmer) and Cubby grew tired of Harry's irregular participation in Bond. Harry wasn't as fast on the uptake, ideas-wise, as Cubby – that was part of the trouble too.' Lewis Gilbert confesses he acted as 'a sort of go-between, keeping the peace' but stresses: 'Once the picture got going [the producers] were terrific. With their vast experience I had people to turn to when I was in doubt, and, good God, at times on Bond you needed support.' During pre-production Broccoli and Saltzman allegedly came very close to dissolving their partnership. They finally parted in 1974, with Saltzman selling out to Broccoli and returning to theatrical management. A very close associate on *You Only Live Twice* says, 'They couldn't stand the sight of each other then . . . and things got worse when Sean's dislike for Harry blew up. It got so bad he wouldn't come on set in Japan if Harry was around. A, he didn't want to be in Japan doing Bond at all. And B, the last person he wanted looking over his creative shoulder was this hard-shelled old driver.'

Roald Dahl, the popular short-story writer who had never written a film, was engaged as an extraordinarily offbeat choice to screenwrite the Japanese film. Perhaps, Gilbert suggests, Noël Coward's observation about Dahl's 'fabulous imagination' with the 'underlying streak of cruelty and macabre unpleasantness and a curiously adolescent emphasis on sex' endeared him to the producers.

Dahl humorously recounted for *Playboy* his early contact with Broccoli. Never having heard of either of the producers and having only seen *Goldfinger* he believed the man trying to reach him on the telephone to discuss a possible commission was one Archie Lockley. Patricia Neal, his actress wife who had answered the phone, insisted, 'This one is Broccoli, head of the Mafia. You'd better watch out.' Dahl wrote his script in record time, ready for shooting at Pinewood in May. There were plot difficulties still, so Dahl and writer Harold Jack Bloom prepared to fly out to Japan in July for revisions.

'There were many, many difficulties,' Lewis Gilbert smiles. 'Apart from Sean's unease, we had a kick-up over casting. Up till the very last minute there was no arch-villain. Harry swore he'd found a superb Czechoslovakian actor, but the man did a few days in Pinewood and we had to let him go. We roped in Donald Pleasence quickly. Then there was the hassle with the girls. These films are prepared on the highest diplomatic level – that's to say, Cubby was getting permissions to shoot at key sites in Japan by approaching embassies and all the rest. So, naturally the Japanese were insistent that certain requirements be met. First we tried to get our Japanese girls in Europe, then Hawaii. But they were too brash and Americanised and all wrong. Then the Japanese people said, in effect, use our girls, or else. So we auditioned and picked two main girls, Mie Hama and Akiko Wakabayashi, neither of whom could speak English. They went on crash courses, but the problem arose when Akiko picked up her English faster than Mie. Mie was lovely, but she just couldn't get her English down. So we decided to drop her, and I took Tetsuro Tamba [Japanese Secret Service chief in the film] aside and told him our situation and asked him to explain nicely to Mie. He was helpful, he took her out to dinner and told her. The next morning he came to Cubby's office and we were having a meeting and we said, "Well, does she know?" "Yes," Tamba said, "I told her." "And how did she take it?" Tamba was very philosophical. He said, "She said OK, if she was out she'd commit suicide. She couldn't go home to Japan and face the loss of honour after all the pre-publicity. James Bond is the king of Japan, and she's got the big role opposite him." Harry and Cubby looked at Tamba with mouths open. Then we all said, "Well, on second thoughts she's not so bad. She can keep at it and we'll fit her in."'

Hama's part, originally to be the larger role of Aki, Bond's agent ally, was swapped with Wakabayashi's Kissy, the pearl-diving island girl Bond later falls for – a part that was less demanding in terms of dialogue.

Connery and Cilento tried desperately to make the three months of location shooting a holiday, attempting to stay close and distance themselves from the usual media-mania. While a chartered jet flew the cast and crew one way round the world, the patched-up couple chose an alternative route, going via Manila. It proved a drastic mistake. In the tiny jam-packed city they were mobbed, pestered in their hotel, ultimately trapped. On arrival in Japan conditions deteriorated fast. The lobby of the Tokyo Hilton was crowded day and night by sweaty, camera-hung newsmen, chattering like geckos in a swamp. The film trail led south, to Kagoshima – and the swelling, surging press followed along. Alan Whicker had accompanied the crew, travelling with his own, more subtly intrusive BBC camera team, and he had the good grace to sip his Kirin beer, play the far spectator and admit appalled amazement. Connery, he noted, had 'abandoned his fierce professional concentration and seemed indifferent to the film's progress'. Cilento in a jaded moment told Whicker: 'He's tried beyond normal limits, because everywhere you go there's always someone coming out from behind a tree . . . photographers follow him into the lavatory.'

After *Thunderball* Connery told columnist Shiela Graham only $2,800,000 plus a high percentage would buy him for another Bond, but when *You Only Live Twice* was over he said: 'I don't want to know. It's finished. Bond's been good to me, but I've done my bit. I'm out.'

'I can understand how he felt,' Lewis Gilbert says. 'If he seemed to be "cruising" in certain parts of our movie it was only because he knew the character was immovably second in line to the gadgets, and that bored him, I suppose. For myself, I tried to give Bond a human dimension. By introducing the emotion when the girl Aki is murdered, for example. But Sean had such a strain to put up with, with the fans. Once, when we tried to do a simple shot of him walking down the Ginza we decided the safest way was to hide our camera, let him slip out of a car and amble past – let him vanish in the street strollers. We *tried*!' Gilbert laughs loud. 'But Sean got out of the car . . . and was just pounced upon by a million fans. It was a nightmare!'

You Only Live Twice, a kind of advanced *Dr No* in storyline, did not sweep the box office as its immediate predecessors had done. The reviews, by now, were token efforts, regurgitated superlatives primed to fill out entertainment pages in journals good and bad. Politically and socially, Bond was now neutral – a labourer with bourgeois style in a high-living, to all purposes apolitical universe. In *You Only Live Twice* Russia and America were testy brothers naturally vexed by the in-flight thefts of their respective manned space shots. The ubiquitous SPECTRE, led by Blofeld (Pleasence), was the real culprit, stealing the space capsules in hope of inflaming East and West to the point of annihilative war. Bond learns the interceptor rockets are being fired from Japan and, with the co-operation of the Japanese Secret Service, he tracks down Blofeld in his volcano mountain hideaway, blows the place up and short-circuits a very unlikely Third World War. Robert Robinson's prognosis on *Thunderball* seemed borne out definitively when Bosley Crowther wrote: 'There's so much of that scientific clatter – so much warring of super-capsules out in space and fussing with electronic gadgets – that this way-out adventure picture should be the joy and delight of the youngsters and adults who can find release in the majestically absurd.'

161

Whatever slender grip the James Bond of *Dr No* had on dramatic reality was lost for ever with the new movie. Connery, therefore, who drew and projected his strength from *real* strengths – from the adverse conditions of his childhood and his assiduous application to the classics – became otiose. James Bond, not Sean Connery, had become a big movie star. To Connery, the option of vacating the role seemed best for everyone. As the movies were going, James Bond could well stand on his own feet. Any hunk who could move, talk and bed a woman could be screen Bond now. 'It could have been different though,' Connery said. 'Had the producers not been so greedy today United Artists could belong to Connery, Broccoli and Saltzman.' But there would have been radical changes had that dream been realised. Financial accommodation aside, Connery made it clear he would have altered the super-structure of 007, re-introduced credible characters and gritty situations, humanising Bond again and broadening the drama challenge for himself.

It didn't happen like that, so Sean Connery pocketed his quixotic dream and set off in 1967 in search of new roles to conquer.

Out of Bondage, Connery had time to contemplate all sorts of unreached goals. His love for golf (which now had him playing off a handicap of thirteen) was one other source of frustration. 'I really adore the game,' he said. 'I considered turning pro, but I'm not sure it would have made me any happier. I'm an actor, and I love my job most.' Always a scribbler, he dabbled with storylines in Putney and started drafting a script he had toyed with for years – 'My own *Macbeth*, to be made in Scotland with Scottish actors . . . I'll direct it myself.'

'Writing, after football and golf, was his big thing,' says John Boorman. 'He liked to write poetry, though he didn't show it around. I suppose he'd read enough bad scripts to make him want to set records right. And, no doubt about it, he had the intellectual capacity to do great stuff.'

The blossoming opportunities of uncontracted idleness

provided Connery with what was to develop into a most satisfying ongoing intellectual stimulus – an outlet for investment, financial and otherwise, in Scotland's future. The outlet came in the person of revolutionary Scottish industrialist Sir Iain Stewart, nationally known in the late sixties for his brave campaigns to reduce unemployment and rejuvenate Clydeside, specifically in his Fairfields Shipyard plan. Connery met Stewart, a Glaswegian, at a golfing society dinner in London. In roundabout chatter, the industrialist detailed his five-year plan for Fairfields, an outrageous labour-management experiment that had started with the support of George Brown at the DEA, Jim Callaghan at the Treasury and Ray Gunter at the Ministry of Labour. The plan, in essence, slackened potentially stifling union regulations and allowed a workers' voice in management. The real viability of the plan was never tested because in 1968 Stewart made the mistake of allowing Fairfields to enter the disastrous Upper Clyde Shipbuilders merger, a scheme that ended in bankruptcy in fifteen months.* But, at the time, Connery was so intrigued by Stewart's rebel dream that he journeyed to Glasgow to examine procedures for himself and, without prompting, decided to make a documentary about the problems of Clydeside.

The Bowler and the Bunnet (a bunnet is the Lowlands Scot equivalent of the flat cap) was written and directed by Connery over a few weeks late in 1967 and shown on Scottish Television. Efforts to sell it to regional independent television, even the BBC, failed, but the documentary was regarded as good of its kind and did serve to highlight the positive progress Stewart was making at Fairfields. Connery was especially proud of his little film because it

* Stewart agreed to go into the UCS merger as deputy chairman because, he said, 'the methods that had been successful at Fairfields would be used and the recommendations of the industry's working party report would be adopted.' This however did not transpire and he resigned after two months, predicting the bankruptcy.

spoke up for Scotland. 'Stewart was doing something at Fairfields that hadn't been done so successfully anywhere in the country, including England. He was bridging that terrible gulf between the bosses and the workers and he was breaking down the petty suspicions between unions. He even had carpenters doing painters' work when necessary and he had union men sitting in the boardroom. It was all working famously and production was going up . . . what the film did for me in personal terms was make me realise that part of me belonged to that kind of background . . . I just couldn't turn my back on it completely.'

The failure of Fairfields in UCS two years later was an industrial and social tragedy, but more than a little good had come from Connery's first personal venture into film-making. The friendship with the sagacious Stewart inspired a concept that was grander than union-management control.

The Scottish International Educational Trust, founded in 1970 to provide bursaries for bright but underprivileged Scots and to supply cash for educational projects like the establishment of a drama chair at Strathclyde University, started life as a modest charity golf tournament set up by Connery along the lines of the famous American Bing Crosby Pro-Am. In 1968 during early preparation for the tournament Connery was announcing that 'part of the money raised is going to be used researching the reasons why the Scots leave Scotland. I've already talked to St Andrews University about the research programme.' At the same time he was declaring his support for the Scottish Nationalists, while confessing he had never actually voted in his life. 'I was reminded of the return of the prodigal son,' says an Edinburgh friend with a grin. 'Sean had never actually got Scotland out of his blood, to give him credit, but he never gave any big indication till then of national pride. Of course everyone here was pleased.' Some interpreted Connery's sudden fervour as an anti-big-town reflex, but it would be naive to think he was recanting some heart-hurting hearsay. 'Sean had wealth and time to do good after Bond,' says Robert Hardy. 'One got the impression he wished to advance himself *and* his causes.'

Following a firm restatement of his allegiance to the Scottish cause on an Eamonn Andrews TV show, Connery was formally approached by the National Party to stand as their candidate at the next election, representing an unspecified constituency. He turned it down because 'I would not be so presumptuous as to sit for any political candidacy without sufficient work, background and knowledge . . . I suppose it would be easy enough to let lieutenants spoonfeed you, but I'm not familiar enough with the details across the country. I'd get found out.' In fact, having dallied with industrialists and politicians for a while – and snatched a good rest – Connery was gravitating back to movieland.

He abhorred boredom and got restless when Cilento's lady friends came to call, or when the children threw tantrums. Charles Feldman's offer to bring him back to the big screen as Bond in the spoof *Casino Royale* was dismissed, as was a clutch of ridiculous 'cardboard booby' spy stories. When at last one offer took his fancy it surprised no one that the subject was a western, intended for early 1968 shooting in Mexico, called *Shalako*.

Edward Dmytryk, the director, chose Connery as 'the ideal' for Louis L'Amour's frontier scout hero, and producers Euan Lloyd and Dimitri de Grunwald granted their blessing with a $1,200,000 cheque (to be cashed in over a nine-month period) plus a hefty 30 per cent of net profits. Connery was childishly enthusiastic about the project, though he cooled slightly when told Brigitte Bardot would be his co-star. Bardot's star-studded ego was well known to be bigger than her going price ($350,000 for *Shalako*, plus a cut in profits), and, true to form, she asked Lloyd to fix a meeting with Connery before she signed papers – 'to test the vibrations'. In his intimate biography of Bardot, Willi Frischauer suggests Connery's initial response was uneasy, but on his meeting Bardot face to face at Deauville champagne flowed and hearts throbbed fast. Gunter Sachs, Brigitte's current husband, 'feared the worst', and cleared out. But within a few days Connery was back in Putney and BB was back in Sachs's arms.

Shalako was not, as Honor Blackman, a co-star, describes it, a happy film. The threat of a labour strike in Mexico forced Lloyd to relocate the shoot in dusty old Almeria and events shuddered to an unpromising start when Bardot delayed filming by arriving belatedly, with snowy Rolls-Royce and entourage of photographers and hangers-on, to take up queenly residence at the Hotel Aguadulce. 'Once Sean was over that bad start he kept out of it,' Blackman says. 'He took a rented villa nearby, where he stayed with his family and made a point of concentrating on doing as good a job as possible under the circumstances.' The circumstances were not conducive to refreshing work. In her personal plot to remain the perennial teenager, Bardot brought to Almeria exactly the kind of press-heavy circus charade that Connery had hoped to see the back of with Bond. Bardot's open rows with former lover, actor Stephen Boyd, made matters worse. Worse again were her threats to quit the location before half her footage was in the can.

'Eddie Dmytryk's patience was truly remarkable,' says Blackman. 'Then, with Brigitte, I guess we all deserved credit.'

Ten years before, the story of a true-as-an-arrow western hero despatched by the army to guide a party of wealthy aristocrats out of raging Indian country would have encouraged Connery to barter his soul. Now he almost regretted signing on. Satisfied enough with his own performance, he was relieved when the picture wrapped up only slightly over schedule. Returning to London, he awarded himself the gift of a new (well, second-hand) Jensen for endurance and self-control beyond the call of duty.

All the publicity promises – 'the most sensuous film BB has ever made', 'Connery and BB, the electrifying twosome' – were not upheld in the final screen cut. Lloyd had shrewdly prefinanced the film entirely by the unusual method of procuring advance guarantees of release from some 27–30 different countries, which was just as well.

Reviewers clashed fiercely, divided between those who thought this first ambitious British western an out-and-out dud, and those who admired the motley of black former football star Woody Strode as an Indian chief, purring over Honor Blackman as the aristocratic faithless wife and Eric Sykes as a French chef. No one said much about Bardot, and she herself conceded, 'Shalako is Sean Connery's film. He carried the whole weight of it on his shoulders.' Marjorie Bilbow in Screen International declined the ritual baton: 'Connery seems so determined to erase all memories of James Bond that he allows the foreground figure of Shalako to fade into middle distance.'

Few kids in the Blue Halls would have been impressed.

13

A Sixties Hangover

With Bond buried and the wound-licking spree of idleness and *Shalako*, the long-dreamt-of western, past, Connery slumped to a career stance that appeared something between defeatism and apprehensive torpor. 'He was, momentarily, completely unsure of himself,' an actor colleague swears. 'Everything he did, he questioned. I remember a friend visited him in Putney, where he'd had this German hot-and-cold shower installed in the basement, and it had cost a few hundred quid. He agonised over it. A few hundred quid was a big deal! In Scotland his dad could've lived for a year on a few hundred quid. Sean wasn't happy, and didn't know how to *get* happy. He tried to give up cigarettes and cut down on his drinking. He tried many things. One got the feeling that here was a man who wanted to retrace his steps, go back to the past – all this was evident in his fixation with doing good for Edinburgh's poor, all that – but he'd lost his way.'

Dennis Selinger, Connery's new agent-manager, replacing Richard Hatton who had retired to go into production, was concerned too. He believed Connery needed to capitalise on the lingering Bond boom, but to work fast to establish himself as a separate, adaptable entity. At round-table meetings in Selinger's office in central London the agent outlined his proposals: Connery must recognise that his non-Bond films had largely flopped and, out of Bondage, he could lose ground fast. He must not sit to wait for offers, he must go out and grab whatever was available, meet directors and moguls, *work*. 'I'd proved this with Mike Caine,' Selinger says. 'If one wants to make international impact the surest system is to make as many films as possible. I told Sean, if one can do four or five movies a year, *one* is bound to hit and that one can up your price and keep you on top. Sean wasn't too convinced. "But *The Hill* won't come along every week," I advised him. "You must get out and at it." '

Very reluctantly Connery shambled back to work, taking on two offers that were to prove atrocious cul-de-sacs – *The Molly Maguires*, directed by Martin Ritt for Paramount, and the Italian–Russian co-production *The Red Tent*. To date, *The Molly Maguires* has lost about $10 million (negative cost, inflation adjusted) and *The Red Tent* about £9 million. Both rate among the twenty biggest box-office losers of all time. Connery had been keen on *The Molly Maguires*, a project first suggested to him by Marty Ritt while Ritt was directing *Hombre* and Connery was visiting his wife. Blacklisted from TV where he started his career during the McCarthyist drive of the early fifties, Ritt was enamoured of the idea of a movie about the abused, impoverished Irish miners in the Pennsylvania coal pits of the 1870s banding together (as the secret Molly Maguires) and taking murderous action against their brutal employers. The story of *The Molly Maguires*, as written by Ritt's lifelong friend Walter Bernstein, revolved round the infiltration of the Irish group by a management agent, McParlan (played by Richard Harris) who eventually befriends miners' leader Kehoe (Connery) and is won over by the sincerity of the oppressed. Though based on fact, the plot is pure fiction and somehow, in its grey-faced telling, reveals all the irksome weaknesses of arty analogy. The critics mostly disliked the film and found little to rejoice about in Connery's unsympathetic character. Many disdained specious crusading, though Connery himself defended the wholesomeness of the venture, seeing it as an extension of his work-for-the-people on *The Bowler and the Bunnet*. The Molly Maguires were the indirect forerunners of free trade unionism, he claimed, and he was proud to be associated with so honest a film.

While the picture was being made on location in Pennsylvania (later at Paramount Studios, Hollywood), *On Her Majesty's Secret Service*, the sixth Bond, was in progress at Pinewood, with Australian newcomer George Lazenby portraying Bond. Connery temporarily declined comment on Bond developments but saw no significant loss of face in his own second-billing on *The Molly Maguires*. Queried about his declining popularity, he said, 'They're paying me a million dollars for this picture. For that kind of money they can put a mule ahead of me.'

In Pennsylavania he was moody, but generally good company. Though he was ready to talk to the press, publicists were advised that questions about a return to Bond were taboo. The weather was good, too good, during most of the shoot and he suffered dehydration – as he had done during the making of *You Only Live Twice* in Japan. The suffering eased some need for purgation within him and he bragged about doctors having to give him tea with whole lemons squeezed into it and salt crackers.

Ritt recognised the failure of his film just about as fast as Connery – though he certainly suffered worse for it. Later he admitted it 'went on its ass, didn't do any business at all, and though I wasn't completely without employment [after it], employment wasn't as accessible to me as it had been – *The Molly Maguires* was quite an expensive film!'

Apart from three slender weeks in Russia on *The Red Tent* early in 1969, employment was no richer for Connery – though this was largely by his own choosing. What followed was a period of film inactivity which lasted almost two years. A colleague opines: 'Part of it was identity crisis, yes. Another part was the general late-sixties hangover syndrome. All the icons were down. The Beatles were hobbling back from the Rishikesh, popping LSD, doing the drab, indulgent trampy thing *Let It Be*. And James Bond was flagging out too. Sean had been on this speeding merry-go-round for six years and when he jumped off everything was swirly. He was trying to get his feet, trying on various masks, I suppose. Like, we saw him for a while as the convert to "serious films" – that was the general impression of *The Hill* and *The Molly Maguires* – but it didn't last.'

In the hiatus, whenever there was a hiatus for the mature Connery, business raised its head. Though part of his continuing association with Iain Stewart's pioneering interests arose from an almost hippie-trendy sense of social duty, many non-charitable, less altruistic investments were explored as well. The Fairfields friendship led to the establishment of a merchant bank, Dunbar & Co, with impressive pannelled offices in Pall Mall, as well as a multitude of large-share interests in other companies. All the time Connery was professing himself a socialist, though not infrequently letting that particular mask slip. 'Golf, food and drink – that's what I enjoy,' he told the *Express*. 'And the only point in having money is to indulge them.' *France Soir*, the French newspaper, was indelicate enough to suggest Mr Connery had gone to seed and had been forced out of Bond by the producers because his waistline had thickened too much. Connery promptly sued. In the High Court David Hirst, QC, for Connery told the judge, 'It was asserted quite erroneously that the producers of the James Bond films had dispensed with his services because he was no longer fit to play the role of James Bond.' Connery had, in his own words, checked his waistline with a measuring tape, recorded an acceptable inch of flab and phoned his lawyer. On 17 February 1969 *France Soir* retracted its statement, apologised for the libel and settled with Connery for an undisclosed sum. Connery was as effusively delighted as he had been when Warners was forced to hand over $50,000 when *A Fine Madness* ran over schedule.

Having holidayed in Australia at Cilento's home and again, living hermit-like, looking after the hundred muscat grape vines just planted on his Spanish farm, Connery progressed to Leningrad and Moscow for *The Red Tent*. He liked Moscow, despite the fact that his hotel room was routinely bugged, but found Leningrad drab. At a top-class Leningrad restaurant he deplored the ineptitude of out-of-step dancers performing to a good balalaika band. They were 'hopeless . . . they wouldn't have lasted ten minutes at the Dennistoun [Glasgow] Palais.' Russia was agreeable, but not the kind of place he'd like to call home. Deciding where exactly home should be became a contentious issue too. Suggestions that he was about to flee Britain and opt for tax exile in Bermuda or somewhere similar were dismissed, as were reports that he banked all his loot in Switzerland and had some personal grand plan for the future. 'Scotland would be as far as I'd consider moving,' he told a journalist, but among friends he aired his angry views on British taxes and weather. 'Because he loved to play golf whenever he could he sought the sun,' Michael Caine says. 'But that wasn't the main reason he'd begun to contemplate emigration. The main reason was money. In Britain, because of the punitive taxes, he believed he was squandering by just sitting on his backside.' Ten years later Connery admitted that his finances during this period 'were in a mess. The accountants were unscrambling what they could. But the practical answer was to get out.'

Before all the vast changes of the early seventies, *The Red Tent* unfurled. In concept an ambitiously mystical film, it failed through heavy-handed direction and a conservative, plodding acting approach that killed all the sense of wonder and intrigue intended. Peter Finch dominated the film as General Nobile, leader of the ill-fated transArctic dirigible expedition, who is visited forty years after the event by the ghosts of the main participants. In the recreated story the dirigible breaks up in a blizzard and the survivors are scattered. A base comprising a red tent and items for survival is set up, but the chances of rescue are slim. Valeria (Claudia Cardinale), Nobile's fiancée, persuades Norwegian explorer Roald Amundsen (Connery) to search for the lost men and, in so doing, Amundsen perishes. Nobile is eventually rescued – before most of his men – and the question of the rightness of his behaviour develops and haunts him. Connery's fee for the film was not large, and though he received second billing it seemed hardly deserved. Roger Greenspun in the *New York Times* observed, 'To have taken a situation with such potential

172

and to have made it as dull as Mikhail Kalatozov has must have taken great ingenuity.'

In November Connery's friend the journalist Roderick Mann was dreamily imagining what a 'splendid year it has been for Mr Sean Connery. Most of it has been spent playing golf. And why not, when you think of it? What's the point of working hard and making money if you're not going to enjoy yourself?' Dennis Selinger was tugging hard in the opposite direction when in between, to universal bewilderment, Connery was declaring his next projects – 'two long-held ambitions' – a stage play he would direct, and his own movie of *Macbeth*.

Diane Cilento was, in the instance of the stage play anyway, the motivational source. It was she who had introduced Connery to the work of Canadian playwright Ted Allan Herman, whose *The Secret of the World* he had hoped to direct after *You Only Live Twice*, and it was she who was first approached to star in the new play of Herman's, *I've Seen You Cut Lemons*. Knowing Connery's admiration for Herman and understanding his restive mood after *The Red Tent* débâcle, Cilento suggested to the producer that he engage her husband to direct the play. Connery accepted and, with Cilento's agreement, invited actor Robert Hardy in as male lead.

'We started rehearsals at a church hall in Putney, not far from where Sean and Diane lived,' Hardy remembers. 'It was, of course, a joy to be working with them because I admired them both for their separate talents – but I must say I accepted the play against my instincts. It was too difficult a work, the odds were heavily against it even remotely succeeding.' The play was a two-hander – just Hardy and Cilento as Canadian brother and sister – which investigated at close-hand the frustrations and passions of two people descending towards an incestuous involvement. At rehearsals in the church hall Connery was never less than positive-minded, but Hardy is not so sure about the director's vision of likely success. 'Sean knew how tricky it would be, but he had a flair that forced the best out of a performance. Once he'd started, there was no turning back.'

Hardy is absolutely clear about Connery's urge to give it his best. 'It's a condition not uncommon in our trade, where stars of great international réclame like Sean decide to go back to their roots. Sean had decided, though I doubt if he saw himself in the long term as a director. He just then felt the need to do it, to rebel against the frivolity of other areas of the business, to work *at the heart* of the craft.'

Prior to the play's opening at Oxford and then going on tour, Connery asked Hardy to stay for a week at his Putney home for further rehearsals. Hardy found 'a big, empty house, quite attractive but with the bare necessities of furniture – though some interesting paintings. We rehearsed hard during the day and talked long into the night. In the end, I think it helped our performances – and, God, we needed what help we could get.'

Every morning Connery allotted a time for Hardy to utilise the house 'think tank', a zinc-lined fully closed-in sentry box which occupied a neat corner in the upstairs study. 'Sean believed sitting in there, totally shut up, concentrated the mind and conserved nervous energy. He used it, and claimed it worked. For myself, well, I didn't rush to install one in my own home.'

I've Seen You Cut Lemons opened in late November to bad notices. The month-long tour took it to Newcastle and Manchester, thence to the Fortune Theatre in London where 'it hit the deck, but *good*!' Hardy was not surprised at all. 'I'd jumped in, eyes closed, nose held tight, feet together. I had the gravest reservations from the start, I suspect many of us had.' After five days the play was handed the Black Spot. Connery expressed only mild disappointment to his cast. 'When word came that we were to close Sean responded in the same positive way he had right through the setting-up. He didn't, like many directors, disappear. Backstage he gave us our little talking to. He said it wasn't our fault, and so on – all the kind things one can possibly deploy at such a sad time. The alternative attitudes and phrases are limited, of course,' Hardy laughs. 'But Sean took it genuinely well. He tried, he failed. I think we had all done our best with very, very tough material.'

Most critics felt the elaborate scaffold-design set by Sean Kenny dwarfed the players ridiculously, and, like Hardy, that the play itself was unfit. Connery received a few luke-warm compliments, but every review, implicitly if not explicitly, called him back to James Bond.

It was a time of disappointments. The radical movie *Macbeth* might have been next, but Roman Polanski suddenly announced his own version, backed by *Playboy* finances. Connery's second major artistic departure was shelved.

Dennis Selinger's insistence on more commercial work to build on Bond finally paid off when Connery accepted a new American movie project to be directed by Sidney Lumet. Of all the directors Connery had worked with Lumet exemplified the qualities he most admired – discipline, efficiency in bringing the work in on time, depth in the script. *The Hill* enshrined Connery's happiest professional memories so now, even before reading *The Anderson Tapes*, Connery was ready for recommitment. Selinger was especially pleased because *The Anderson Tapes* was to be a light caper movie aimed at a wide audience, as opposed to the usually lofty Lumet fare. 'It was the kind of renewal he needed,' says Selinger. 'Plus I think he needed to laugh a bit at himself at that time.'

The Anderson Tapes, shot on location in New York to the tightest of schedules, was a resounding hit, rocketing Connery back into the American top ten box-office draws for 1971, a feat that might have seemed unreachable after *Shalako*. Once again, Lumet and Connery drew the best from each other and the same Roger Greenspun who had damned *The Red Tent* in the *New York Times* rejoiced in 'Sean Connery's laconic, attractive, beautifully subdued John Anderson' in a movie where 'the quality of professionalism appears in rather lovely manifestations to raise a by no means perfect film to a level of intelligent efficiency that is not so very far beneath the reach of art.' Despite this, Greenspun accurately pinpointed the fact that *The Anderson Tapes* is a 'minor story': John 'Duke' Anderson, recently released from jail, visits his former lover Ingrid (Dyan Cannon), interestedly digests her new surroundings – a luxury apartment block where she is residing with a sugar daddy – and reckons the entire building constitutes one abundantly stacked safe for the cracking. He gathers a team of experts and, over a Labour Day weekend, attempts, almost successfully, to outwit police chief Delaney (Ralph Meeker) and strip the joint of treasures. For Greenspun the 'multiplicity of life' yielded by small characters made the movie, and indeed the best fun comes in flashed vignettes, where the racy wit of Connery's Duke points up the hilarity of everyday life.

But even before the June 1971 première of *The Anderson Tapes* the astounding announcement of a return to Bondage had been made. In March, out of the blue, and catching even close friends by surprise, a press release stated that Connery had been talking with Broccoli and Saltzman again and a deal had been reached: Connery would return to the mink-lined harness of 007 for a fee of $1.2 million, plus a percentage. Every cent earned would go to the newly formed Scottish International Educational Trust, which had Sir Samuel Curran, Vice-Chancellor of Strathclyde University, as its chairman, Iain Stewart and Jackie Stewart, the racing driver, among its trustees, and had had its first financial kiss of life the previous summer with the Connery two-day pro-am golf tournament at Troon. The personal bait for Connery, it was stated, had been the bonus offer of United Artists' support for any two films of his own choosing, to be made after this single, final Bond.

Connery's very closest friends were stunned. One colleague says, 'He never told me. I read about it first. Did it seem out of character for him to reverse the pledge he had so solidly made a couple of years before? Well, put it this way: it had nothing to do with [George Lazenby's] failure as Bond. It could never have happened the year before. Sean had things to work out of his system – and the exercise strengthened him. He resumed Bond, I believe, with two equally important motives – to help his charity and to restore his market position.' In the clear light of the aftermath of holiday and experiment, then, Connery assessed

176

Tommy Connery, aged 10. 'We were poor, but I never knew how poor till years after.'

Fet-Loa Amateurs soccer team 1949–50. Connery stands third from right, middle row. 'In that game you're old at 25. I wanted to go on a bit longer than that.'

Top: Connery with the beautiful Janet Munro in Disney's *Darby O'Gill and the Little People*, Connery's first Hollywood film, 1959.
Middle: The breakthrough: filming *Dr No* with Ursula Andress in late January 1962 at the private beach of Minnie Simpson in Jamaica. Mrs Simpson was a fan and neighbour of Ian Fleming.
Bottom: With Daniola Bianchi in *From Russia With Love*, which opened in America in May 1964, heralding the Bond boom.

Alfred Hitchcock directs Connery in Winston Graham's *Marnie* (1964). Hitch 'wasn't convinced' that Connery fitted the Philadelphia gentleman role, but paid $400,000 for Connery's services anyway.

Connery arrives at Nassau Airport for *Thunderball*, March 1965. Tired of Bond, he was also fighting marriage problems. Cubby Broccoli is on Connery's left. Kevin McClory is on his right, with director Terence Young behind.

At Pinewood Studios, spring 1965, rehearsing *Thunderball* with Molly Peters and director Terence Young. Molly Peters found Connery full of humour and 'brotherly'.

With director John Huston on location in North Africa for *The Man Who Would Be King*, 1975. The movie is widely rated as Connery's best of the Seventies.

March 1965, Nassau, Bahamas. Diane Cilento swaps
the trials of life in Acton for a place in the sun.
Connery is in costume to battle the villainous Largo in
Thunderball.

Claudine Auger – Miss France 1958 – became the
requisite 'Bond Girl' in *Thunderball*. She and Connery
enjoyed a harmonious relationship on what was to be
the most financially successful of the Sixties Bond
movies.

With second wife Micheline, whom Connery met on the golf course. Micheline designed their Spanish home and helped redesign Connery's lifestyle.

Connery with son Jason in 1982. Jason's acting career started with *Aladdin* in Perth, before graduating to *Robin Hood* and beyond.

Top: Brian De Palma's *The Untouchables* (1987), based on
the famous American TV series of the Fifties and scripted by
David Mamet, won Connery an Oscar that many
felt was overdue.
Middle: Connery's greatest popular success since Bond came
in Steven Spielberg's *Indiana Jones and the Last Crusade*,
for which Tom Stoppard helped him develop the character
of Jones's dad. Here with Harrison Ford on
location in Spain, 1989.
Bottom: The Hunt for Red October was Connery's first
movie after a sudden health scare in 1989. His voice was
unusually gravelly but his performance was confident.

Connery today. 'Time has been good to me.'

his values and saw that Selinger and other advisers were right: everything, even his philanthropic concern, was dependent upon the manipulation of his standing and that meant maximising the Bond-based success.

Playing the long-haired poet with the Zapata moustache and the zinc-walled-hideaway was a happy diversion, an extension of the madman of *A Fine Madness*, an extension of tearaway Tommy. It would always live within him, but it would, from now on, be secondary to the discipline of moving *forward*.

It was a transformed Sean Connery who late in February 1971 signed with Eon, and UA's Bond fan-in-residence David Picker, to make *Diamonds Are Forever*. Gone was the pale-faced tension just the word 'Bond' had induced, the recalcitrant urge to row with Saltzman and Broccoli, the lion's mane of thinning hippie hair, the confusion of purpose. Gone too was the pretence of permanence in the relationship with Cilento. It was change, all change. At the High Court trial two years before Connery had given his address as Curzon Street, a side-track of some significance to those who knew him. Now, he was open in his feelings about the marriage. He told friends it was over, that he had true respect for Cilento, but they could never be compatible. He bought a flat overlooking the Thames at Chelsea Embankment, in a block where once Hitler's ambassador von Ribbentrop had lived, and removed all his possessions from Putney. It was a whole new lifestyle. Casual acquaintanceships with women friends were more actively pursued, and Connery unapologetically told an interviewer, 'Sex is still important to me.' Nothing more was confided. Nothing more would be said. His private life, as he always insisted, was nobody's business.

Contrary to the apparent consensus of jaundiced gibing, *On Her Majesty's Secret Service*, had not, without Connery, fallen on its face. True, in the series to date it was the slowest earner at the box office. But then *You Only Live Twice*, its predecessor with Connery, marked a decline from *Thunderball*. Furthermore the kind of invidious comparison fledgling George Lazenby was subjected to, especially in the lesser journals, advanced a reputation for the film which related not at all to its achievements. Far and away the most human Bond story, rich in pathos and irony, *OHMSS* surefootedly took its place alongside *From Russia with Love* as a triumph of British cinema – all credit to breakneck direction by former editor Peter Hunt; Lazenby, excelling by instinct; and the splendid, endearing Diana Rigg.

As eulogy and lament for all that was best in Bond, indeed in sixties cinema, *OHMSS* would, everyone knew, take some beating. Moreover, its storyline effectively completed a Bond cycle: Richard Maibaum had started *Dr No* with the raw material of a boisterous, not-too-far-from-juvenile fist-fighter policing the lions' lairs of the world. By *OHMSS* Bond was flawed, weathered, weakened by the business – a weary man given to melancholy, ultimately settling for the emotional shield of marriage. Guy Hamilton, who had been signed by Eon to make *Diamonds Are Forever* before Christmas 1970, was amply aware of the need to construct a brand-new James Bond persona.

'I was under the impression we were going with a new actor after *OHMSS*,' Hamilton says. 'John Gavin was a possible, and there were others.* Myself, I suggested an affable gent called Burt Reynolds, but the producers said no, he's only a stunt man! Anyway, I worked on the script a little in London, and then dear Tom Mankiewicz [the writer] was called in to redevelop this Bond character. So, off to America we went – we knew America was to be our setting, having considered France and a few other places – and got down to some hard rebuilding. After *OHMSS* which was slow and had lots of overage [overtime expenses], we needed a fresh type of story – yes. By the

---

* John Gavin was contracted for *Diamonds Are Forever*. When Connery decided to return he received a pay-off fee of \$50,000. Roger Moore was, according to Hamilton, 'in the offing right through the negotiations'. But he was contractually tied to Sir Lew Grade for the TV adventure series *The Persuaders*, co-starring Tony Curtis, at the time.

time I was told Sean had signed with David Picker and Eon, the script was already there, finished. Sure, it was quite a departure from old Bond. Above all the others it was larger than life, zany. But Sean came out to America in April and we had just a day or two before we started shooting, and he looked over what we had and agreed it was good. He did suggest alterations – attitudes and a line here or there – but fundamentally he agreed that Bond must be exaggerated, expanded, after the kind of saturnine presence of before, especially *OHMSS*.'

Diamonds Are Forever was the first American Bond, ostensibly based at Pinewood but, because most of the shooting was in Nevada and California, utilising Universal Studios in Hollywood also. In part, Eon's selection of America was motivated by the opportunity for widest media cover. And the strategy worked. On the heels of Connery's arrival at Las Vegas came the old bandwagon, journalists from everywhere (yes, even Japan again), this time fattened by the dark gossip that had surrounded the enigmatic personage of 'Bond' in retirement. Connery was strangely amenable, prepared to talk to most about anything – but there was some speculation among the discerning about the straightness of his replies. Though everybody knew his well-aired views about the decline in Bond script values he announced, straight-faced, that this was 'the best script I've ever had' – curious, that, because *Diamonds* positively emasculated the character as never before. Questioned about future prospects in light of the extra two-picture deal that went with Bond he stated, 'There's no doubt that Bond made me a success, and made it possible for me to do other things. But I won't stay an actor, that's for sure.' To others he mused on the possibilities of pursuing *Macbeth*, even in competition with Polanski, and to the few journalists who were old sparring friends he confided his business plans and great hopes for the Educational Trust. Baring his soul to Peter Evans he admitted that *Diamonds* was an act of enriching exorcism which would help his charity, help his businesses and, with luck, aid his career. He did not, he stressed, wish to make for himself 'another fortune – I don't want that kind of maniacal power'. Essentially this Bond was the key catalyst. 'With this picture I'm finishing part of my life. I will have accomplished quite a few things . . . and bought a bit of breathing space to look at my life and decide what I'm going to withdraw from, reach for, what I really need.'

Guy Hamilton found Connery very relaxed and clear about his acting future. He had laid down laws about this Bond with David Picker – the shoot must not run longer than sixteen weeks: if it did a further $145,000 per week would be added to his salary – and he was anxious to progress to other films, intelligently conceived popular films like *The Anderson Tapes*. Confident of the coming success of the Lumet movie Connery arranged a special private viewing, pre-première, in Vegas during the first weeks of *Diamonds*. Chorus lines from all the big Vegas shows were invited, as were many top-bill stars. Anyone who indulged reservations about Connery the actor in the wake of *The Red Tent* discarded them. All agreed *The Anderson Tapes* displayed brilliant wit and timing.

As on *Goldfinger*, Hamilton's fine-art technique of knowing what he wanted to shoot and going unwaveringly at it satisfied Connery. 'With a limited number of days,' Hamilton says, 'one can't "have a bash", one has to clearly perceive the thing. All our problems were worked out before we shot a foot of film.' Saltzman and Broccoli prudently steered clear of the set and Connery was put up in the Presidential Suite of the best hotel in Vegas. 'Golf was his only outlet,' says Hamilton. 'We almost had it written into our contracts that we had this one day off per week to take a helicopter and fly to one of the great courses nearby. Sean unwound there. As for gambling, he didn't do much – threw a few dice maybe, tried the one-arm bandits. Basically he was there for the job, and his sights were set further away.'

Rumours about a romance with Jill St John circulated, but both stars assiduously avoided compromising off-the-set photographs by dining in private. St John had originally been assigned the part of Plenty O'Toole, a peripheral character devised by Hamilton, who would be Bond's only minor fling beyond the heroine, Tiffany Case. Hamilton then decided she was wasted as Plenty, but just right for the 'brassy, hard-nut Tiffany'. Some rejigging ensued and Lana Wood, raven-haired sister of Natalie, was placed as Plenty while St John took the big role.

'The chemistry between Sean and Jill was undeniably interesting,' Hamilton reckons. 'And that was important to me. One of my interminable gripes about Bond concerns the women. I've always felt Sean especially needed a strong co-lead, a woman who could answer up to him, appear equal in talent anyway.'

After nine weeks in America cast and crew made for Pinewood and location work in Europe. Connery remained cheerful, though tired from the unrelenting schedule he had set himself. On the studio floor he looked slightly bored, slightly overweight. His toupee was streaked with grey and his eyebrows bushier than usual. He looked, one film worker commented, like 'Bond getting set for pension', but he was placid enough. As time ran out the schedule tightened and Hamilton speeded up. Journalists were ejected and concentration fixed. Having forked out more than a million of the seven-million-dollar budget to their lead star, UA was unwilling to draw out the chequebook again. A record of a few days towards the end of filming indicates the pressure.

Thursday	7.14 a.m. :	Car picks up Connery from home to take him to Pinewood.
	8.30 a.m. :	Filming of Metz' laboratory sequence starts.
	16.00 p.m. :	Filming completed. Connery, St John, Saltzman, Hamilton depart for Heathrow to fly to Frankfurt.
	19.55 p.m. :	Arrive Frankfurt. Greeted by press and fan crowds.

Friday	7.00 a.m. :	Make-up and wardrobe call at hotel.
	8.00 a.m. :	Filming on set at Lufthansa jet at airport.
	14.00 p.m. :	Film complete. Connery and St John lunch aboard jet.
	16.50 p.m. :	Depart for Amsterdam.
	20.30 p.m. :	Press conference in Amsterdam.
	22.00 p.m. :	Off duty.
Saturday	12.00 p.m. :	Connery's call – after lie-in and late breakfast.
	12.15 p.m. :	Filming Connery's drive to rendezvous with Tiffany.
	16.30 p.m. :	Daylight shooting finished.
	21.00 p.m. :	Night-time scenes outside Tiffany's apartment filmed.
	Midnight:	Filming completed.

In John Boorman's words, brilliance often arises from adversity, but in the case of *Diamonds* an unblended script of disparate elements made the task impossible for Connery and Hamilton. About three chapters of Fleming's novel formed the basis of the movie and clearly much more could have been effectively used. Instead, a cocktail of tawdry razzmatazz and unctuous humour inflated a windbag story. Here, Bond masquerades as a diamond smuggler, assisting another of like kind (St John), with the intention of unravelling the mystery of a diamond pipeline leading from Africa to middle America. He discovers Blofeld (Charles Gray), his old enemy, to be masterminding yet another scheme to dominate the world, this time wielding the untouchable weapon of a laser-satellite powered by diamonds.

Though the film did come in on schedule in August, set for Christmas release, pressure fractures were evident, even beyond the storyline. One continuity error that has a stunt-car driving down a narrow alley on two wheels, going in balanced left and coming out tilted right, was laughable for all the wrong reasons. Yet even this glaring abuse of what Bond once was skipped the uncritical, Connery-drunk fans' notice. Reviewers were less gullible. *Commonwealth* magazine pined for pure Fleming, while welcoming Connery, the essence of the series' success, back: 'The new film is . . . a bit early to have camp appeal . . . and scriptwriters Maibaum and Mankiewicz, along with director Guy Hamilton, seem unsure why they are making another Bond feature just now. Their one fresh idea is to throw in some self-parody . . . not much relief from almost two hours of Bondage . . . but all the film has to offer.'

By the time such reviews were circulating Connery was too deeply involved in other matters – the promotion of *The Anderson Tapes* and preparation for a great new departure, to be much bothered. David Picker and Eon weren't much alarmed either. *Diamonds Are Forever* opened simultaneously in America and London at Christmas and caused tremors that shook box-office records everywhere. Film history was made when £6 million was grossed in twelve days worldwide. In London alone the picture took more than £34,000 during the first week at the Odeon, Leicester Square. Po-faced newspapers reported staff arriving for work early in the morning finding 700 fans already queuing. 'The theatre telephone has been permanently blocked,' *Films Illustrated* recorded, 'and police have frequently been on the spot to cope with fisticuffs started by anti-queue jumpers.'

Historians and cynics agree: Bond had crested with *Thunderball* in which he was the neo-establishment rebel-or-hero (whichever you may choose) of sixties society. Outdated, jaded and back-tracking, the impossible had yet been accomplished: the ghost had risen in Las Vegas, rolled the bones and hit jackpot again. Nobody doubted that this freakish new success was entirely due to the contribution of Sean Connery, token playing or not.

Declared box-office champion of 1971, the movie world once again lay like a carpet at Connery's feet. Older and wiser, he could now reshape his image in whatever way he desired, with guaranteed UA backing to begin with. Predictably, to smash type, he turned, too soon, to an offbeat classic.

14

Micheline on Course

It was, for Connery, the best of times and the worst of times, these mellow days after *Diamonds Are Forever*. The press allegations that the Educational Trust fund was a tax dodge device – which had naturally upset him more than a little – were exploded by the patent advance of the cause. Connery's insistence on having *The Anderson Tapes*' European première in Scotland brought £5,000 into the Trust and the Troon golf tournament had totted another £17,000. This on top of the hefty $1 million had already begun to assist young artists in need and, more ambitiously, had padded the backbone of a new social and industrial experiment of Sir Iain Stewart's. A new town in Scotland called Glenrothes in Fife, population 30,000, expected to rise to 75,000, was the site of investment. Money from the Trust, it was announced, would finance a training college for trade unions and management within the estate, the main object of which was to break down the barriers which can disrupt industry. A seminar at Glenrothes in which the plan was forged created so much interest that the Labour Party and the Tory government sent representatives north to examine Stewart's and Connery's device.

Whilst stating he was still a socialist with nationalist interests at heart, Connery was eager to extend open arms to anyone keen on promoting his beloved Trust. 'If a good idea comes to the Trust I don't give a damn whether it comes from a Tory or a Communist.' Lest anyone doubt his true loyalties he expanded: 'I'm in favour of fragmentation in general. I don't believe in the Common Market or the United States or the Soviet Union – because there'll always be national differences and skirmishes . . . so Scotland should pull away somewhat after hundreds of years taking second place to England.'

While remaining active vice-chairman of the Trust he did not neglect his businesses. Dunbar & Co, the bank, thrived and, among other new investments, he became part-owner of a London garage. On the movie front he readied himself for the project he had chosen as the first of the UA-guaranteed twosome – a film version of John Hopkins's stage play *This Story of Yours*, a Royal Court success in 1960, which Connery had been planning anyway to revive for stage. He also formed a production company, Tantallon Films, and scouted for further properties. Everything was suddenly tinged with activity, optimism, hope . .

But at home there were regrets and heartbreaks. Quietly preparing for divorce from Cilento he reflected on 'years of failure. What we had to do was step back and see just what we were doing to each other, to our lives, and the lives of our son and daughter. Our careers were incompatible, not us. You were offered a part you wanted to do but suddenly there are a hundred questions to settle: What is she doing? What is he doing? Who will look after the kids? Can they come? Who will look after the house? Interminable.' The split was amicable, with Connery arranging reasonable financial support through his own bank. All that really concerned Diane and himself, he made clear, was the effect of the break-up on the children and 'making sure the future works for them . . . fortunately they know the situation, they're great.'

Hot on the heels of the divorce agreement came the shock news in a phone call from Neil that Joe was dead. Less than four years before, Connery had at last urged Effie and Joe out of Fountainbridge – and then only because the brewery had started demolishing next-door properties. They had settled in a pretty gadget-equipped house in the quiet Edinburgh residential district of Newington, a considerable distance from the good memories. In retirement

Joe had been endlessly restless: some days he went to the pictures, often to see his son on screen, on rainy days he stayed in bed. 'He'd never been really sick a day in his life,' Neil says. 'Right up to the end he looked fine of fettle. It was custom for Mum and Dad to join myself and family for Christmas lunch. But this year Dad had phoned and said he'd a touch of 'flu, and wouldn't be round. I offered to bring food to their house, but he said no, he wasn't hungry. A few days later he was hospitalised for tests . . . then a doctor called me aside and spilled it out. He said, "Your father's got cancer, and he hasn't too long to live." At the time I just couldn't believe it. He was only sixty-nine, it seemed impossible.' Once informed, Sean Connery wanted to arrange the best medical care for Joe, if necessary moving him from Scotland. But the doctors advised that no better treatment could be had anywhere – Joe had no options.

Within weeks, too few weeks, Joe was dead. By mistake the night sister phoned not Neil but Effie, now living alone, to break the sad news. Neil was appalled. 'It took mother from midnight till two in the morning to ring over the word – she was so distressed. The hospital had blundered with phone numbers, it was very unfortunate.' Roderick Mann, interviewing Connery a short time after Joe's demise found him 'quietened down'. Connery attributed the change to the events of the last year or so, especially his father's death. 'That was a great stopper for me,' he revealed. 'More than I can explain. I never thought it would happen. . . . The Masai tribe say that you're not a man until your father dies. They may be right, but if it's true it is a pretty stiff price to pay.'

Joe's funeral interrupted production work on the new film, a venture that UA had grave doubts about underwriting. Ian Bannen, Sidney Lumet, Trevor Howard – all old friends of Connery's – were signed by Tantallon Films, steered by executive producer Denis O'Dell. 'It was a cracking play,' Bannen says, 'but presented problems in terms of commercial cinema. We – the people working on it – loved it, but it would be foolish to say we expected it to have anything like a Bond impact.' John Hopkins, who had once penned some twenty episodes of BBC's *Z-Cars* in two years, worked closely with Connery and his team. Over months the title switched from *This Story of Yours* to *Something Like the Truth*, finally, unsatisfactorily to most, *The Offence*.

Connery detailed his outlook to Tony Crawley: '*The Offence* was *the* reason for going back to the Bond films . . . the premise was a picture that people [like Lumet, Bannen] could make and *participate* in . . . it was a sort of downbeat theme but the last forty minutes of it, quoting John Huston, is some of the best he's ever seen. . . . It was the study in the disintegration of a policeman and his mind – aided by the terrible things policemen are exposed to, and a really destructive marriage. Sidney made a fantastic job of it, but I think he got a bit European on us.'

The Offence was a rogue movie, styled and performed miles from the mainstream of current cinema. A daring choice for a star actor at any time, but downright insane, on the face of it, after so big a popular hit as *Diamonds Are Forever*. Connery seemed to take fiendish pleasure in indulging himself at the expense of UA, declaring later that he had never imagined the movie would make a profit. United Artists had allotted $1 million to the movie, which came in $80,000 under budget. In August 1981, eight years after release it first showed a profit.

In *The Offence* Connery played the unstable Detective Sergeant Johnson, a man tainted by the cruelty of the criminal world, who breaks down while interrogating a child molester (Ian Bannen) and, in a mindless frenzy, kills him. Parallel with the story of the inner struggle which erupts into violence runs the account of home life, a strained, furious partnership of habit with Maureen (Vivien Merchant, impeccably self-controlled). Paradoxically, though *The Offence* was chosen with the serious intention of neutralising Bond identification, Connery's portrayal of Johnson, so large and verbose and strong he looms, produced an illusion of heroism – soiled perhaps, but no less honourable. In killing the rapist, in cracking up,

Johnson is seen to be doing the decent thing: the subtleties of the dialogue exonerate him. In that slight but significant way, Connery's purpose was frustrated with *The Offence*, though the movie itself displays a crystal, uniform brilliance that gave him much satisfaction.

Bannen remembers, 'We rehearsed it like a stage play, very tightly, then started a fast shoot at Twickenham. Sean was worried about only one aspect of the production: time. He wanted to bring the thing in in twenty-eight days and save money. Otherwise, he was pleased with Hopkins's script and all the technical and acting people he had round him. There was a family feel, which was good, and I thought it one of his finest performances . . . though in that last scene of mine I suffered his true-to-life playing!' (Bannen, as criminal Baxter, is beaten to death by Johnson in a graphic, detailed scene: Bannen was heavily padded beneath his clothing.)

Though Connery defiantly pretended indifference to the world, he was hopeful that *The Offence* would take money, some money, *and* be seen too as an artistic success. As with *The Anderson Tapes*, he arranged a special showing at his business office near St James's Palace, to which he invited important friends, as well as cleaners and porters from the building. 'I tried to find out how people would react,' he said. 'The film's story is probably difficult to take. The cleaners and porters all said they liked the acting, but were not too forthcoming about the subject,' For Bannen, everything was right, barring the title. 'In Italy or somewhere I saw it go out as *In the Mirror, Darkly* using the Shakespearean clip, and I thought that was much better. *The Offence* spelt out grimness.' Connery felt the film was maybe fifteen minutes overlong, but he trusted Lumet's decision on what to leave in. Because he had had huge creative control, he enjoyed making *The Offence* more than any movie to date, but he was enraged when UA released the movie 'through the toilet', making no effort at all to push it on its most likely receptive markets (the film was never shown, for instance, in France).

Critically *The Offence* scored. Sydney Edwards of the

Evening Standard admired it, and Connery. Marjorie Bilbow liked the 'well constructed script and finely controlled acting. When any two characters are locked in spoken combat the film is both moving and intellectually stimulating.' But the box office was awful and those, like Selinger, interested in Connery's development, were worried. 'I think the fear might have been that Sean would persist in trying to mock Bond in the rest of his work,' suggests Selinger. But Connery was really only interested in assembling sound credits that would be a foundation for wider acceptance. After shooting *The Offence* he flew to Spain to unwind and take in some golf, but he brought a mountain of script treatments with him, leaving Selinger in no doubt that he was intent on working fast, as prescribed, to 'build on' Bond. 'He was interested in a possible comedy,' says Selinger, and Connery himself went on record cataloguing his priority choices: comedies came first. 'The only movies I never miss are the *Carry Ons*.' Spy stories did not interest him; John Hopkins had written, on commission for Tantallon, another screenplay, based on the life and adventures of the explorer Sir Richard Burton – but the second $1 million from UA would not cover such an expansive film. Connery had also contacted Germaine Greer and asked her to try a script – her idea was about Australian Aborigines, and was instantly chucked aside. Connery quite liked Greer but found that 'her mind worked on that outer cog. I feel the Aborigines were there thousands of years before us and they seem to have survived . . . so let them get on with it!' Politics in movies, apparently, left him cold. 'He saw himself as an entertainer first,' says Selinger. 'No question about that. He respected all the old theatrical thespians, but he considered himself more a man of the people, if that doesn't sound too pretentious. He really had a grasp of his craft. It was just a question of getting off his ass and *doing more*.'

At this frantic time of project-searching, something entirely unexpected happened. At a golf tournament in Morocco Connery met a tousle-haired blonde artist called Micheline Roquebrune, an avid golfer and multi-linguist, and found immediate, unique friendship. Born in Nice and brought up in a wealthy family in North Africa, Micheline was 38, with a young son and a failing marriage. On their first meeting Connery won the competition he was playing in, Micheline won hers. The shared passion for golf was the binding force of that early friendship. Very soon afterwards Connery pursued her and told her, 'I'm very serious about this. I don't play games.' Which appealed to Micheline who found herself inescapably attracted to 'his masculinity and his honesty'. They were inseparable during their first summer together in Spain, but friends doubted the relationship would survive Connery's determination to stay single. 'His feelings about marriage were very mixed,' says Ian Bannen. 'From week to week he contradicted himself. Now he wanted more children, now he wanted total freedom.' Connery himself told the press: 'I don't seem to have the equipment for marriage in terms of the contract as it exists today. But I'd like more children. And of course I'd want them to be by a woman who would bring them up properly. Who knows what will happen?'

For a year, in the eyes of the press and public, almost nothing happened. Over Christmas 1972 Micheline and Connery grew closer, but when he returned to Britain to launch *The Offence* he played his cards close to his chest and gave little hint of the lifestyle changes already on the horizon. On the spur of the moment he accepted an offer from adventurous director John Boorman, based in Ireland, to lead his futuristic fantasy movie *Zardoz*. Burt Reynolds, the director's first choice after their superb pairing on *Deliverance*, had cried off because of a hernia rupture, but Connery was overjoyed to be asked anyway. 'I located him on a golf course in Spain,' says Boorman, 'and sent out the script. Sean doesn't shillyshally. He read it over a weekend and agreed to do it immediately. He was in Ireland, sitting down with me for script talks within a couple of days. He was extraordinarily imaginative, supportive, assured. I knew instantly I had netted myself a bonus.'

Zardoz almost defies description in its unshowy but truly cosmic concept. Its strange, voyeuristic slant on a far future world where inhabitants of the bubble-covered Vortex cherish the secret of eternal life senselessly owes much, Boorman reckons, to his six years in America, where he directed smash-hits like *Point Blank* with Lee Marvin. 'It's about immortality being a fairy tale,' he says simply. 'And in America, in that crazed consumer-land, one sees this obsession with imagined permanence, this desire to perfect life and extend it.' After the success of *Deliverance*, with which Boorman won an Oscar nomination, Boorman approached Warner Bros for finance. On the basis of his synopsis and demand for total artistic control he was turned down. Columbia also rejected *Zardoz*. Finally Twentieth Century-Fox agreed a deal – 'not great, but one accepts and adapts oneself to restrictions in this business. Greatness often comes from adversity. In *Zardoz* we ended up on a shoestring, but the pressures brought out the best in everyone, especially Sean. It was no hardship for him.'

As Zed, exterminator by decree, Connery plays the balancing spirit incarnate of nature, who breaks into the time-locked Vortex to confound the immortal élite and reintroduce the threat of their mortality. He has come from the polluted, ravaged world beyond the Vortex, and appears at once as god and demon to the Vortex people. Consuela (Charlotte Rampling), among others, is eventually swayed by Zed's promise of natural ageing and death, and joins him in escape from the bubble world. They live, breed and die together.

'No one part of the filming was harder than any other,' says Boorman. 'It was an enormously difficult film to do, with effects and all the rest. Because there was so much running round, it was physically taxing for the actors, particularly Sean, who was half-naked all the time. The final sequence, however, caused a stir. It involved a long, messy make-up sitting in order to show Sean and Charlotte growing older and older, till they die. Sean was very good and patient, but after the first make-up and shoot we found the film stock was faulty, so that necessitated a complete re-run. Sean was less philosophical about sitting through the make-up process again, but he held out. And we shot

191

the sequence again, and it turned out fine. Then some young boy we had at the Studios accidentally exposed the film, destroying it. So I came to Sean and told him. His reaction was hilariously frightening. I mean, he took off! The poor kid was cursed to death. "Where is he?" Sean demanded to know. "If I get my hands on him I'll break his fucking neck!" And this boy was scuttling round the Studios for days, whispering, "Where's Connery? For God's sake, have you seen Connery?"' More seriously Boorman relates, 'Sean had no patience with people who behaved unprofessionally. His goal was fulfilling the ambition of the movie, fast and competently.'

Connery's Zed, given the dazzling distractions of photographic and directorial wizardry, was masterful, and inspired Jan Dawson in the *Monthly Film Bulletin* to wax eloquent about the ferociously concentrated energy which imposes the character as 'both a physical and moral force and does much to dispel one's doubts about the apparent loose ends in the philosophical tapestry'. Dawson also saw the film as primarily 'visonary – its images speaking both louder and clearer than its occasionally pedantic dialogue'.

As with *The Offence*, Connery found the stimulating artistry and relative critical success of *Zardoz* satisfaction enough, though again he was mildly disgruntled by the bad box office. *Zardoz* he judged rightly, to be ahead of its time, but he did not regret a moment of the ten weeks he had spent in County Wicklow making the picture. On the contrary, Ireland had galvanised him into reorganising his domestic life. Before *Zardoz* premiered he was flying back from Spain to arrange the sale of his Chelsea Embankment flat and finalise divorce proceedings with Cilento. 'My decision to sell was a pollution thing,' he told the *Express*. 'After spending all those weeks in Ireland and then being in Spain, London seemed pretty ropy when I came back: all those car exhausts spewing out muck.' Allusions to another marriage were evident: 'Who knows? Permissive society or not, it's a rare bird who'll stay with you year in and year out if you don't marry her.' And a telling secret emerged: in London he had started Spanish language lessons, attending classes in a school above Dunbar & Co. The fact that Spanish was Micheline's second language was significant to many.

A sense of anti-climax, suffused the next films Connery hurried into during the winter and spring of 1973–4, though their popular targeting was unquestionable. *Ransom*, for Finnish director Casper Wrede, was a pedestrian affair in which Connery played a security chief in Oslo pitting his wits against a terrorist group led by Ian McShane, which is holding a Boeing aircraft and the British Ambassador against the release of six political prisoners. The plot incidents, ranged like bean cans on a supermarket shelf, were eminently forgettable, the direction sadly weak. Connery was efficiently heroic, stiffly assured – but little else. Snowbound Oslo seemed to excite Wrede more than his actors' potential. Actor Chris Ellison felt, 'Wrede wasn't living up to whatever one might have expected from the man who made *One Day in the Life of Ivan Denisovich*. We, the cast, figured we were on an average movie, with average chances.' The schedule ran over, due to, among other unavoidable intrusions, acts of God. The snow melted too soon, and thousands of tons of salt-mix had to be brought in for continuity. Connery grinned and bore it. Minor altercations brightened the lives of snow-blinded actors longing for London. At one Stage Connery threatened to walk off the picture because the canteen food was so bad. On another occasion his wit, honed by adversity, lit the gloom. At a private showing of *Ivan Denisovich*, attended by cast principals and Wrede himself, no one knew that Alexander Solzhenitsyn, author of the book, was seated in the murk at the back of the theatre. As the film ended Solzhenitsyn stood up and applauded. Everyone turned to cheer the great man in turn. Connery watched the squat, bearded figure approach, the high domed forehead fringed with black stubbly hair. As the Russian drew almost into earshot Connery cracked, 'He's got this fucking head on upside down.' Wrede did not appear to hear, or chose not to. As for Solzhenitsyn – 'the Scots drawl probably saved him,' says Ellison.

In April Connery repaired to Elstree Studios to embark on Agatha Christie's *Murder on the Orient Express*, a thirties' crime thriller immaculately dressed and costumed by Tony Walton. Sidney Lumet was the unusual choice of director, and as ever Connery attained his near-best under his old friend's control.

As Colonel Arbuthnot of the Indian Army, en route home with his lover (Vanessa Redgrave), Connery becomes a suspect, along with a dozen others, for the vicious murder of Ratchett (Richard Widmark). The redoubtable Hercule Poirot, played to definitive perfection by Albert Finney, finally discovers a conspiracy of no less than *all* the suspects to murder the man they held responsible for the death of a child many years ago. Though the film was a sizeable hit – 'a splendidly frivolous gift wrapped in glittering silver foil and tied with a big satin bow', in the eyes of *Screen International* – Connery did not benefit as he might have done. The movie was star-heavy, featuring Ingrid Bergman, Anthony Perkins, John Gielgud, Michael York and others. So, Finney apart, even the most distinguished character acting assumed no better than cameo impact. In a BBC radio interview during filming Connery assessed his recent career frankly, curiously expressing no disenchantment. He recognised the fact that most people still linked him with Bond, though Roger Moore had already taken over the mantle with reasonable success in *Live and Let Die*, and agreed that some of his post-Bond work had flopped. Work satisfaction was monumentally important to him. But he was learning to enjoy leisure without guilt. Future plans, he said, were vague – though that confession seemed not to bother him. Actor colleagues who met him on *Murder on the Orient Express* found him fit and tanned from frequent months in Spain and, in the words of Bannen 'very bloody smug'.

Though officially still domiciled in Britain he had taken residence in Monaco, was applying for citizenship to ease tax pressures, and had swapped his farm in Spain for a villa, the Casa Malibu, near Marbella. 'It was all a very calculated process,' says an acquaintance, 'which, in retrospect we can see was leading up to a second marriage. Sean had lawyers working here to sort his affairs out, and Micheline standing by in Spain. His close friends, if they could be described as "close", were golfing people like Tommy Cooper, Bruce Forsyth and Jimmy Tarbuck. Eric Sykes, saw a fair bit of him too, and they played together very regularly in Marbella.' To all intents, he was married to Micheline already, though he was loath to discuss any intimate business with any journalist, friendly or otherwise. Gigi was sixteen now, and going her own way in Diane Cilento's footsteps, but Jason and Micheline's younger son Stefan were settling in Spain, at the villa, called Casa Malibu. Within a year of the divorce from Cilento, Connery was snugly back in a family unit, drawing fresh profound strengths from the stability of a peaceful home.

In the autumn he started work in Almeria, comfortably close to Micheline, on John Milius's *The Wind and the Lion*, earning his biggest cheque since Bond and his finest chance to achieve wide audience appeal. Privately he was happier than he'd been in a long time but, fearful of any disturbances of the secret calm, he presented a stony uncooperative face to the press. When the *Daily Mail*'s Ann Kent visited him on location she discovered a sober, defensive man who 'gives you his "that's another stupid question you asked me" look'. He did, however, confide some surprising news. The lawyers working to 'sort out' his affairs in Britain had disentangled him from *all* his business concerns. 'It's the easiest thing in the world to start a business empire,' he groused, 'but it creates a chain reaction of secretaries, minutes, meetings . . . it just never stopped. I found I was a mogul without a structure to support my empire, every decision had to be mine and it became too much. Now I am dropping everything except the Trust and my film interests.'

Many old buddies were surprised by the suddenness of the volte-face. Increasingly, through his thirties and early forties, Connery had prided himself on his ability to turn over a quick buck. Increasingly in the press he was 'businessman-actor', and it was popular knowledge in the City that most of his investments, properly structured or not, had turned good. The warm friendship with Sir Iain still flourished. . . . So why the sudden departure?

Some found Connery's continued movie choices just as confounding. David Quinlan, the film writer, thought him miscast in *The Wind and the Lion*. Here Connery was a noble desert warrior, the last of the Barbary pirates . . . speaking with a broad Scots burr. It was breezy fare, but the likes of Quinlan hungered for another *Offence*. Theoretically Connery could have been making another *Offence*. United Artists' proffered $1 million was depleted by inflation, but the fund still stood to back a small film of Connery's choice and though Connery often denied it, there were obviously plenty of modest properties around. Acquaintances began to speculate that Micheline was the force behind the changes – that Micheline had urged her man out of time-draining business management and had started to work on his career. But Connery retorted: 'I've never had a confidant, I've never needed one. Even when I was married I made my own decisions, by myself.' This remark had raised some eyebrows in Cilento's circle of friends. Had she not nurtured and advised the young movie-struck Connery? Hadn't she been responsible for his taking on Bond? Suggestions were made that Connery's spiky references to a friendless past arose from remarks Cilento had been making to the press about their years together. When they divorced Connery had phoned Diane and asked that neither should talk about their past. Though this was agreed, Cilento had given interviews subsequently which irritated him. Connery told Ann Kent that it was unlikely he would marry again, which further confused the situation for inquisitive friends.

Whichever way, Micheline's setting up home with Connery, coinciding with his abandonment of business concerns, assumed some importance in light of *The Wind and the Lion*. John Milius, famous for telling the cinema tales of *Dillinger* and *Jeremiah Johnson*, designed the movie as mass-market pop fodder, applying by *Photoplay*'s reckoning, 'all the elements essential for big screen

196

entertainment . . . there is romance, drama, large-scale battles, pageantry and, above all, heroes.' In spite of the clutter of the production, Connery's Berber leader Mulay El Raisuli, holding America to ransom by kidnapping an American woman (Candice Bergen) and her children, towers like a colossus, a character creation universally admired. Marjorie Bilbow saw it as 'relax-and-enjoy-it gusty entertainment to be taken no more seriously than a game of cowboys and Indians', while Vincent Canby in the *New York Times* contemplated what was possibly 'the most sappy movie ever made, as well as one of the shrewdest . . .'

By the time *The Wind and the Lion* opened in May '75 Connery was at work on another 'local' picture, the John Huston epic, *The Man Who Would be King*, shooting across the Med from home, in North Africa. For it too the signs were good. In the way of the movie business, though Milius's picture had yet to be judged at the box office, word had it that he was focused again, ergo hot again, and his fees were up. The tiny aberration that succeeded *Diamonds Are Forever* was as good as forgiven and the fan mail was pouring in once more. The sideline business distractions were gone, the bachelor drifting was over. Dennis Selinger was happier, and Connery and his Micheline had special reason to smile too. At Christmas, in secret, in good old Gibraltar, they had tied the knot.

15

Hits

The Man Who Would be King was a watershed in many respects. Crucially, it marked the end of critical assessment of everything Connery did in terms of transmutations of James Bond. In the film, playing adventurer Danny Dravot who becomes king of a remote Himalayan tribe, Connery finally outpaced Bond and created his richest character. In work terms, the movie was the milestone of altered outlook. With it he began an intensive spate of varied, non-stop mass-targeted projects that has lasted to today – a Selinger-and-Micheline-inspired unflagging campaign that has yielded quite a few superb movies and huge box-office business. Connery clearly recognised the dividing line. 'The definite swing', he told *Men Only*, started when Joe died. 'It really hit me. I changed offices, agents, accountants, lawyers, secretaries – even my wife!' Micheline became comforter and guide, but Connery still harboured resentment about a variety of wrong decisions over the last years. Quietly, from the serenity of life with Micheline and work with the much-admired Huston, the lingering bitterness was vented. Those few journalists who got past amiable film PR man Brian Doyle heard Connery's bald account of wasted years. Staying loyal to Britain, for starters, had cost him dear. On reflection, the colossal taxes he had paid for ten years enraged him. Only very lately did he realise the need to 'get out from under the umbrella of parasites headed by people like Healey – and if not him

Barber, when he was Chancellor'. He expressed no admiration of British accountants either. 'People have said I'm worth three or four million pounds,' he told writer William Hall, 'but that's rubbish.' He went on to outline losses in shares and anticipated the likelihood of being 'worth a million' once all affairs in Britain were sorted. His future, he made clear, would now be films, films, films.

The Man Who Would Be King was a $7 million version of Kipling's boyish yarn which John Huston had originally developed more than twenty years before with the hope of getting Bogart and Gable together in rebel-ridden India. 'It kind of sat on a shelf,' Michael Caine says. 'First Bogie died, then Gable, and John didn't know what to do with it. Then, after all those years, John brought it to Dennis Selinger, saying he wanted Sean and me, because we were the big British names and I suppose he thought that would be nicely fitting for Kipling.' Selinger was more excited by the script than anything he had read in years. He contacted Connery and Caine immediately, confident that 'this was an important picture for Sean, something of real substance that could give him one hell of a spurt.' Connery liked the idea of working with Huston, and with his buddy Michael Caine. The added factor that location work was planned for Morocco, next door to Micheline, appealed too. Fees were negotiated – not great, but not bad by current standards for actors trailing the American élite of Redford, Hoffman and Brando. Connery and Caine were given a quarter of a million each, plus a percentage.*

Work began in the foothills of the Atlas Mountains, in an atmosphere of harmonious joy. 'Sean had married Micheline shortly before,' says Brian Doyle, 'and he reluctantly decided to announce it to a Scottish journalist during the film. In a matter of hours, of course, Fleet Street had it

---

*Connery and Caine sued Allied Artists, the production bosses, for proper percentage returns in 1977. They won their court action and were reported enriched by $250,000 each. The countersuit for $22 million, claiming libel, failed. Had it succeeded, Connery was in no doubt, it would have all but destroyed him.

and there was a mighty fuss that didn't please him. It was like Bond all over. He'd say before a press conference, "Look, no questions on Bond, OK?" But that only incited them. That's all they wanted to talk about . . . and now he found it all a bore again, and he let it show. He was really for the most part quite pleasant with journalists, but the myth of the surly, difficult slob was perpetuated, based on scraps.' Connery severed with Bond bluntly in a chat with William Hall. 'I say no (to a return) because I don't feel a great passion for it myself. If it was something that would give me a *zing* then I'd do it.' No mention of Kevin McClory or the upcoming collaboration with writer Len Deighton was made; at this point in time Bond was a fringe interest, no more. He had other, bigger fish to fry.

After two weeks of intense rehearsals under the African sun, the cameras were ready to roll. 'One of the things that worked right was the relationship Sean and I had as Danny and Peachy,' says Michael Caine. 'It was based, if you like, on the way we got on. There was humour in the script, but we wove in our own. Back at the hotel at night, or just before shooting during the day, we'd work out together some bit of business and go to John [Huston] and present him with it. More often than not he'd accept it, and say, Yeah, that's better than the script, do it. For instance, there's the little soldier routine we do at one point, marching into the palace, one-two, one-two, all haughty disdain – that was Sean and me injecting a bit of ourselves.'

Huston was also impressed by each actor's confidence in the other. 'We decided we'd play to camera, emphasising each other's best lines – so in that *we* orchestrated movement. And Sean was particularly good at that – anything physical, anything to do with grace of movement, he was terrific. . . . He was great – a great *person* to work with, not only an actor. He had no time for the appurtenances of success, none of your whose-dressing-room-is-biggest? I think the biggest hit element the movie had going for it was the *genuine fun* of the whole escapade.'

Shakira, Caine's wife, was in the film too, and, with Micheline, they made a happy foursome after hours. There was much laughter and Huston thought the experience rewarding beyond expectations. Six years later, when the director was critically ill and believed to be dying, Caine and Connery visited his bedside. 'It was uncanny,' Caine says. 'He recognised us but he called us Peachy and Danny. He'd loved those damned characters so much, he'd lived with them in his head for so long.'

Huston, assisted in the writing by Gladys Hill, had considerably expanded Kipling's short story, embodying the author as narrator in the parable of two former Army sergeants, half-literate, striking a 'contrack' to cross the Himalayas and become the first Europeans to set foot in wildly primitive Kafiristan, where they will set themselves up as kings. Duly succeeding, they ultimately lose their hold over the tribesmen by revealing their humanness. Danny, the king, is killed trying to escape, and Peachy (Caine) survives to recount the adventure to Kipling (Christopher Plummer). In the *Monthly Film Bulletin* Tom Milne drew comparisons with Orson Welles's planned production of Conrad's *Heart of Darkness*, thematically similar. Though Welles would doubtless have explored the parables more fully, Milne opines, Huston 'does bring the conflict ignored by Kipling (sympathy for the underdog combined with support for imperialist authority) into the open. . . . Here the film is beautifully served by the performance of Sean Connery and Michael Caine, very funny as twin incarnations of typically endearing Kipling ranker-rogues . . . identical in their sharp-witted, foul-mouthed opportunism.'

From the moment the film opened in December it was a clear hit. *Photoplay* judged Caine and Connery 'inspired'. *Screen International* blared, 'Here's richness! A splendid all-rounder'. The *New York Times* agreed: 'Mr Connery and Mr Caine are two of [Huston's] nicest discoveries. The movie . . . looks lovely and remote and has just enough romantic nonsense in it to enchant the child in each of us.'

This definitive success, totally removed from Bond, excited Connery's energies in yet more ambitious efforts. After the briefest snatched holiday waterskiing from his own beach at Marbella with Jason and Stefan ('actually I find the sport quite boring – give me golf'), Connery signed for Richard Lester's proposed tragicomic *Robin and Marian* to be shot entirely on the Plain of Urbassa (doubling for Sherwood Forest) near Pamplona, Spain – a favoured site Lester had picked and used to supreme advantage with his *The Three* [and *Four*] *Musketeers* the year before. 'Filming in Spain was suddenly important to him,' says Selinger. 'It reflected his new mood, the settling down thing. He had decided on a new life with Micheline and he'd had enough of Britain and so it became a factor: if a producer wanted a better than average chance of Sean taking his project on it had to be Africa or Spain . . . I don't think Hollywood was much on his mind, as such. He was big enough everywhere, I suppose, and he had no love for the bullshit of LA anyway. . . . So these new movies were like working at home, in your front garden.'

The Wind and the Lion and *The Man Who Would be King* had been made back to back, so by the time Connery encountered Lester's film he was unusually tired. Still, he perked up when he read James Goldman's script. He was also stimulated by the prospect of exploring a new relationship with Lester, whose avant-garde qualities immortalised the Beatles on film in *A Hard Day's Night* and *Help*. For his part, Lester was inspired by Connery's recent work and eager to cut new ground. 'Not having worked with Sean before I can't say I imagined at all what his reaction [to the initial approach] would be,' Lester says. 'He wanted to see the script, naturally, but his response revealed no tiredness. He took it, read it and . . . he was enthused, as I had been four years earlier when the idea was offered to me.'

Years before, a Columbia executive had come into Lester's Pinewood office with four cards on which were scribbled synopses of potential films. Riding high on the strength of the Beatles hits, Lester had an embarrassment of choices but – 'I jumped on the *Robin* one. I told him that was the picture I wanted to make and if he could go away and fix a deal, I was in.' Months later Goldman's script – 'beautifully done, and scarcely tampered with at all in the shooting version' – was submitted, and financing arrangements made. Lester thought of Connery first for the part of Little John (eventually played by Nicol Williamson). 'I thought that might be fun, off-centre casting, but then the notion of his taking on Robin Hood grew and grew. The quality of innocence he can so well portray was food for thought.'

Competition from other Robin Hood productions in planning threatened Lester's movie. Polish producer Wieslaw Kliszewicz was in discussion with British director Sidney Hayers to shoot a version starring Patrick Mower in England. In Hollywood Mel Brooks was at work on a TV series. Undeterred, Lester planned 'the consummate version' – and to that end secured the participation of Audrey Hepburn, agreeing to return to the cinema after seven years' absence, to play Maid Marian. That coup effectively quelled competition, and proved decisive in winning Connery's signature. Conclusive for Connery too was the quirky slant of Goldman's text. Though Lester's imprimatur assured a popular film, Connery was unashamedly attracted to 'a story about death, and dying. I had to find out what kind of man *is* Robin? Considering his later days will be something new . . .'

Micheline obviously approved, as did Selinger. But not everyone was as convinced about this dark new script. 'So Sean's making a picture about Robin Hood dying?' a film executive at Pinewood is alleged to have said. 'How long will it take? He was ninety minutes dying in *The Offence* . . .'

Lester completed his film in an astounding six weeks, entirely on location. 'I don't think I made many mistakes with it,' he says, 'but I regretted Ray Stark's [executive producer] decision to alter our working title. Our title was *The Death of Robin Hood* and should have been left as such. In changing it we were inviting the kind of mindless technique many critics have of evaluating your movie *by the last one you made*. To me, *Robin* was not comedy – yet people asked me where were the jokes? Yes, there were humorous moments. Sean is an actor who looks for humour in his parts, to humanise characters – which is quite right. But *Robin* was straight, all of us saw it like that – and because of the connotations of the changed title it prompted the wrong reaction.'

Nonetheless *Robin* was sufficiently strong to complete for Connery the hat-trick of critical successes begun with *The Wind and the Lion*. Despite kind critiques, however, the film failed to ignite the American market. The heart of the story, Connery himself squarely judged, was wrong for America. American films favour fountain-of-youth heroism. But Lester's Robin is in decline, returning disillusioned from the Crusades but wearily ready to do battle again with the Sheriff of Nottingham (Robert Shaw) who, by order of King John (Ian Holm), is rounding up all higher clergy for exile. Maid Marian (Hepburn), now the abbess of a priory, is due for imprisonment so Robin's wrath is fired and he frees her, reactivates their love affair and finally tackles the Sheriff in single combat. Robin is gravely wounded and Marian sips poison to die by his side in a tragic but unsentimental concluding scene. American reviewer Vincent Canby was ready to concede that Hepburn's and Connery's screen presences 'are such that we are convinced that their late-August love is important and final'. Others found the movie maudlin and overlong.

Connery had mixed feelings and, in hindsight, wondered about Lester's basic approach. 'There were elements that hadn't been foreseen,' he told journalists at a press conference. 'Principal of which was the Catholic response. She [Marian] was guilty of committing many sins by committing suicide, killing me and living in sin.' Another difficulty for Americans was that 'their philosophy is very much in terms of solving problems, and that the good guy should never be over the hill, never in a state of deterioration'.

This American failure didn't unsettle Connery because the movie, more than anything he'd recently done, won him the admiration of many people whose opinions he valued. John Boorman admired it. Robert Hardy considered his contribution 'a personal best' and took the trouble to write to Lester when he couldn't contact

Connery. Pauline Kael in *The New Yorker* was effusive in her praise: 'Sean Connery – big, fleshy, greying – is the most natural-looking heroic figure. He seems unrestrained, naked: a true hero . . . he's animal-man at its best.' Fred Zinnemann told me in conversation, '*Robin and Marian* drew my attention to Sean. His authority was memorable.' Frank Rich of the *New York Post* was greatly generous too, believing Connery and Hepburn 'epitomise ideals of glamour and sophistication that have since passed out of our lives'.

Connery had not, however, abandoned his vagrant fondness for selecting oddball projects as the next movie script he accepted demonstrated. Lester stated that he wanted to use him again – 'as quickly as possible, as soon as the right script turns up' – but Connery went immediately for the unorthodox with Richard C. Sarafian's *The Next Man*, a low-budget film whose plot, funding and distribution were shaky to begin with.

Sarafian's filmic vision is best demonstrated by his earlier arcane *Vanishing Point* (1971), but *The Next Man* unfortunately combined all his sense of riddle irony with liberal doses of derivative tomfoolery. The 'humanitarian plot', with its agreeable dressing of high-risk intrigue, obviously engaged Connery's interest, but unending rewrites spelt trouble from the start. Connery played a visionary Saudi Arabian minister determined to sign a pact with Israel for the co-production of petroleum and its by-products for distribution at cost to poor nations. Sexy blonde Cornelia Sharpe was Nicole Scott, callous and amoral as Bond himself, assigned to kill the good Arab after first seducing him. The preachy tone of the hokum encouraged Vincent Canby to slam the makers as people 'whose talent for filmmaking and knowledge of international affairs would both fit comfortably into the left nostril of a small bee', and, for the first time ever, a Connery movie found no willing distributor in Britain. *The Next Man* was finally seen in Britain on Independent Television network in January 1982.

Sarafian and Connery were equally irritated by the critics' reaction. Much earnest labour had gone into the picture, and $4 million had been spent location-hopping from Nassau to London to Ireland to Munich, Nice and Morocco. But, after a gloomy opening at the Rivoli and other New York theatres, the movie died. Cornelia Sharpe, with her 49 costume changes, token nude scene and antagonistic cool took the brunt of most criticism. Deservedly: the script's attempt to maintain her at star billing was agonisingly obvious, and the film would have been better had her role been played with subtlety. Connery might have granted that, but he would not truck with one New York journalist's style of criticism. In America to discuss offers with his Los Angeles agents, he read a review which boldly stated that Sharpe was only cast because she was the producer's girlfriend. Connery wasted no time in contacting the journalist by phone and threatening, very eloquently, to push her words down her throat. 'What did she say?' Roderick Mann later queried Connery. To which, without batting an eye, Connery replied, 'Nothing, she was speechless.'

This commendable quality of loyalty – if a bit fiery – had always won Connery friends in the film business. Even those directors who stopped short, for whatever reasons, of using him, held him in high regard. John Schlesinger, whom Connery had approached in 1971 for a part in *Sunday Bloody Sunday* (Peter Finch was already cast, so Connery was turned down), frequently loaned out his Beverly Hills home to him. Others went out of their way to enjoy his company. But, as Guy Hamilton says, 'Sean is not a social animal – though once admitted to his circle, people are inclined to stay there. Sean's ability to call a spade a spade makes him valued.'

In Hollywood, during the aftermath of *The Next Man* Connery re-evaluated his American market position and dined and drifted with Michael Caine, the writer Stanley Mann and a few notable expatriates. 'His strategy was a gut one,' says Caine. 'The truth is he wasn't a great guy for advisers and all that stuff. But he was your typical canny Scot. Nobody's fool. Every time he reached a career dead spot – or a hot spot – he took time out, a day here, a day there, to reconsider and ask himself: Where do I go from here? I think Sean is a great career planner. He hides it, but he is.' This time – perhaps smarting from the poor press for *Robin* and *The Next Man* – Connery wasn't particularly warm to Hollywood, nor energetic about his chances there. Spain, he told Caine and others, was the dearest place on earth to him, Hollywood was good only for the best beef and lamb in the world, and Britain – well, Britain had its values all mixed up. He told Roderick Mann that he regretted not having been able to attend the premières of his last three movies in Britain but 'the tax laws just won't allow it. If I stay in Britain for more than ninety days I'm subject to those crazy taxes. It's self-defeating, the government's making a big mistake. [The tax problems] only serve to discourage major film-making in Britain. No big star will agree to risk a movie there that might conceivably overrun and land him in it. It's unfortunate, but I just don't want to know.'

Back in Spain, too far from the risky realities of London and LA, Connery signed quickly for Joseph Levine's mammoth production of *A Bridge Too Far*, a $25 million reconstruction of Operation Market Garden, General Montgomery's controversial attempt to terminate the Second World War in a single co-ordinated thrust. Sir Richard Attenborough had signed to direct, and the prestige ring of the endeavour, along with the quarter-million-dollar fee, convinced Connery he was onto a good thing. He was, in fact, the first of some dozen international stars to be signed and he was appalled when, weeks before shooting commenced in Holland, he read a newspaper account of Robert Redford's negotiated $2 million fee. Connery's response to this discovery reveals his perception then of his own market value. 'At first I thought it was a mistake,' Connery said. 'Then I learnt it wasn't. Now, considering the size of my part in the picture, the salary I'd agreed on seemed fair. But when I found out how much others were getting – for the same amount of work and with no more acting ability – it became unfair.'

Connery's role was that of Major-General Roy Urquhart,

whose job was to command the Rhine bridgehead at Arnhem, hopefully – but tragically not – with the support of General Horrocks's (Edward Fox) XXX Corps ground force. The part was meaty, and Connery vied for screen time only with Anthony Hopkins (as Lt-Col. Frost, the fighting hero of Arnhem Bridge). Incensed by what he suddenly saw as the privileges commanded by the Hollywoodites – James Caan, Elliott Gould and the others – Connery met with Joe Levine and demanded fairer status. 'It had nothing to do with egotistical arrogance,' Ian Bannen contends. 'One of Sean's slogans after Bond had always been, pay me what I'm worth. Naturally he gathered that since Levine priced Redford so high, he deserved more. No slick-ass producer, however well disposed towards him – and Levine was a pal – would deny him his worth.'

Levine agreed to increase Connery's salary by fifty per cent rather than lose him and the units moved to Deventer, 40 kilometres north of Arnhem, to commence a massive shoot. The logistical problems of mounting the film – assembling the 300-man production team and more than a hundred actors, buying aircraft, tanks, guns from all over the world – were monstrous. But the end result, with superlative post-production – dubbing, music, cutting – made the undertaking worthwhile. Unlike *The Longest Day*, this movie (also based on a Cornelius Ryan book) knitted smoothly. Where Zanuck had corralled stars for 'star effect' in *The Longest Day*, Levine had employed the instantly recognisable faces as a means of punctuating the complex fabric of the story, making them, in their identifiableness, the keys to narrative coherence.

While at Arnhem Connery had no time for the usual golf. 'When I'm working this hard I miss the golf . . . though I find ways to get round that.' When the production finished everyone, even Micheline, expected him to rest in Marbella but the experience of 'Hollywood games playing' on *A Bridge Too Far* seems to have chastened him and, of his own volition, he wanted LA again and the chance to reaffirm his status at the core of the industry. 'He seemed to grab the first juicy studio script he could find,' says Bannen. And on 31 October he swooped into the muddy mire of *Meteor*, $15 million of unmitigated disaster, directed by Ronald Neame, all about the attempts of an American and a Russian scientist (Connery and Natalie Wood respectively) to divert an earth-strike by a meteor. Elaborate special effects delayed the completion of the movie – which did not open till November 1979 – but Connery wasn't bothered. Before a quarter of the picture was shot at MGM Studios the cancer of defeat was about.'It was one of those movies where you have to *try* hard,' commented an actor afterwards. 'When you have to try *that* hard, you know there's something amiss.' The expat community he usually sought out found Connery tired from three years of unbroken work, but coolly philosophical. He stayed again at Schlesinger's house, but this time had the company of Micheline and the children. When he wasn't working he often sat late into the night, his talk frequently nostalgic. En route for this trip the family had stopped off in Britain, where Connery had treated the boys, and Micheline, to a saunter down memory lane. He had collected Effie and driven to Fountainbridge to glance over 176 before the wrecking cranes moved in. To his surprise, he himself mirrored something of the boys' reaction. Fifteen-year-old Jason found the place just 'interesting', where Stefan, two years his junior, thought it awful. 'I wanted them to see it,' Connery mused, 'but it really was a dump. A terrible place. No hot water, gas mantles on the landings . . .'

Micheline, who had had the comforts of a wealthy African and French upbringing behind her, was horrified: 'What a dreadful place!' Effie had just smiled and hugged her son and whispered that it was really quite nice, unchanged. She didn't have to close her eyes to imagine what it was like all those years ago, with Joe out till all hours, toiling at the rubber mill, and Tommy stealing away, too young for dreams even, to kick football on the biggie.

In the Hollywood Hills, in the spring of 1978, Connery relaxed and ruminated on the grey harsh past. Watching Micheline working with her oils and easel, painting Shakira

Caine, the children, the scenery; dining with welcome visitors Ian Bannen and Richard Burton; snatching an hour's golf in gentle sun. . . . In many ways, remembering Fountainbridge, the new, secured life was hard to accept. He certainly had more than he'd ever dreamed of. The ups and downs of his Bond fortunes were over. By his own planning he had made the million he'd intended when he quit Britain for good – and well more. His career was stable, his services in demand, his company sought. So much had changed. And yet, and yet. . .

'In himself he remained basically the same,' Michael Caine says. 'Always a bit of the decent working man about him – like the time we were at a club in Los Angeles and this crowd of loudmouths started to heckle the performer on stage. Sean wouldn't have it. He didn't call the manager or anything. He just did the bold thing and had a go at 'em. Very brave. But, you see, he wasn't offended himself – it wasn't that his cosy night out had been interrupted. He was upset for the performer on stage. He just couldn't take those rowdies, so he gave them a dose of their own medicine. Like any noble working man.'

In Hollywood writer-director Michael Crichton and producer Dino de Laurentiis offered Connery *The First Great Train Robbery*, which he agreed to do, but withdrew from when informed the shoot would be at Pinewood. Schedules were reshuffled, Ireland's National (formerly Ardmore) Studios, was judged to be the ideal substitute, where Connery's tax status would not be compromised, and a two-month filming run began in the summer of 1979. Just before shooting started, mulling over the new script at Schlesinger's house, Connery showed old loyalties again by inviting Ian Bannen aboard. 'Crazy,' says Bannen. 'It was about two o'clock in the damned morning and Sean threw me the script and said, "See if there's anything in it for you. I can't see it, but have a look."' Bannen perused Crichton's racy script and declined. 'Sean was a very astute reader,' says Ardmore director Sheamus Smith. 'He had a conversational range, an intelligence, an intellectual capacity that one might put on a par with, say Peter Ustinov. He read all the time he was in Ireland. Whenever I saw him he had a book in his hands, not some trashy paperback, always something substantial. His way with scripts was remarkable, too. He could glance over an offered script and establish immediately whether it was right for him, or whoever. He was never brash, when one submitted something for his evaluation, just utterly, intelligently decisive.'

The First Great Train Robbery was a good choice at a good time in Connery's career. Crammed with images resoundingly redolent of Victorian life, it told the story of the incorrigible crook, Pierce (Connery), who devises a plan to steal £25,000 of bullion being shipped to the troops in the Crimea, on the first leg of its journey – by train to Folkestone. Abetted by his mistress Miriam (Lesley-Anne Down) and Irish safe-cracker Agar (Donald Sutherland), Pierce gathers the four keys necessary to open the bullion safes, then tackles the train. The resultant episodes, where Pierce performs hair-raising carriage-top stunts on the moving locomotive, are among Connery's best action moments since James Bond. They were eminently memorable for Connery too. Sheamus Smith recalls: 'Micheline wasn't around for all the shooting, and had she been there would have been trouble over the stunt sequence. Sean wanted to do it, but he was under the impression, as was Crichton, that the train which was an original 1870-built steam model would travel no more than about 30 m.p.h. Of course, when the shooting was over the helicopter pilot who'd been covering the shot flying alongside said, "No, mate, my instruments aren't likely to be wrong – and you were doing more than fifty!" Sean was, needless to say, shaken and stirred.'

After location shooting in Meath and Cork, Crichton moved his cast to Pinewood for two London sequences, carefully limited so that Connery would not spend too many days 'under the umbrella'. Sheamus Smith followed on to watch progress and observed that Connery demonstrated 'remarkable stamina. One found it impossible not to admire the gusto he put into the picture. When Micheline wasn't around he doggedly kept his head down at golf. He ate well, enjoying good grub, and drank mostly wine. I got the feeling here was a contented man, ideally suited to the rigours of his chosen career.' Confusion of identification with Bond no longer troubled the mellow Connery. Smith recalls 'an awful, rainy afternoon, late-lunching with him at Pinewood's restaurant. The manageress came in, having picked up her children from school. Sean was off-duty, wearing a dirty anorak, bearded, without his toupee. But the kids instantly recognised him and came darting over, asking, "Can we have your autograph, Mr Bond?" Sean paused – and grinned. He seemed delighted to be recognised and cheerily responded to these children with their awestruck expressions.'

Crichton's film lived up to all its promise, mixing pure escapism with visual sumptuousness, providing a fitting colourful epitaph for cinematographer Geoffrey Unsworth, whose last film it was. Gordon Gow in *Films and Filming* crystallised the specialness of the movie when he wrote 'charm is uppermost in this breezy film', and though *Time* and other notable journals picked out Lesley-Ann Down for the scene-stealing awards, Connery received his fair share too. Looking back on his recent career, *Films Illustrated* called him 'the most improved British actor of the decade' and everyone agreed that Connery had much to look forward to in the immediate future. 'He wanted to direct,' Sheamus Smith says. 'Everybody knew that was a desire he'd long held. But he genuinely adored acting, and the parts were there for the taking like never before.'

'I haven't made too many mistakes,' Sean Connery told a press conference in 1981, 'but I made one with *Cuba*.' Late in 1978, just weeks after finishing Crichton's film, Connery hitched onto Richard Lester's new project, a love-and-war story about the last days of Batista's Cuba. By any reckoning he was due a break but aspects of his last movies bothered him. Before he saw a frame of it he felt *Meteor* was a dud. This misjudgement annoyed him, as did the growing signs that United Artists had no intention of heavily promoting *The First Great Train Robbery*, a movie he believed in. *Cuba* was an urgent compensation device.

But in *Cuba* he blundered, settling for the two things he was instinctively most wary of – an unfinished script in the hands of an unsure director.

'Confidence is an actor's lifeblood,' said Robert Henderson. 'Take it away and you've got an actor in trouble.' Connery's choice of *Cuba* was to take him from the smoothest, happiest plateau of his career to the brink of disaster.

16

Misses

A considerable amount of Connery's undoing with *Cuba* was his own fault. Ever since the Bond days he had resisted long-shoot commitments on movies, believing a shorter, intense schedule allowed one the emotional intensity plus a detachment which made one more likely to achieve interesting screen results. The film most wasteful of time and energy had been the penultimate Bond, *You Only Live Twice* – a memory which still rankled. As late as 1981 Connery was still cribbing that 'that took six months of my time, after two or three postponements – which meant it was almost a year out of my life . . . and if one film takes six months and the people who are supposedly producing it are so stupid they cannot programme it properly, then it leaves no room for flexibility [to make other movies].' Dennis Selinger's tactical scheme of fast-filming had shown itself worthy over four exciting years – and now Connery was emphatically agreeing that 'the more diverse the parts you play, the more stimulating it is and, in turn, the wider the experience, so there's even more you can play.' But speed-of-light transition from role to role entails real dangers – the very least being the on-screen exhaustion which showed itself during the mid-sixties; at worst, misconceived, rushed mishmash when the actor has too much control because of his stature.

Richard Lester had been eager to work with Connery again after *Robin and Marian*. Motivated by a loyalty principle similar to Connery's, Lester believed he had 'come close to something really good' with *Robin*, but had failed commercially. Intending to make up to the actor he greatly admired, in 1977 he commissioned his friend the writer Charles Wood, 'a gifted character creator' who had worked on ten Lester films, to write something special for Connery. Inspired by conversations with producer Denis O'Dell, mutual friends of Connery's and Lester's, who had himself spent some weeks in Cuba during the Castro takeover in 1960, the director chose this 'truly remarkable period' as the basis of what would be the Connery epic to end epics of the seventies. In a phone call outlining the proposal, Connery expressed enthusiasm. He thought the originality of the concept striking. It seemed 'extraordinary' to him that no film-makers had raked the Cuban revolution in twenty years. Once excited, and trustingly fond of Lester, Connery was in. Once in, he was hurrying. The first treatment Charles Wood submitted he liked, and though he felt uneasy about the unfinished screenplay, he felt far more unhappy about the prospects of *Meteor* and the damage that might do. Very fast he negotiated *Cuba* with Denis O'Dell and production supervisors Alex Winitsky and Arlene Sellers. On the strength of recent achievements his fee rocketed to a fat million dollars, his biggest in some time. He gave Lester a deadline: the film must start while the weather was right in southern Spain, which would double for Cuba. September–October would be a good time.

But by October Wood's script was still unready. 'It was constant re-evaluation,' says Lester, 'because I felt we weren't reaching the proper balance between foreground characters and background history. We were risking falling between a romantic story involving uninteresting people, and a documentary-like survey of a ridiculous, fascist, sin-ridden mafia-controlled city undergoing total change in a three-day revolution. I was under pressure to get rolling, but I was terrified of trivialising this fascinating time in recent world history.'

Connery himself claims he postponed shooting twice because the script was not satisfactory. Eventually, 6 November was announced as a start date – 'because we were running out of weather' – but this was again cancelled. Logistically, for Lester, the film was a nightmare. As on *Robin*, there would be no studio work, just ten weeks at 78 sites, ranging from the famous old cities of Jerez de la Frontera (where the sherry comes from), to Cadiz and picture-postcard Seville. The crew, organised under a plethora of assistant directors, numbered 160 – their job being to utilise multiple camera techniques in order to speed up the shooting and vary choice of sequences for editing, all designed to make the film fast, explosive and innovative. Finally, Connery's patience was spent. The umpteenth draft of the script was deemed acceptable, though Lester had reservations and was still scribbling amendments when filming started on 27 November. The singer Diana Ross had been first choice for Connery's love interest, but had dropped out late in the day, to be replaced by a coquettish but rather young-looking Brooke Adams, cast by Lester before he even met her.

The opening of *The First Great Train Robbery* in Britain a few weeks into shooting did nothing to cheer the glum mood on location. United Artists had, as Connery anticipated, spared much on promoting *Robbery*, even though notices were excellent. Unfortunately UA would also distribute *Cuba*, which wasn't encouraging. On set Connery was gruff and irritable, refusing to join a party of British journalists who had specially flown out for informal drinks after work. 'But there were no tantrums,' Lester insists. 'Sean is too seasoned, too professional.' Good relationships with fellow actors Jack Weston and Brooke Adams ('He's hot, he's so hot!') were formed and, day by day, problems were overcome. 'But those problems, script apart, were too numerous,' Lester confesses. 'Problems like borrowing military hardware from the Spanish government, and it being taken back at the last minute. A key plane, the only one of its kind in Europe, crashing on us. The train for the last big sequence blowing up on *the first take* . . . We were just snowed down.'

By January the rumours of chaos were widespread in the industry. Allegedly *two* different endings were to be shot and *Screen International* reported that 'Lester can often be heard speaking about fear. It seems that when he wakes up he is terrified of what lies before him. He worries about all the things that might go wrong.' At the same time Lester was putting a confident brave face on his difficulties. The open-ended script was no cause for alarm: 'It is lovely when films have their own organic growth,' he said from location. 'You let it develop and sometimes marvellous things happen.'

Sometimes.

Cuba had Connery looking more Bondish than he had done since *Diamonds*. His hairpiece was thick and neat, the Gable moustache cropped to insignificance on his leaner, fitter face. The story is of a former British Army Major (Connery) hired by Batista's people to teach the troops counter-insurgency as the storm builds in Havana. The Major meets a woman, Alexandra (Adams), with whom he had an affair fifteen years before. They are swept into the chaos of revolution but cannot agree on its likely outcome. While filming progressed the separate endings had Connery persuading Adams to leave as Castro takes over, or, against his convictions, deciding to stay with her to face the music. In the end a compromise was struck: Connery flees to Havana Airport to get out of the country, leaving an air ticket for Alexandra, should she choose to follow. The effect was unfortunate after two hours of genuinely gripping action, after the intimacies, almost a cop-out. Marjorie Bilbow fairly castigated the whole, whilst admiring 'the way Lester keeps the pace going, fits the jigsaw pattern together, contrasts the squalor of poverty with the smug elegance of wealth'.

During the filming Connery never once complained of developments to Lester. 'I'm not a director who runs rushes, so there was nothing, in that way, to be discussed,' Lester says. In fact, work apart, the two men spent little time together. Throughout the shoot Connery drove home whenever possible to Marbella, taking the wheel of his own Mercedes, refusing party gatherings. Quinn Donohue, the publicist, urged him to co-operate more fully with the press but his regular reply, bundling golf clubs out of the car during afternoon breaks, was 'Give me a break, eh? I've done my bit.'

Cuba came in on schedule and on budget, a laudable accomplishment in the eyes of those who knew. Connery saw a rough cut, the unfinished edited version, but did not reveal his feelings to Lester. 'Only later did it come back to me that he wasn't happy,' Lester says. 'He never said it to my face, but he was cross and he held me responsible for all that went wrong.' Lester emphasises that he is not sorry he made the movie. 'It works on a superficial level, the character interplay, all that, but the profundity I envisioned went out the window. There just wasn't time to get it.'

Unreasonably Connery judged *Cuba* a waste of time. Unforgiving, and admitting no blame himself, he dubbed it 'a fatal error . . . a case of patchwork'. In his opinion, he stated grimly, Lester 'hadn't done his homework'. Lester was understandably aggrieved and confessed to me that he doubted the breach of friendship was repairable. 'I haven't heard from Sean about the picture, but I take it his feelings are very strong.'

A shock of disillusionment – or just plain tiredness – rattled Connery after *Cuba*. Its consequence was the first long period of inactivity since 1972. Speculative projects were announced – a possible role in James Clavell's *Tai-Pan*, to be directed by John Guillermin for Filmways Productions (originally announced to star Steve McQueen), another possible in *Shogun* for ABC TV. All fell through, lost under another secretive blanket of business reshuffling. After a row with his Los Angeles agents, Connery quit Dennis Selinger and ICM's management advice. Michael Ovitz now became his LA representative and career guide.

In the spring-cleaning that followed, Connery unearthed astounding miscalculations, bad judgements by himself, bad advice, unwise investments throughout the seventies. He told the *Express* writer Victor Davis that while founding the Educational Trust and seeking ways, with Sir Iain Stewart, to improve the industrial atmosphere between men

218

and management he had mistakenly assumed himself to be rich. The regretful irony was, that when he was writing over his $1 million-plus to the Trust, he himself was almost broke – 'thanks to mishandling, the fortune had turned out to be all figures and no substance.' Having rebuilt the nest egg during the relentless Spanish and American interlude, he swore that this time he would oversee everything personally and trust no one completely. 'Nowadays I handle contracts myself – and I have a good lawyer. I think it was Erica Jong who said the difference between making a lot of money and being rich is a good lawyer.' In Los Angeles he purchased an apartment, and in Iowa a 600-acre pig and cattle farm. 'His intention,' says Caine 'was to resettle a part of himself near the hub of the film world. On *A Bridge Too Far*, for example, he had suffered the remoteness of Marbella. Everyone else was raking in their millions while he was playing innocent golf, thinking, 'Oh, they won't try to swindle me . . . Sean always had that interest in the American scene. He knew like I knew that you had to do it if an international reputation was to be maintained.'

Much as he guessed, Connery was in trouble, reputation-wise, when *Meteor* finally opened in November 1979, followed weeks later by *Cuba*. The panning both movies received reverberated through the industry, amplified by the sad story of sadder takings on *The First Great Train Robbery*, whose progress around America was funereal. Connery sprang into action, confronting United Artists first of all for its weak-spined promotion of *Robbery*. He didn't need any agent to speak up for him – 'after all, it was me who made the film' – but went and saw the publicity-distribution people himself, pounding desks and demanding explanation. 'No satisfactory explanation came . . . United Artists owe me a bit, but I owe them some too, I suppose. I never did make that second picture for them, after *Diamonds* . . .'

With Natalie Wood, uninterestedly, he toured to promote the dreary Columbia *Meteor*, but was glad to get back to his LA apartment to see Mike Caine and chat, in Caine's words, about 'anything but the bloody business'. He spent a few days at the new farm in Iowa, and resolved to put Stefan and Jason to work there for a spell, to toughen them up. Dining with his friend the writer Roderick Mann, he would not be drawn on the failures of *Robbery*, *Cuba* and *Meteor* – nor the prospects of playing Daddy Warbucks in the upcoming film version of *Annie*, offered to him by producer Ray Stark. Yes, he liked the idea of hoofing in a musical again, and was taking singing lessons to loosen up the chords last fully tested with 'There is Nothing like a Dame!' – but that was as far as he would go in committing himself. Instead, he wanted to chit-chat and, as always lately, his idle talk was about the fortunes he had wasted. Did Mann know, for instance, that the Chelsea Embankment flat had gone for £60,000? Too little – it was worth £300,000 today. But it wasn't all bad news. Dunbar & Co. was still flourishing, still dear to him – and he held 80,000 shares. Plus shares in 'a number of banks in the Mid-West'. Mann noticed, as others had, that the balancing act – and the motivation –was a dovetailed combination of business and movie–making. Success in one area was still as important as success in the other.

Peter Hyams, celebrated new whiz-kid director who had scored a massive pop hit with *Capricorn One*, at last urged Connery out of what Caine called 'this mini-retirement', with the offer of the big budget sub *Star Wars* venture, *Outland*. Connery was thrilled by '. . . the story, the whole story. The setting of it and how it was [to be] constructed and designed and, obviously, as with any film, it had to be a viable part that I'd find stimulating . . . it was.' With surprising native loyalty he persuaded Hyams to relocate the shooting, planned for Hollywood, to Pinewood – 'partly because the technical facilities are so superior there' (where *Star Wars* was made), but also 'because I haven't fully made a film there since 1974'.

While waiting for the start date Connery snuck in a few days in a cameo role in Terry Gilliam's *Monty Python*-esque *Time Bandits* – an episodic bag of jokes, awkwardly interlinked but full of invention, which told the story of a boy's odyssey through holes in the fabric of time. As King

Agamemnon, Connery was, predictably, the heroic colossus at the centre of the film, battling masterfully with the Minotaur till saved, by chance, by the boy (Craig Warnock). *Time Bandits* was convenient because it was shot in Morocco, next door to Aloha Golf Course and the stress-saving opportunity to bang a ball about with good pals like James Hunt, now in retirement and living nearby.

Hunt saw Connery principally as 'a man's man', but observed too the deepening spiritual relationship with Micheline. Micheline's great quality was an ability to share his daily routines while allowing him the space and privacy he craved. Her devotion to him was beyond question but, says Michael Caine, 'she never cramped his style'. At the ritzy Marbella Club Hotel, where Loren and Bardot stopped off whenever cruising through, Connery was an occasional visitor, usually in male company. Jackie, wife of high-living Prince Alfonso, the hotel owner and casual friend of the Connerys, commented, 'Dozens of the most beautiful women dally and flirt with him, but he doesn't give them the slightest chance.' Micheline, quite clearly, was the ideal mate. Golf continued to unite them, though he baldly confessed that he preferred male competitors – which just made Micheline laugh. 'I like to win too – that's the trouble,' she told Caine. Together they played his favourite golf courses – she off handicap seventeen, he now off a confident nine. The relationship thrived, Michael Caine believes, because it was founded on deep, abiding mutual respect. Connery's brazen honesty Micheline loved, and her personal confidence was such that it didn't at all bother her when Connery said, 'I couldn't possibly be with someone night and day . . . Whatever your situation, you should be parted for a lot of the time. I'll tell you why: if you've been away acting, painting, whatever, it's that marvellous exchange when you get back that counts for so much.'

After sixteen months of film inactivity Connery particularly enjoyed the challenge of *Time Bandits* and preparations for *Outland*. But he was upset that the usual 'games' of tax penalty avoidance were once again imposed

221

on him. Because he had, for the last four years, insisted on visiting St Andrews and other Scottish courses for BBC TV pro-celebrity matches, his allowance for work days in Britain was reduced – hence, despite the fact that through his efforts millions of pounds of American investment was once again coming to Britain, *Outland* commenced under the rigours of time restrictions. A friend says, 'It really fucked him off. He hated the games. He is a very black-and-white man who has felt at times utterly abused by the system. He pays his dues. He has contributed millions to the UK economy. His 007 movies reinvented British international cinema . . . but at times he feels shortchanged by the system.' *Outland* was a complicated endeavour that looked likely to swallow every minute of Connery's permitted ninety days, so at weekends he was forced to fly out of Britain aimlessly, to return for work on Monday morning. This 'nonsense handicap' appalled him, and he aired his views aloud. He told anyone who would listen that he had proudly given employment to a hundred Pinewood technicians and he resented the 'paradoxical law that makes it difficult for a man to work as hard and often as he chooses to do. They [the government] seem to be more flexible [with] villains who break the law.' Connery wasn't one for aimless moaning. He had, he believed, a solution to this injustice. The ninety days' tax concession should be a personal one. Beyond it stars like himself, Caine and Roger Moore should be encouraged to bring what work they could into Britain, and then be taxed on their earnings on that specific production. No one listened, so Connery shrugged and turned back to *Outland*.

On set, opinion was divided among those who found Connery 'shaky, unsure of himself when disasters struck' (a fellow actor) and those, like the script girl, who greeted 'a feeling of strength when he's around'. Peter Hyams, whom Connery admired for his 'working to programme' – unlike the Bond producers – found 'an actor so consummate that he can convey a breaking heart without his head [moving] an inch to left or right if the technicalities of the scene forbid it'. The sets, techniques and story of *Outland* were unusual in the realm of sci-fi. In telling his lean tale of the manipulation of labour by drugging workers on the futuristic mining base Con-Amalgamate 27, on Jupiter's moon Io, Hyams employed new film devices like Introvision, and a story principle purportedly based on Fred Zinnemann's *High Noon*. Where Gary Cooper was the moral marshal single-handedly confronting corruption and cowardice in the Wild West in Zinnemann's 1952 film, Connery was O'Neil of the Federal Security Service, investigating the labour unrest on Io and challenging the might of mine boss Sheppard (Peter Boyle). Some late sequences of *Outland* mimicked *High Noon* visually, but Fred Zinnemann took exception to the publicity campaign launched by Warner Bros which traded the movie as an updated *High Noon*. 'It was ill-advised and wrong,' Zinnemann told me. 'I saw *Outland* and naturally observed similarities in isolated incidents. But the pictures were *totally* different in mood and meaning.' Connery himself, as he had done before, tripped into the hyperbole. After filming he was, he said, 'most conscious of the *High Noon* aspects' and that Hyams had not tried to disguise the fact that his picture was based on Zinnemann's.

'What was clever,' Connery said, 'was setting it in space – a new frontier town. *That* was what appealed to me in the first place.' Connery vocally supported the *High Noon* promotion for a variety of honest reasons, not least of which was his desire to hype the project and make it work at the box office, thereby regaining lost ground. 'But he truthfully believed in it,' says film writer Tony Crawley. 'He set out to promote it more actively than anything he'd done in years because, he said, it was a novel and worthwhile space venture, a new cinematic departure. He greatly admired what George Lucas and Spielberg had been doing in their movies but he made a big point that here (in *Outland*) was a space movie *he* could understand. His kind of futurology.' Connery asserted: 'Space fantasy doesn't appeal to me . . . in the end I get lost among all those laser beams and hurtling spaceships.' He believed, he said, that what was depicted in *Outland* was 'a logical extension of human technology'. He also appreciated the way Hyams dealt with human issues in a world of technology run amok.

Connery's creative input in *Outland* was far greater than in any movie, with the exception of *The Offence*, to date. He participated, with Hyams, in set design and vetted all the actors, deeming it vital to 'have mainly people with good faces [who] had a certain look about them . . . rather like Western pioneers.' He wanted Collen Dewhurst for his assistant Dr Lazarus, but she was working in theatre so he settled for Hyams's choice of Frances Sternhagen instead. Introvision, the complicated camera effects technique related to simple old back projection, and launched by Tom Naud, John Eppolito and former giants RKO, made an impressive début at Pinewood's Stage J, creating the illusion of vast backgrounds and lending the picture a deep space dimension hitherto unseen.

Connery's pride and delight in *Outland* was evident when he enlisted immediately for two more major films – one American and one European based. The main attraction, in these instances, was the directorial name. First up was *Wrong is Right* (later retitled in Europe), directed by Richard Brooks, whom Connery knew socially and whose work – sometimes dramatically successful, like *In Cold Blood*, sometimes politically indulgent – Connery admired. Brooks's reputation was an oddball one – 'boisterous,' John Boorman called him – and Connery was not embarrassed about asking to preview the screenplay. Brooks agreed, and went a step further. To Connery's delight, Brooks invited his collaborative help in redrafting the overlong 208-page script.

While this pleasant business was afoot in New York Fred Zinnemann made his approach. Zinnemann, one of cinema's true legends, liked Connery in *Robin and Marian* and thought he might suit the special part of a mountaineering doctor in an upcoming movie that Zinnemann called 'my all-time pet project', *Five Days One Summer*.

It was mid-1981 and though Connery was beginning to experience the upswing of new demand in important quarters there remained some muted frustration. 'I believe it was all about money,' says a producer associate. 'Yes, he was doing OK, but he hadn't managed to break any records in the last few years. His best run was around *The Man Who Would Be King*. He wasn't progressing in any significant way and I think he knew he could exhaust himself for ever with these lofty, classy pictures. I believe he wanted an Oscar, or respectable recognition at any rate. But I believe his fee status was equally vital to him. I think it was then, when nothing seemed to be particularly exciting in his life, that he seriously looked at Bond again.'

Approaching the twentieth anniversary of the *Dr No* breakthrough, it seemed the right time to recap. Being at Pinewood again had, he told friends, given rise to happy nostalgia. It was there, on Stage D, that James Bond had first introduced himself to the film world. From there the journey to wealth and wisdom began. And yet, all these years later, he had to admit he had never actually sat through an entire completed Bond movie – other than those demanded of him at the few premières, and the two Roger Moores he had sneaked in on. Once in LA, he told Roderick Mann, he did arrive home after a night on the town with Richard Burton and Mike Caine to find *Dr No* running on TV. He took a beer from the fridge, kicked off his shoes and slumped in a chair to watch it alone. He liked it well enough . . . but fell asleep half-way through. For the admirers, Connery-Bond was an institution, the epitome of hedonism, the enviable face of high living. For Connery, Bond was . . . confused memories, old hopes, triumphs, tears.

Box-office anaemia struck *Time Bandits* around the time of the European première of *Outland* arranged by Connery for Edinburgh again, with proceeds to the Trust, in August. In Europe especially *Outland* did well, aided by a fan press that loved sci-fi and admired Connery as a stoutly moral hero. In America, by contrast, the movie bombed, seen as an anachronistic, tired fable that paled alongside the spectacle of *The Empire Strikes Back*.

By now Connery was in Switzerland, toiling with Zinne-mann, but he interrupted the shoot to help promote

Outland. To Alan Ladd Jr's chagrin, Connery allowed only three press interviews in Edinburgh. Then it was back to the Bernina Range of mountains, round the corner from St Moritz, for five months of snowbound toil. Ladd didn't complain too much: his new company was funding *Five Days One Summer* as well.

For Zinnemann, a double Academy award-winning director with a thirty-year record of excellence, Connery was 'never less than remarkably professional. He was not difficult, had no star ego, no moods. One felt he had only one objective – to get on with the picture and do what was best for it.' Typically, nothing of the creeping insecurity that was the legacy of so many recent hapless choices revealed itself to Zinnemann. As a young man Zinnemann's favourite pastime was hiking through Europe's mountainland; for countless years he had tried to mount this cherished project. 'Sean was my first and only choice of actor because no one else could undertake the hazardous exercise required, and yet was mature and yet again *could* act,' Zinnemann asserts. After the Richard Brooks film wrapped in June Connery had immediately begun mountain climbing training at Pontresina. From there it was plain sailing. As with Brooks, Connery requested script participation – a precondition of all his movies now – but Zinnemann found no problems in agreeing. 'Sean was constructive,' the director says. 'The story was one I'd read, in a short-story form, thirty years before, and it needed quite a lot of development and imagination to make it work for cinema. We had a very fine young writer, Michael Austin, but Sean had thoughts and concepts, ninety-five per cent of which were worthy of assimilation.'

Betsy Brantley, the North Carolina newcomer, cast to play the young woman obsessively in love with the married doctor 25 years her senior, posed inevitable problems. 'Obviously there are difficulties when you place an actor of Sean's experience opposite a girl without the range, like Miss Brantley,' Zinnemann says. 'I can best explain the problem by telling you that the second film I ever did had to do with a detective and a senile dog. The detective had trouble learning his lines and needed seven or eight takes. The dog, on the other hand, was only good for one take – then he ran away to hide. All this had to be done in four weeks. So one learns to gear one-self against such disparaties and *make* things fit. Sean was as helpful with Betsy Brantley as could have been expected of him. He's a very fine actor, and he didn't let me down.'

The stresses of coping with arduous, freezing rock climbs and inexperienced actors were pushed aside again when, three weeks after Edinburgh, Connery attended the Deauville Film Festival on a $15,000 expense chit from Warners, to beat the drum about Hyams's film. *Outland* opened the festival and attendants were later treated to a retrospective of Connery's earlier films, coincidentally side-by-side with a Lana Turner retrospective. Turner showed up to queen over the event, and even dined with her former close friend. They were pictured together brushing shoulders, grinning wide – but neither would comment on their controversial and mysterious past. 'Through Turner's stay and her packed press conflab,' wrote Tony Crawley, 'she gave the kind of glitzy performance that can only be described by one of her film titles: *Imitation of Life*.' Connery, for his part, was life itself – an accurate embodiment of all that had been whirling round him professionally and personally these last tough months. He was curt but courteous, impatient but grimly dedicated, voicing concern but brave-faced throughout.

To discerning onlookers at the Connery Deauville press conference it seemed that here was a star actor who was floundering, but hanging in.

17

Facing Back

At Christmas 1981 Sean Connery came home for his first serious break from work in almost a year to ponder the question that had been on the lips of half the world's movie-goers for nine years: would he don the Savile Row mantle of James Bond again? Home, 'the sanatorium rancho' by his wife Micheline's definition, was the place to be after the rigours of Switzerland. Balmy in December as a good May in Britain, with hibiscus and lime trees to spice the air, San Pedro de Alcantara, next door to Marbella, has the peaceful spirit of a quiet fishing village all year round. The Casa Malibu, the Connerys' immaculately neat ranch there, had increasingly become the haven and hideaway in the troubled times. By the early eighties the Connerys had an embarrassment of choices of places to call home. Apart from Spain, there was the luxury apartment in LA and a large house perched on the edge of Lyford Cay golf course in the Bahamas. But the Casa Malibu, designed by Micheline and now encompassing an outhouse bungalow where Connery worked in his moments of seclusion, was always first choice for privacy and rest.

That Christmas Connery's mood was rocky. Sheamus Smith spoke often to him and described him then as 'restless'. John Boorman knew why: the potential of reviving James Bond was preoccupying him, and troubling him.

There were other distressing distractions. A court action by a former ally, trusted film accountant Kenneth Richards, greatly upset him. Richards sued for monies he claimed Connery owed – totalling more than £100,000 and an ongoing 2 per cent of some thirteen films Richards had worked on, which, with court expenses had Connery's countersuit failed, would have amounted to a massive sum. Richards lost his claim, but Connery was shaken by his misreading of a key professional associate and by what was, not only on the face of it, a close-fought battle. A measure of his anguish about the November row was reflected in a *Daily Telegraph* headline – CONNERY NEAR TO TEARS AS HE WINS BOND FILM FIGHT – and the concurrent spray of articles that spoke of his torment and delight. 'It was certainly an ordeal,' Connery confessed just before Christmas. 'Something I don't want to go through again. It's much better on the film set.'

But on the film set, since *Meteor*, things were anything but good. *Meteor, Cuba* and to a lesser extent *Time Bandits* had all proved major disappointments. All fared badly at the box office, *Meteor* worst of all, with a recorded loss of $15.8 million two years after release. In his attempts to reorientate Connery had taken great care in choosing *Outland* and *The Man with the Deadly Lens* (the retitled *Wrong is Right*) but they too lost money and faded quickly from view. Fred Zinnemann was the obvious potential saviour, but *Five Days One Summer* attracted weak notices and weaker business, despite its handsome playing and memorable scenery.

By Christmas Connery sensed a professional cul-de-sac. 'He ran aground,' Ian Bannen believes. 'I think there are stages and ages an actor goes through. Sean was past fifty and, maybe in somebody's view, past his prime. So he was poised for a different *kind* of role. I think it all becomes quite muddled for a lot of actors, around that time. I think Sean is no different. He wasn't a young man. He wasn't a grandad. What exactly was he? How would he cast *himself*?'

Bannen goes on to say that Connery was 'much disappointed' particularly by *Outland*. 'He prizes his instincts, you see, and he had seen the success of *Star Wars* and accordingly thought that space-age *Outland* would make a fortune. I believe it continued to matter to him that he succeeded with a very wide audience. He had set himself that standard, and now it wasn't working so well.'

Connery understood the dilemma of age. He understood too how professional inertia is insidious and potentially fatal, how rock-solid superstardom frequently gives way to petrification. Richard Burton in his heyday could be farmed out to junk, Richard Harris to parody his own manic raucousness, Olivier to all comers. A star is not for ever.

Through December, Connery found himself particularly reappraising the question of Bond, the career cornerstone he loved to hate. Various Bond projects had been pushed his way over the last few years and he had always brusquely distanced himself. Now, in the face of an apparently viable new Bond project that did not involve Cubby Broccoli, he was tempted to reconsider. Could Bond restore his flagging market appeal? Certainly, without doubt, he could hike Connery's 'purchase' price. The deal on his last Bond, *Diamonds Are Forever*, had never been matched: $1.2 million from United Artists, plus a percentage and a choice of two further movie projects. Connery's recent fees had been nearer half a million, often somewhat less. Apart from elaborating the super-draw profile, what could 007 offer Connery in compensation for the risks and difficulties – at 52 years of age – of revival? $2 million? More?

The businessman in Connery was stirred by the factors working for a return to Bond at this time. Above all, the proposed new project, offered by producer Jack Schwartzman, was in direct competition with the Cubby Broccoli–Roger Moore Bonds. The course and purpose of the recent Moore Bonds was manifestly confused and audience indulgence was waning. *Moonraker* (1979), undistilled kids' fizz, grossed massively by turning tail totally on trademark Bond. Its successor, *For Your Eyes Only* (1981), limped through twelve months without showing a remotely Bondian profit. But still Roger Moore could cruise on *Moonraker* and demand, as he did, $4 million for the upcoming Broccoli venture, *Octopussy*. Fine by Connery. If

Moore was good for $4 million while the pre-sold Bond market was quivering uncertainly, Connery could bat against that figure and look for more.

What of the quality of the new Bond property, though?

'Quality never came into it, not in the purest sense,' Ian Bannen opines. 'I think Sean was crazy to give up Bond in the first place. When he quit he was riding high, but he could have gone higher. He could have done a Bond a year and said, To hell with it. Great, it's done, now I can go on and do Shakespeare or whatever I like . . .'

Typecasting apart, Connery himself felt that Bond at his best was something to be proud of. With their multi-layered scripts, inventive direction and extraordinary production values, those early Connery–Bonds minted a brand-new cinema genre and Connery, once you scratch the surface, has always relished his achievement. The great frustration, he often felt, was that so few understood how much acting and art went into making Bond a world-beater.

Schwartzman's Bond had all the indications of the pedigree best. Schwartzman himself for a start was the kind of producer Connery liked to deal with: by reputation forthright, scrupulous, a fast decision-maker. He had been associated with Lorimar, producers of the TV hit *Dallas*, and had masterminded Peter Sellers's subtly wonderful *Being There*. Schwartzman's essential intention was to remake *Thunderball*, the rights of which, alone in the Bond corral with *Casino Royale* (made as a spy spoof and sullied forever by Charles Feldman and Jerry Bresler in 1967) did not belong to Cubby Broccoli's Eon Productions company. The circumstances that brought about the availability of *Thunderball* rights are today still in debate. When Kevin McClory sued Fleming for copyright infringement on the original *Thunderball* storyline part of the settlement granted McClory the movie rights. These he later shared with Eon in a funding deal to make the 1965 hit movie. Specific in the arrangement was the condition that all rights to *Thunderball* would revert to McClory after ten years. This remarkable clause either demonstrates the shortsightedness of Eon or the bargaining strength of the blarney-rich McClory. Whichever way, as Bond sailed soundly into the seventies, the Irishman was left with a solid gold property – the script and characters of the most widely successful of the sixties Bonds. Duly, early in 1975 when Connery was in America overseeing post-production on *The Wind and the Lion*, McClory presented his first revival idea. Connery demurred. But McClory wasn't to be put off so easily.

'He asked would I be interested in contributing in any way,' Connery explained later, 'with all the experience that had been gained in the six previous ones I'd done. I thought about it and said, "It depends who you've got writing it."'

Blockbusting novelist Len Deighton, living in tax exile ninety miles away from McClory's Southern Ireland home, was lured in, Connery was appeased and an agreement reached. Connery, Deighton and McClory would write a new Bond. Connery flew to Ireland and took up residence at McClory's sprawling country mansion in County Kildare. 'Sean was keen,' McClory told me. 'Bond was still in his blood because, after all, he made Bond. But we kept it all a close secret.'

After a year's work, a full-page advertisement in *Variety*, the sacred showbiz chronicle, announced production preparations for McClory's *James Bond of the Secret Service*, a Paradise Film Production. The electric addendum, 'One of the most exciting screen plays I have ever read', signed Irving Paul Lazar, the top American agent, stamped marketworthiness on the whole thing. Speculation still flapped around Connery's possible portrayal of Bond (he was, says McClory, ready to play the role), then suddenly McClory and Paradise Films fell silent. The cause, quite simply, was Eon's wrath. Many claimed McClory was suffering the most fundamental problem – financial difficulties. But McClory is quick to remind you that the original *Thunderball* was the biggest ever Bond grosser. In its cinema tour it took $27 million – allowing an inflation adjustment factor, an equivalent today of $67.5 million (against a budget of $4 million). And the law of the cinema is what rakes once will rake again.

Connery himself defended the financial solidity of McClory: 'So many people were wanting to contribute to the picture with funds and what have you. There were no problems financially. But I was under the impression that it was totally clean. Free from any litigational problems. When we started to talk quite seriously about the possibility it became so complex. Och, the lawyers came out of the woodwork by the hundred. . . . The legal factors were harder to face than making the film. Then the publicity started to work on it and I said, "That's enough!" And I walked away. . . .'

Walking away entailed some anguish because 1975 was, for Connery, the ideal time to contemplate swooping back as Bond. At forty-five he was still fit and fast enough to appear credible with Berettas or in the boudoir. And the clutch of interestingly diverse and artistically successful pictures he had just made distanced him sufficiently from a too-ready character identification whilst allowing the challenge of developing Bond with some continuity. Roger Moore, then commencing his third Bond for Broccoli, was consolidating a personal following, just enough to whet Connery's competitive appetite. 'Professionally there's no more fierce competitor than Sean,' says Michael Caine – and Moore's challenge was, then, the happiest of motivations.

But Eon and United Artists, the Bond series' distributors, would allow McClory no leeway. Clearly they recognised Connery's power, resurrected at any time as Bond, to scotch their films. Court action began. Arthur B. Krim, head of UA, insisted that nothing other than a verbatim rehash of *Thunderball* was permissible, that a new script using 007 was illegal. McClory resisted, detailing his speculative screen work with Fleming back in 1959, before Bond ever hit the big screen. *Thunderball* was not his only Bond treatment. There was *Latitude 78 West*, *Bond in the Bahamas* and others – any of which could legitimately be used as the basis for a McClory Bond film.

It was a borderline case but McClory's intentions were eventually seen to be honourable and legal enough, and

Broccoli's intentions designed – for understandably commercial considerations – to obstruct and delay. Early in 1980 an Appeal Court decision in America cleared the path for McClory and in July of that year, while Connery's Los Angeles agents were negotiating *Outland*, British newspapers announced that the actor had at last signed a contract to return 'for a small salary, most of which will go to charity'.

In reality Connery had signed nothing. McClory had his clearance to do a Bond but, exhausted from wrangling, was beginning to offload. Already he had invested and lost a considerable sum in defending his Bond rights. Enter Schwartzman, fresh from the triumph of *Being There*, with a favourite writer, Lorenzo Semple, Jr, formerly of *Batman*, latterly *Three Days of the Condor* fame. Protracted talks followed before a deal was settled upon, late in 1981. Schwartzman inherited the Fleming–McClory concepts and the Deighton–Connery script and hefted the lot onto Semple's desk. Around the same time Schartzman, in McClory's wake, decided only one actor could revive this Bond: Sean Connery. Before the respective producers' signatures had dried on what was then widely known as the *Warhead* contract, Schwartzman had Connery on the telephone – and Connery wasn't saying no. The initial response was equivocal but encouraging enough for Schwartzman to start shuffling together a distribution deal and investments of the highest order which would afford Connery the kind of welcome the penny-conscious Scotsman was never likely to refuse. Schwartzman might have thought Connery could be seduced by $2 million. But Connery's vision of the movie marketplace and his value in Bondage was always sharper than others'. $2 million would not be enough.

From Connery's viewpoint 1975 might have been the ideal time to renew Bond, but 1982 was a workable second best – possibly, from a financial angle, if managed properly, the key time, the pension paymaster.

Without doubt Connery carefully monitored Roger Moore's negotiations with Broccoli for increased Bond fees over Christmas and during the early part of the New Year.

Broccoli incurred Moore's expensive anger by scouting for a possible new Bond – Superman Christopher Reeve was considered as, reputedly, was Broccoli's daughter's boyfriend, an unknown American actor. Moore continued to up the asking price for *Octopussy*. Finally, sensing multi-millions slip away from him with Broccoli's impatience, Moore settled for a salary of $4 million – ample enough to cover his daily consumption of Monte Cristo cigars at $9 a smoke and jet-hop trips back to Gstaad for family reunions when the din of Pinewood's sound stages wore thin. Connery now had a target fee to pitch for and let it be known that he wanted more. Schwartzman continued to court Connery and, in April, it was announced that Irvin Kershner, one of Connery's favoured directors, had been signed to direct.

'Sean might appear to be endlessly sitting on the fence with this,' a close colleague told me during the spring of 1982, 'but you can bet he's involved on every level. He knows they *need* him, and he knows he probably needs this too. He'll have the measure of everything working for and against him. He'll be aware of the Broccoli plans, and every aspect of Schartzman's finances.'

To understand Connery's continuing procrastination one is drawn back to his resentment of Broccoli and the Bond makers' meanness. In 1981 a conservative estimate put Connery–Bond movie earnings at around $260 million. It is unlikely that Connery, the very life's breath of the series, would have netted a fiftieth of that. Connery understandably felt aggrieved. Bond was not one lucky-dice throw for him, rather a continuing commitment over nine years. He nurtured Bond, he styled it; others made their contributions, but Connery *was* Bond.

There was nothing of meanness in the bartering for several millions to play Schwartzman's Bond. Connery simply weighed his position past and future, watched Moore and judged his own worth. Then he stuck by it. In part, Connery had always been a financial hoarder. From the time he left school at fourteen to take up a first shaky fulltime occupation as a milk-roundsman he had been

235

saving for inevitable Edinburgh rainy days. In the sixties he had been incautious and had lost money. In the seventies others had manipulated and stolen from him. Now he would be nobody's fool.

Underlining the difficulty of keeping things in proportion as the stakes got higher throughout his career, Connery once told the *Daily Express*, 'Funnily enough I worry much more about small sums than big amounts. Blood and tears go into parting with £10 on the golf course – ask any of my friends. But when something like £40,000 is involved I am much more objective.'

John Boorman believed Connery simply enjoyed the professional sparring. 'He knows this business and he can be properly cynical about it. I think he got great fun from standing up to certain people and certain demeaning, dehumanising situations which are often part of this business, and winning out.'

According to sources in Marbella, a positive commitment to do Schwartzman's film was signed in Los Angeles by Connery on 18 May, a few weeks after *The Man with the Deadly Lens* opened. Location shooting was scheduled for the Bahamas and Ireland but this was changed when the Irish government closed its Ardmore Studios late in the summer. Kershner flew to Britain and studio time was booked at the EMI Elstree complex, not many miles down the road from Pinewood where the whole Bond business had begun and where, on 16 August, Roger Moore knuckled down to start sixteen weeks on the rival *Octopussy*.

Kershner, Schwartzman and Connery stayed tight-lipped about fee arrangements but, presumably, Connery was happy. Late in July when I questioned a major director friend who holds Connery's confidence I was told, 'I won't say Sean's madly looking forward to Bond, but he's looking forward to the $5 million it will earn for him.'

Once decided, Connery threw everything into the Bond comeback. 'It was unequivocal commitment,' a friend said. 'A lot of the driving force was Micheline. It was she who thought up the movie's title, *Never Say Never Again*, which was brimming with irony and wisdom. Sean loved it. . . . She groomed him for it. She even trimmed those bushy eyebrows again. It wasn't a wishy-washy effort. It was Now, let's show Broccoli and those bastards how to do the *real* James Bond.' With echoes of the dance-movement studies of the Cilento days, Connery decided to engage a dance instructor to improve his agility. Peggy Spencer, the sometime BBC *Come Dancing* judge who trained Nureyev for Ken Russell's *Valentino*, took charge, relentlessly working him through his paces and teaching him, among other things, a mean modern tango.

Reactivation brought him back to Scotland, too, for happy reasons and for sad ones. In the run-up to Bond Lord-Provost Kenneth Borthwick asked him to participate in a film to promote Edinburgh tourism. Andrew Fyall, in his capacity as Edinburgh's Director of Tourism, came aboard and was flattered by Connery's generosity. The budget was £100,000, mostly funded by the British and Scottish Tourist Boards, but Connery didn't ask for a penny. 'He started by agreeing to do a voiceover, then gradually dominated the thing,' says Fyall. 'It was utter commitment – from seven a.m. on location at Edinburgh Castle, till seven p.m., when he took the crew out to dinner. He was a gem to work with.' For the film Connery returned to broken-down Fountainbridge as he would do, again, in 1991 for Fyall and Ross Wilson's STV documentary. The time was well spent and the resulting very personal film received excellent notices and bookings for special screenings at the Commonwealth Games in Brisbane in the autumn, as well as in Melbourne, Auckland and Sydney where Connery was, and remains, one of the best-loved international stars. The film premiered at the Edinburgh Film Festival, of which Connery was enduringly proud ('He abandoned his golf at Gleneagles to drive down for the première,' says Fyall), but his proudest moment that summer came when hometown Heriot-Watt University bestowed an honorary Doctor of Letters degree. Connery was modestly silent but old pal John Brady said, 'I know it moved him. He never got the education he wanted, because of the circumstances of his childhood. That sort of honour recognises his intelligence and the intelligence of his achievement as an actor, which is no small thing. I mean, how many actors are given doctorates like that? It doesn't happen to the folks from *Coronation Street*, does it?'

But it wasn't all good news. On 27 September location filming of the new Bond started in Villefranche, near Nice in France. Connery appeared content, in the words of journalist Margaret Hinxman of the *Daily Mail*, 'shooting his cuffs with deceptive nonchalance'. Though Schwartzman and Kershner's presence was conspicuous, it was clear to most that Sean Connery was in command on this movie. Co-star Barbara Carrera said, 'It was Sean's picture, Sean's choices.' One of Connery's first decisions was to avoid banter with the media. Even at this late stage Broccoli was still attempting to halt the film, this time engaging the co-operation of the trustees of Ian Fleming's estate. Connery was worried and, according to one visitor to the set, 'bullish in his apprehensive mood'. But Broccoli's action led nowhere. In London Mr Justice Goulding rejected Broccoli's request for an injunction on the basis that it would be unfair to hinder a production so far advanced. The judge acknowledged the plan for a further High Court action but ignored the plea by Mr Sam Stamler QC that a victory for Eon then would be useless, 'merely closing the stable door too late'. Effectively, Broccoli's opposition was over.

Margaret Hinxman was one of the few journalists Connery allowed on the Bond set. He told her curtly: 'Bond's an interesting character. There's a lot more I can do with him. I'm fifty-two. There's nothing particularly daring about playing your age. I've done it before – in *Robin and Marian* and *Murder on the Orient Express*. It's absurd to cling to what you were in your youth. It's the difference, say, between Burt Lancaster and Kirk Douglas. Lancaster plays his age, looks his age and has given some memorable, fine performances on the screen. Douglas strives to stay young. But he seems gaunt, a shadow of his former self. It's a little sad.'

In fairness, there was something a little sad about Connery – who otherwise embraced middle age – attempting to re-create superfit, devil-may-care 007 in an era that positively buzzed with macho young bloods like Travolta and Stallone. Though few would dare to challenge his or Schartzman's wisdom on such matters, the grooming and make-up aspects of new-age Bond left much to be desired. Though Connery was light-footed as ever, it was hard to miss the thickening of his features and his wig particularly seemed misjudged. Rather than opt for a shaggy, upswept *Goldfinger*-like hairpiece, Connery chose a flat, near crew cut wig that was reminiscent, said an actor, of George Burns's. The 'special make-up' too (by Ilona Herman) was disastrous, offering blue-eye-shadowed doll-like features which looked particularly ridiculous in the action sequences.

After France, *Never Say Never Again* went on location in the Bahamas where McClory's Paradise Island home, 'Pieces of Eight', became Bond's native base. Here the brooding atmosphere was augmented by foul weather. After a week of monsoon-like rain Connery was edgier than ever. Richard Schenkman, the founder of the international Bond fan club, visited and observed, 'Irvin Kershner was under a black cloud and was trying to save a schedule knocked all to hell . . . Connery's glib humour and creative interest can quickly turn to vociferous anger if he thinks that people, including the director, are being inefficient or uncommunicative. He blew up when he realised that ten minutes of rehearsal time had been lost because Kershner hadn't told everyone that he had changed his mind about something.'

Kershner, for his part, remained loyal. He had grown to admire Connery when he directed him in *A Fine Madness*. The admiration was unshaken: 'He had done some wonderful things . . . *The Man Who Would Be King*, for instance. Unlike so many American actors of his status he isn't afraid to take risks.'

On reflection, with the perspective of time, *Never Say Never Again* was a no-win gamble that Connery probably shouldn't have undertaken – at least not as an actor. Warner Bros' advance publicity offered the earth – and delivered very little. The 'event extravaganza' premiered in New York on 7 October 1983, and in London a fortnight later. Business initially was excellent and the general press write-ups good. When the dust settled, though, the hardcore reviews were distinctly lukewarm. *Films and Filming* damned the 'tide of improbability and slack script', but went on: 'What does it matter, though? Anticipation of this cinematic return has provided much of the fun.' In the same article Brian Baxter lamented the updating of Connery-Bond, deriding his appearance in bicycle shorts and boiler suits. 'For myself I would be a lot happier to see the *real* actor develop. Anyone who has waltzed so successfully through masterpieces like *Robin and Marian* and *Marnie* . . . should not need to tango. Let's say never again.'

Never Say Never Again lost the box-office war against the Roger Moore contender *Octopussy*. By 1990 the US rental grosses on Connery's picture were listed as $28 million. *Octopussy* had taken $34 million. These were suitably fat Bondian figures, but they paled against other megahits of the eighties. The relative failure of Connery's revised Bond seemed apt: the movie really did display chronic weaknesses and misjudgement and Connery must take the burden of blame. He told Marjorie Bilbow: 'I had script approval as well as casting approval, director approval and lighting cameraman . . . the idea of lighting it with a first-rate man like Dougie Slocombe gives it so much prestige and substance.' In fact, most notably in the camerawork, the movie falls far short of competent. Slocombe's photography is unimaginative, minimising as opposed to maximising the beauty of the French and Caribbean seascapes. The camera framing, for example, is consistently tight, as befits TV shows in which limited budgets mean small sets and claustrophobically narrow 'dressed' areas on location. This critical failing is especially noticeable in scenes like

Bond's arrival at Nice airport, perhaps the prettiest of all Mediterranean airports. The camerawork never 'opens up' and rarely moves away from close-ups of an over-made-up Connery.

The fault isn't entirely in the camerawork. Kershner's focus is unsure. In the same scene a key female character is introduced – unforgivably – without a single close-up shot to establish her. In subsequent scenes she imparts crucial impetus to the plotting, yet is usually unidentifiable. Elsewhere, the movie music (by the normally reliable Michel Legrand) is entirely inappropriate and the action coordination wooden. Two areas normally triumphant in Bond movies are plainly undernourished: the set design (by Philip Harrison) and the theme song, an absolutely silly ditty by Alan and Marilyn Bergman and Legrand.

Connery initially pushed the film, making talkshow guest appearances worldwide. But within months of its opening he was bickering with Schwartzman and publicly regretting the experience. (He launched a lawsuit against Schwartzman for, said *The Times*, 'loose change'; it was settled out of court.)

Connery went on record: 'There's nothing I like better than a film that really works, providing you don't have to deal with all the shit that comes afterwards in getting what you're entitled to. But when you get in a situation where somebody who is totally incompetent is in charge, a real ass, then everything is a struggle. There was so much incompetence, ineptitude and dissension during the making of *Never Say Never Again* that the film could have disintegrated. It was a toilet. What I could have done is just let it bury itself. I could have walked away with an enormous amount of money and the film would never have been finished. But once I was in there I ended up getting in the middle of every decision. The assistant director and myself really produced that picture.'

Micheline told journalist Pat Tracey that the movie had been 'a nightmare' and that Connery would *never* re-do Bond 'for love nor money'. She went on: 'It was the last time. He's too old now. And I am glad that Roger Moore is quitting too. He has been marvellous, but no one can go on for ever . . .'

Connery's personal hurt ran deep. His back firmly turned against Bond, he would have nothing more to do with him. He was, he told persistent enquirers, just too old. It had become an unfunny joke. A measure of his antipathy was reflected in a harsh remark on Michael Aspel's TV show. He was too old, Roger Moore was too old: 'It was rather silly on Roger's part to have done the last one . . .'

More than one old industry hand felt the same about Connery's swansong.

18

Enter Oscar

Five million dollars better off but spiritually exhausted, Connery reacted to the trauma of Bond by withdrawing into semi-retirement. For almost three years he refused all scripts and vanished from the public arena. According to Micheline, the reason was 'the upset' caused by the less than decent management of the Bond revival. 'Sean has such high ideals. He is always being shocked by people. I have tried to teach him cynicism. Don't be shocked, I say, the world is like that.'

But there were shocks in store. In the autumn of 1982 as he worked on Bond Effie suffered a stroke in Edinburgh and was admitted in a critical condition to the Infirmary. Connery left location to fly to her side and was saddened by what he saw. A friend says, 'She was the rock at the core of his childhood. No matter what, the fame never touched her. He thought her invincible – and now she was fading away. Joe was gone – so much had changed in his existence in the seventies. Neil was still in Edinburgh but Sean was never *that* close to him. So I think he felt something slipping away.' Another friend from Edinburgh points out that Micheline and Neil were never more than 'cool friends' but that Micheline always acknowledged the key role Effie had in Connery's affections. When it was clear that Effie's active days were over, the friend says, 'Micheline grew even closer to Sean. It was a time when he was jaded and she was there for him, at home when he needed her, on the golf course when he needed her. Without the family security Micheline and the boys gave him then, I think he would have been in trouble.' Connery's relationships with stepson Stefan and son Jason grew warmer but the friend points out, 'He was hardly a conventional dad . . . there was a definite distance with Jason . . . but I think this was reasoned out, that he didn't want Jason to become over-dependent, to assume the role of a rich man's son.' Jason's progress in acting briefly horrified Connery, finally delighted him. After schooling at Gordonstoun, Jason first trod the boards in *Aladdin* in Perth before graduating to minor movie playing alongside his mother Diane in Australia. Later success in the UK starring in HTV's *Robin of Sherwood* brought bigger film roles and, ultimately, perhaps inevitably, the role as James Bond's creator in *The Secret Life of Ian Fleming*, an American TV movie that attracted wide attention. 'I've never felt in competition with him,' Jason later said. 'And he's never made me feel I get work through him, or that I have to prove myself to him. There are a lot of unhappy people with famous parents, but he's never made me feel uncomfortable about who he is. I'm proud of who he is.'

Connery arranged the best medical treatment for Effie, who would linger for a few disabled years, visited daily by Neil who fed her soup and kept her abreast of family news. A close friend says, 'Sean rang me constantly with messages for the doctor, or for Neil. He may not have been on the spot, but he was close to everything that was happening. He adored her, but there was nothing more he could do.' When Effie died, on 2 April 1985, she was cremated at Mortonhall on Edinburgh's southside and Connery joined a close family group for what Andrew Fyall describes as 'a traditional Scottish wake' at the North British Hotel. 'There were lots of old Connerys there,' says Fyall. 'Distant uncles mostly, and the younger generation was really just Neil's daughters. There were no celebrity guests. It was a very personal sadness that touched Sean deeply.'

The blows fell thick and fast. The disillusionment of *Never Say Never Again* fortified Connery's determination to wring whatever he could from Broccoli and Eon for past services unrecognised. In the summer of 1984 he unleashed his worst, filing a federal action against Broccoli, Eon, Danjaq SA, and MGM/UA for unreturned profits on *From Russia with Love, Goldfinger, Thunderball, You Only Live Twice* and *Diamonds are Forever*, amounting to at least $1.275 million. Connery's companies that took the action accused Broccoli and his companies of 'fraud, deceit, conspiracy, breach of contract and causing emotional distress'. Damages sought amounted to $225 million. The hearing early in 1984 in Los Angeles revealed much of the intimate background of Connery's early Bond deal-making. For *Dr No*, it emerged, he had been guaranteed one per cent of all gross monies in excess of $4 million received by backers United Artists. For *Goldfinger* it was five per cent, with an additional five per cent on profits for *You Only Live Twice* outside UK, Ireland and North America. Connery also claimed he was entitled to, but received nothing, from the vast merchandising of his face and image as James Bond.

The case was thrown out by District Court Judge David Kenyon on the basis that the defendants' action did not constitute a violation of the Securities Exchange Commission. Connery had no comment to make but Broccoli professed himself 'pleased' while his lawyer, Norman Tyre, announced that his client had not made any plans on whether to sue for false accusations.

A very low-key Sean Connery re-emerged on movie screens in the final aftermath of the 007 débâcle in two broadly differing movies. Stephen Weeks's Arthurian mess *Sword of the Valiant – The Legend of Gawain and the Green Knight* earned him $1 million for six days' work and generated no excitement at all. In the States it was hardly seen and even in its subsequent video distribution proved a failure. The film had been through various hoops of development over ten years and the muddle of the script and quasi-moral message show why. The *Monthly Film Bulletin* called it 'an unsatisfactory crossbreed of Robin Hood and Monty Python'. The recovery plan was Russell Mulcahy's *Highlander*, another costume part, this time a grand $12 million feature shot in Scotland that had more, perhaps, in common with *Zardoz* than anything. Connery seemed briefly enthused – though friends attributed the Scottish distractions, not the work, to the smiles on the set. Connery's publicity profile was next to non-existent, but Russell Mulcahy welcomed 'a pro' who 'loved the costumes'. If the film's publicists hoped to galvanise Connery as the project matured, they were bound for frustration. Connery obviously liked the role of Juan Sanchez Villa-Lobos Ramirez, the time-travelling immortal who is Christopher Lambert's spirit guide in his own immortal quests, but saw no reason to analyse it. His best contribution was: 'The dramatics take care of themselves if you get it right. The humour you have to find.'

Denied the tub-thumping, *Highlander*'s publicists could only watch wistfully from afar as Connery helicoptered across Scotland from golf course to location, or larked on Loch Shiel with co-star Lambert and Micheline, lustily enjoying the role of tour guide, expounding the legends and beauties of his beloved Scotland. In his one longish but insubstantial interview of the time Connery seemed unfazed by what he himself judged to be professional mistakes, and resilient in his independence. 'I somehow never fit into the scene in the United Kingdom, or Hollywood, or Spain, or anywhere for that matter. The only group I ever belonged to was the Navy. Rightly or wrongly I've always made my own decisions. But given today's climate, to continue to be in demand for a wide spectrum of parts means I must be doing something right.' Second billing to Christopher Lambert or anyone else didn't bother him in the least. 'I am also an actor not concerned with age. I do not have to stay within the confines of leading man.'

'Sean has never had that vanity *per se*,' says Guy Hamilton. 'But his *presence* leads him in a certain direction. Bond was gone. But he had to replace him. He isn't complacent in any area of his life. So I would say that the urge to score big again kept him on his toes. I imagine that drove him.'

Highlander had cult success but was seen by the highbrows as an unmitigated failure. 'A mess,' *Sight and Sound* reckoned – though Connery was allowed to pass unscathed. In America the film was released in a much-shortened version, which helped repair some of the plodding historical point-scoring in the original. But the *Monthly Film Bulletin*, among the many, saw through the ruse: only on the surface, said the *Bulletin*, is the film 'periodically exhilarating'.

Once it was clear that Connery intended to bury Bond and re-establish himself as an actor everyone who knew him expected role choices as radically varied as possible. One friend says, 'That was the most telling time of his life. There were all sorts of mumbles circulating that, if he got $20 or $50 million from Broccoli he would simply give up and play golf for the rest of his days. Sean sometimes encouraged the gossip. He'd tell the guys he played with at clubs like Las Brisas [in Spain] that golf was *everything*. Showbiz was a drag. He wanted out.' Connery didn't get the court settlement he wanted but he was still an immensely wealthy man and, once recuperated, keener than ever to push himself as an actor. He told Michael Aspel: 'I couldn't just play golf. My God, I'd *kill* someone.'

His next film choice – immaculately timed – was a gruelling test: the austere, excellent *Name of the Rose*, based on Umberto Eco's modern classic. From the start Connery gave it his all, displaying a candour and commitment beyond the norm. When *Rolling Stone* visited the freezing Rome location in February 1986 it reported with surprise that Connery was more socially active with director Jean-Jacques Annaud's team than anyone had previously observed. After an exhausting week traipsing over the wind-lashed Roman hills, clad only in the coarse smock of the fourteenth-century Benedictine monk-detective he was playing, Connery was in no rush to go to any golf course, nor did he hide himself in the comforts of his suite at the Savoy Hotel. *Rolling Stone* reported: 'Tomorrow, Saturday, [the crew] will all get together for a feast at the local trattoria, a tradition with this group. Even Connery . . . will perform magic tricks, tell jokes and cheer as Annaud dances a fiery flamenco . . .'

Connery was, in fact, elated by the quality of this subtle,

brilliant project. It was *the* tonic. Eco's book, serpentine and elusive in its linguistic adventures and semiotic discourse, thrilled him and challenged that aspect of his intellect formerly fed by the likes of Henderson and Cilento. He flitted and prowled through the book, constantly teasing new dimensions from his character, Brother William of Baskerville, who is appointed to investigate a string of grisly murders at a remote monastery. The character is multi-faceted and Connery especially enjoyed the subplot device of his relationship with a young novice, Adso, played by sixteen-year-old Christian Slater. Adso narrates the movie as an old man reviewing his youth, and Annaud and Connery enjoyed the best of working relationships with the new star. '[Adso] is the student and Sean Connery is the teacher,' Slater told *Rolling Stone*. 'It's pretty much what's going on here in real life.'

Annaud reported Connery relentlessly pursuing the *truth* of the part and 'inspired' by the thoroughness of the production's homework. The shooting script, for example, was a *fifteenth* draft, on which four very experienced writers had worked. Connery's greatest pleasure, it appeared, was maintaining the reality of authentic medieval life. Not only was the actor studying ritualistic and hierarchical accuracy but he was disciplining his own every move – 'how close you stand in relation to each other, how much obeisance to give, who sings . . .'

There was further motivation for Connery, Sheamus Smith believes, 'in the deprivations and awfulness of the locations which took him back to his own lean, mean days.' Connery might have been reminded in some oblique way of Fountainbridge when he proudly detailed life in 'a monk's outfit, thermal underwear and moonboots': 'All those rats you see underfoot are real. They had them ready in polythene bags, hundreds of them. I was walking on a carpet of rats. I killed about fifteen of them in my sandals and bare feet. I was sorry about that, but there was nothing I could do about it.'

In every way *Rose* was the opposite of the reprised Bond movie, and its purity and thoroughness wrote a blueprint for

Connery's future movie outlook. As Annaud tells it, the movie was prepared with an enormous, sensitive passion. There were no cheap concessions to commercialism, no half measures. In the beginning, Eco himself had resisted the idea of a Hollywood-big movie. RAI, Italian television, initially owned the rights but Annaud – with a Sorbonne degree in the Art and History of the Middle Ages and Greek behind him – met Eco and persuaded him that an international, large-scale production was essential in terms of maintaining fidelity to the book. 'When I was a kid I was impressed by the magic of castles and old churches,' Annaud said. 'There was something very romantic about those old stones, their smell, the humidity.' Eco swooned, the deal was done and Annaud commenced the daunting task of reconstructing 'a fully honest' Middle Ages. The movie's interiors were shot at the Kloster Eberach, near Frankfurt, a twelfth-century home of the Cistercians unchanged in eight hundred years. Exteriors proved more difficult and no match for the monastery and tower described in Eco's book could be found in Europe. Annaud then employed Dante Ferretti to construct a real Romanesque church with a 210-foot tower, mostly cast in real stone. The props, too, were mostly real artefacts which, Annaud claims, helped the confidence and posture of the actors. Attention to detail was relentless: all the casting was 'authentic'. 'In the Middle Ages people were malnourished, semi-crippled – with disastrous skin conditions in some cases.' Therefore backgrounds were filled with real people, local farm-folk, hand-picked special extras. During the shooting day Annaud even forbade the wearing of foot-warmers and socks, despite the often sub-zero temperatures 'because people sit differently when they are cold'. Later Connery called this 'over-realism'.

Annaud confessed that the movie's $16 million budget might easily have doubled in Hollywood but there was no way this film could be made with integrity in LA and he was satisfied to take the half-price fee he was offered to do it as it was done.

The Name of the Rose garnered wonderful plaudits

worldwide throughout 1986 and restored Connery's confidence and good humour. *The Monthly Film Bulletin* applauded Connery's Brother William as 'a quite remarkable construct'. *Photoplay* called the movie, and Connery, 'masterful'. Others concurred. The movie became that rare beast: an honest intellectual endeavour that scored at the box office.

Sheamus Smith, now Ireland's film censor, delighted in Connery's choice when I attended the certification screening of the film with him in Dublin. 'This is a turning point,' he said.

Prophetically, as it turned out.

'I was never that interested in the Academy Awards,' said Sean Connery. 'I used to watch them thirty years ago, but I never knew how to join. I thought you had to put your nose in the door to be considered. Guys like Jack Nicholson and Dustin Hoffman are entrenched in that scene, but I'm not. I don't know. I suppose all the lawsuits helped . . .'

For twenty years stalwarts all across the industry had predicted an Oscar for Connery. In 1982 John Boorman openly mused on the reasons for the Academy's neglect: there was no denying that Connery had produced supreme characters beyond Bond, in hugely diverse movies like *The Offence* and *The Man Who Would Be King*. 'But then many other notable achievers got left out: Cary Grant, Burton, lots of them.' Lewis Gilbert wondered if Connery wasn't his own worst enemy in his projection of invincible roles, what writer Neil Sinyard called 'the acceptable face of heroism in an anti-heroic age'.

True to his guns, it was for his portrayal of conventional, square-chinned heroism in Brian De Palma's gangster movie *The Untouchables*, Connery's first true Hollywood picture in five years, that the elusive Oscar nomination finally came. In the film Connery played a street-wise cop who is guardian angel (but second-billing) to Kevin Costner's Eliot Ness, the scourge of Al Capone. De Palma, whose bloodshedding reputation was forged on hits like *Carrie* and *Dressed to Kill*, approached the project with his

250

usual thunder and re-created 1930s Chicago with the aid of 400 guns and 50,000 rounds of ammunition.

Michael Caine had starred in *Dressed to Kill* and highly commended De Palma to Connery. What doubtless appealed to Connery too was the pedigree of David Mamet, the Pulitzer Prize-winning screenwriter. Mamet grew up in Chicago and schooled across the street from the very spot where the St Valentine's Day Massacre occurred. As a child he had fed on the stories of gangsters, and of Capone's terrifying power. But the facts of gangsterdom, the writer believed, weren't enough for great cinema. 'That something is true,' he said, 'doesn't necessarily make it interesting. There wasn't any real story. So I made up a story about two good guys: Ness and Jimmy Malone.'

True or not, De Palma left no stone unturned in depicting the real terrors of mob rule. 'The photogenic qualities of gore are very apparent,' one reviewer wrote – though others criticised De Palma's historical exaggeration. The plot centred on Fed 'untouchable' Ness's efforts to eliminate Capone and his mob. Ness seems bound for success in the movie but in reality he never met Capone, never killed his enforcer Frank Nitti (as he does in the movie), never succeeded in quelling the rackets. Nonetheless, the day-to-day activities of agents like Ness were accurately depicted, coached in fact by a surviving 'untouchable', 85-year-old Al Wolff.

On the face of it, *The Untouchables* was Costner's picture. But the movie hadn't premiered when the preview writers were signalling a breakthrough for Connery. In the *Sunday Mail* Dermot Purgavie spelled it out. He acknowledged a great screenplay by Mamet and the brutal ingenuity of De Palma. 'It is [all] memorably diverting but it is the informed performance of Sean Connery, judiciously working for a percentage of the profits, that carries the film . . . and he is widely expected to get an Oscar for his portrayal of the cautious cop who keeps a sawn-off shotgun in his gramophone, a bottle of whisky in his stove and a medal of St Jude, the patron of lost causes, in his pocket . . .' To top it all, the distinguished Pauline Kael likened Connery's performance to Olivier's.

In some ways Connery's 'tutor' role in *The Untouchables*

echoed his part in *The Name of the Rose*. Here, again, he was the oracle, wisdom incarnate, the old moraliser. In *Rose* he triumphs. Here, poignantly, he dies – though his wisdom is delivered and absorbed. Through Connery's Malone Costner's Ness is indelibly changed. The upright incorruptible Fed man surrenders his values, loses his innocence but will, we know, go on to win.

The heroic tragedy of *The Untouchables* decisively won the Best Supporting Oscar for Connery. Prior to the ceremony Connery refused to participate in anticipatory interviews but was, says Caine, 'anxious'. When he won, the walls of the Shrine Auditorium in downtown Hollywood came down. Six thousand industry guests rose to their feet *twice*. Compere Cher, in an all-revealing clinging chiffon-and-spangles gown, dominated the evening up to that point. When Connery's win was announced the room became electric with excitement. 'It was something I had never seen before,' Michael Caine emphasises. '*Two* ovations – it just doesn't happen.'

Connery, with Micheline clutching his arm, had tears in his eyes then – and at Swifty Lazar's traditional bash afterwards. There were plenty of high flyers in the other awards for the evening – Michael Douglas was Best Actor for *Wall Street*, Cher Best Actress for *Moonstruck*, Bertolucci Best Director for *The Last Emperor* – but Connery undeniably had the centre stage. With touching modesty he told NBC: 'I don't know why they gave it . . . I suppose it was recognition for a body of work.'

There were those who lamented Connery's Oscar, declaring it 'second rate', insisting – nobly and probably rightly – that he belonged at the peak: as Best Actor. Certainly his consistent performances over the years outranked newer players like Costner colossally but, as he himself averred, there is a pecking order in Hollywood, a visible 'club', and it is notoriously difficult for infrequent visitors like Connery to break through.

Though Connery ranks today as one of the few always-bankable Hollywood imports, his forays into 'West Coast' movies have been few. Some years ago actor Robert Hardy said: 'I cannot see Sean and Hollywood settling down as long-term partners. There is a rebel element within him that would not fit, I think. It is such a pity, in ways, that the theatre didn't hold onto him. Because the method of his approach is not lightweight or conventional.'

John Boorman says, 'Sean is inside the system and outside it. He remains his own man at whatever cost. He is not an actor who will ever conform to what Hollywood routinely expects.'

Connery isn't shy about denouncing the limitations of 'the system'. Whilst referring to the likes of Roger Moore and Costner as 'good friends' he criticises freely when he feels it is due. 'Actors like Costner are very much tied to American audiences. But I've been making films all over the world for the last thirty years and I have a very strong international foundation. Outside the United States there isn't an actor who gets better exposure or success ratios in any country than me.' ('When you are with Sean you learn pretty quickly your place in the galaxy,' Costner once told *The Sunday Times*.)

After Oscar, inevitably, Connery was flooded with American offers. He took his time in selecting the best, and exercised a new tactical planning that would gradually bring him into a position of greater executive power within the Hollywood system.

He turned down a succession of major movies, the Peter O'Toole role in the disastrously unfunny comedy *High Spirits* (1988) among them. Terry Gilliam tried to get him for *The Adventures of Baron Munchausen*, offering him the zany role of King of the Moon, not much different from the Pythonesque *Time Bandits* part. Connery was amused but told Gilliam, 'It's not really a role.' Gilliam agreed, and booked Robin Williams.*

---

* The roles Connery missed – or rejected – make interesting reading. Producer Mel Ferrer wanted him as Audrey Hepburn's husband in *Wait Until Dark*. Director Terence Young did not. He was also Tony Richardson's first choice to play Captain Nolan in *The Charge of the Light Brigade* – David Hemmings replaced him. He was in line too for *Boom*, *The Last Hard Man* (Charlton Heston wanted him), *Ladyhawke* (Rutger Hauer replaced him), *Air America* and *Sleeping With the Enemy* (as the proposed first choices, he and Kim Basinger proved too expensive; Patrick Bergin and Julia Roberts replaced them).

Connery opted to stay in Hollywood where he made four major movies over the next two and a half years – his longest unbroken American spell. First up was old pal's Sidney Lumet's comedy, the gravely miscalculated *Family Business*. Here Connery again prematurely embraced old age to portray Dustin Hoffman's dad and Matthew Broderick's grandfather in what was essentially a crime caper designed for the mass market. Connery was Jesse, head of a reformed hoodlum family in New York's Hell's Kitchen, who joins with his grandson in a bungled heist very much against his son's wishes. Writer Vincent Patrick adapted his own novel and Lumet imparted what significance he could to tangential observations on class and generation conflict and the dichotomy between morality and the law. But ultimately the story died in its levity. Connery's comedy was deadweight and did little to revive memories of *A Fine Madness*. In London *Time Out* threw it out. After *The Untouchables* it was a major let-down, 'a forest of clichés and contrivances'.

Connery wasn't stopping for analysis. He appeared to have a grand plan and was determined to get on with it. With the guidance of agent Michael Ovitz he negotiated superb deals on three other Hollywood megamovies in rapid succession: Peter Hyams's *The Presidio*, Steven Spielberg's *Indiana Jones and the Last Crusade* and John McTiernan's *The Hunt for Red October*. All these movies were in the mass-appeal category, all lavishly budgeted and peppered with American stars. All brought Connery huge fees, dramatically enhanced as they were by the Oscar success. A colleague says: 'These couple of movies earned Sean ten million dollars clear. No one ever called Sean a dumbo – right? Well, look at his position. He had been thirty years trying to get there, at the top where Hollywood was chasing after him. When Bond happened he was either too tired or too distracted or maybe too immature. This [situation after the Oscar] was similar to the impact of Bond. But now he was older and wiser and not about to lose out.'

Living out of his LA apartment (but skipping home to

Spain when he could) Connery knuckled down to a relentless Hollywood schedule. *The Presidio*, like *Family Business*, failed him. A straightforward murder mystery in which Connery plays a US Army Provost-Marshal engaged to assist the San Francisco police in finding the murderer of a military policewoman, the movie laboured through red herrings and subplots and showed all the plodding weakness of Hyams's earlier *Outland*. High style, low content.

But in Spielberg, at last, Connery found a winning action formula befitting the man who made James Bond. Indiana Jones was already vastly popular on the basis of Spielberg's first two movies, a calculated phenomenon to challenge Bond. As a teenager growing up in Arizona Spielberg revered 007. Later he confessed to the influence of the Bond movies and a lifelong appreciation of Connery. When it came to planning his third Indian saga Spielberg grew excited by the notion of using seminal Bond as a foil for Indiana's Harrison Ford. But when Connery first met up with Spielberg and producer George Lucas the signs were not good. Spielberg had firmly in mind a middle-aged professorial-type character who might be Indiana Jones's father. George Lucas, Spielberg's partner in the project, wasn't too sure. There seemed little flesh on the idea anyway, Connery later reported, and when he asked to read the first draft script Lucas refused him. That initial meeting seemed a time waste. The talk was circumspect, and Connery left Spielberg's suite feeling 'there was a reluctance on the part of George for me to play the part'.

Steven Spielberg admits that Lucas was wary. 'George wasn't thinking in terms of such a *powerful* presence. His idea was for a doting, scholarly person, an older British character actor. But I had always seen Sean Connery. Without a strong, illuminating presence I was afraid that Harrison Ford would eradicate the father from the movie. I wanted to challenge him. And who could be the equal of Indiana Jones but James Bond?'

Connery was briefly resting in Marbella when finally Lucas forwarded a script. He hated it. '. . . It was all very serious and there wasn't any jazz in the part, so I said, "It's not for me." Steven couldn't understand why, so I went to America to discuss it. My idea was to base a lot of him on Richard Burton, the nineteenth-century explorer. He'd been quite selfish and intolerant. So we called Tom Stoppard to rewrite the part that way and he came up with things like the dialogue where Indiana says to his father, "You never talked to me", and he replies, "You left home at nineteen, just when you were becoming interesting." And also the business about the father and son sleeping with the same girl, which is a good gag.'

Stoppard was the glue that made it work (though his written contribution received no screen credit; screenplay credit went to Hollywood resident Jeffrey Boam). What followed was a thrilling, absorbing shoot in Spanish desert locations that Connery found 'more fun than I've had in a while'. Especially gratifying was the growth of his character. What started as a few incidental pages in a fat script grew to occupy half the story. Subsequent audience response validated the approach. 'It gave him particular pride,' says a friend. 'In Bond he dominated. Indiana Jones was a phenomenon like Bond. Harrison Ford had made it his own. Sean likes to compete. So he competed with Ford and he blew him off the screen. Nobody could ask for more . . .'

At this high point Connery suddenly faced the greatest shock of his life. During the summer he was in high spirits, commuting to Spain, golfing in Scotland, counting his luck. He was, in the words of the *Sunday Times*, one of the most sought-after actors in the world: 'the star who grew and grew'. Steven Spielberg had judged him 'one of only seven true movie stars alive'. The friendship with Stoppard that grew from the Indiana Jones success was flourishing and Stoppard had asked him to star in his own upcoming directorial début, the classic *Rosencrantz and Guildenstern Are Dead*. Connery was keen, and his agents were happily negotiating when the blow fell.

For some time Connery had been suffering a dry throat. Often, in the din of a loud scene in *Indiana Jones*, his voice would fail him. When the movie wrapped, he reluctantly consulted a specialist at UCLA clinic. The doctor stuck a probe into his throat and said, 'Oh-oh, there's some trouble here.' Connery later said, 'They found three little white dots on the right side of my larynx . . . like most people, medical matters are a mystery to me and a lack of knowledge makes matters worse.'

Connery was, in his own words, 'absolutely terrified'. He had seen old friends like Jack Hawkins die before his eyes, savagely worn down by throat cancer. On *Shalako* Hawkins was seriously disabled and, though he put up a game show, all his lines were dubbed by Charles Grey. His presence had been, said Honor Blackman, 'agonising'. Now Connery's doctor was advising that the 'angry patch of tissue' was 'probably benign'. Connery could choose a biopsy, laser surgery – or perhaps a prolonged rest of his vocal cords might repair the problem. Connery wasn't satisfied. 'Sean always was a bit of a hypochondriac,' says Michael Caine. 'You didn't dare ask how he was because you'd soon get the picture: "I've got this stiff arm and my back has been killing me and, funny you should mention it, I haven't been feeling too hot . . ."'

Now, however, there seemed genuine cause for concern. Connery consulted other specialists and was advised to try thirty days of complete silence and rest. It was possible the spots would disappear. It was possible they were benign polyps resulting from the vocal stress of acting.

Rosencrantz and Guildenstern was the main casualty. In his terror of the possibility, however, remote, of throat cancer, Connery had decided to keep the situation from the media. He instructed his agents confidentially to withdraw from Stoppard's movie, now just three weeks away from shooting. Stoppard, his agent, the producers, the fellow actors were stunned by the unexplained reversal. Stoppard was livid and believed the withdrawal had to do with the small fee on offer. The movie's budget was a tiny $4 million. Connery had agreed to accept $75,000 – his lowest fee in years. But now he was crying off. Stoppard's agent Gordon Dickerson was naturally upset, but kept a brave face. On 13 January 1989, announcing the cancellation he dodged: 'There has been a problem over conflicting dates . . . it's now up to the producers to solve.' Robert Lindsay, Sting and Jeremy Irons had been announced to star opposite Connery, who would be the Player King. Now the legal threats started. Connery abruptly bought himself off the movie . . . for $300,000. 'Tom was annoyed,' he said later. 'But he got it all wrong. I could have fought it in court but – who needs another lawsuit? So I just paid my way out.'

In LA Connery's agent denied to *Today* that the star was ill. But within weeks the British tabloids carried the scream headlines: CONNERY CANCER SCARE.

'Once those inaccurate rumours started circulating, I couldn't deny them. I didn't know what was going to happen until I went back to UCLA a month later . . . I have to admit the effect on me was awful . . .'

Under a cloud, Connery flew back to Spain with Micheline quietly by his side. The word 'cancer' haunted their days and nights. 'Other things in your life take second place,' Connery later said, 'and whatever you are doing that nagging worry is always at the back of your mind.'

In the privacy of the Casa Malibu all they could do now was sit on the terrace and watch the sea, and wait.

19

Untouchable?

'It was a *pill*,' said Connery wryly. 'I had this pen which I wore around my neck. And every time I wanted to say something I wrote it down on the back of old scripts. I wrote hundreds of pages and I should have kept them, because it was so crazy. It was lots of non-sequiturs, like you never knew the question. Like there would be "How the fuck do I know?" . . . Anyway, I printed up these cards saying "Sorry, I cannot speak. I have a problem with my throat. Thank you". And everyone would look at the card and say, "Why, what's the matter?" . . . And then I would write out what I wanted to say. Half the people would take the pen and write their answers back. You realise very quickly the world is full of idiots . . .' Micheline underlined the anguish: 'You should have seen the *way* he was writing . . .' Connery confesses: 'I cut through the paper.'

Rigid with fear as he was, Connery refused to surrender to depression. A friend says, 'He kind of cut himself off. It was something he shared with Micheline, Stefan, Jason. It wasn't something he wanted dragged round .. . because, in his case, it was the most debilitating thing. I mean, how could he answer these morons? By showing a card saying, like some cripple, *I cannot talk*? He had to bite the bullet . . . and he tried to keep smiling . . . but it was his darkest hour.'

Connery returned to LA to bad news: 'I was told that the month's silence hadn't worked and I would have to have the biopsy anyway. You can't imagine how I felt. The

259

terror returned. But I got three opinions before I settled for this supposed expert who is the top man in UCLA. It was very hard to make a calm judgement in such circumstances. Other things in your life take second place, I'm afraid.'

He finally had one bout of laser surgery in LA, but the results were inconclusive so he checked into London's Royal National Throat, Nose and Ear Hospital under the alias of David Martin. The *Sun* and the other tabloids had him rumbled overnight and, rather than face the fray of journalists camping in the street, Connery checked out just hours after cancer specialist David Howard performed another minor laser operation. One more minor operation followed before Connery was at last given a clean bill, with a recommendation for six-monthly screening tests.

Connery got his final clean bill in LA in April and opted to stay there when *The Hunt for Red October* was offered to him. Klaus Maria Brandauer, his old adversary from *Never Say Never Again*, had been signed by Paramount to play the hero Soviet skipper who defects in the film version of Tom Clancy's bestseller, but had dropped out at the last minute to accommodate a German movie in Europe. Connery was offered $4 million – his biggest cheque since Bond and, perhaps, justification for doing Bond after all. He dallied, taking careful medical advice, before agreeing in late April. The movie was six weeks under way, with hotshot John McTiernan at the helm, before Connery joined the cast at Parmount Studios on 22 May.

During the in-between weeks Connery spent frequent hours in LA with Dr Lillian Glass, a former Miss Miami and university lecturer based in a Beverly Hills clinic who specialised – for $95 per half-hour session – in speech therapy. Glass's regulars included Dolly Parton, Rob Lowe and Mickey Rourke and she addressed herself, in Connery's case, to restructuring his voice. Glass said, 'Sean came to me every day for weeks after the operation to remove the nodules . . . The story that he had cancer was a lie. He is a very healthy man. It's his bad habits that caused the trouble. I could find examples of these in the early James Bond films when he said "My name is Bond . . . James

Bond." His voice sounded as though it was clenched in a ball. It sounded sensuous, but it was very damaging. Now his voice is even more sensuous because it is open and flowing.'

Connery's refusal to discuss his throat problem created a lingering mood of suspicion on the set. As one actor explains, his arrival on *Red October* was shrouded in mystery. There was talk of his illness everywhere and 'Sean really couldn't be bothered going over old ground . . . he kept himself to himself but in this business that kind of silence encourages speculation . . . not that I suppose he gave a damn.' The first knowledge the cast and crew had of Connery's positive role in the movie came when, in late April, shooting a Washington scene, the image of the skipper of the submarine *Red October* flashed onto a monitor during a top-level government briefing. Sean Connery's face was superimposed on the skipper's body. When Connery eventually arrived on set to play defecting Soviet Captain Ramius, all eyes were on him, wondering, prying. Connery countered with a solid, disciplined performance that won everyone's admiration and discouraged gossip. One observer remarked: 'He was hoarse, that's for sure. You see it in the screen cut. The voice is quite different, lower, more gravelly. He also doesn't *boom* like he usually does, in the tense moments.' Connery responded: 'It's the first time I've been able to do a movie without losing my voice.'

The Hunt for Red October was a seriously flawed but very engaging movie whose timing was unfortunate. Tom Clancy, the author, published his technically heavyweight account of a Soviet defection in 1984, prior to *glasnost* and *perestroika*. The book was a publishing sensation, not least because Clancy gave it to a little-known academic publisher, the Naval Institute Press of Annapolis, instead of one of the leading commercial houses. The Naval Institute had helped Clancy in preparing the book and the 116-year-old establishment expected nothing other than a modest popular success. But *Red October* proved a runaway bestseller, its appeal vastly heightened by the unfolding changes in

Moscow. The Institute made a killing, and scored again almost immediately with Stephen Coonts's *Flight of the Intruder*. Though the Institute disputed rights with Clancy – and prompted him to go elsewhere with his follow-up novels, *Red Storm Rising* and *Patriot Games* – the author was paid handsomely by producer Mace Neufeld for movie rights. The plan was to develop the novel's American CIA agent Jack Ryan (Alec Baldwin in *Red October*) as a series character. Clancy was overjoyed but suspected, rightly, that *Red October*'s topicality might present problems. The speed of change within the Soviet Union and Eastern Europe that would see, within a year, the fall of the Berlin Wall and, shortly after, the collapse of Communism and the USSR as a political entity, made the movie an anachronism before its completion. Though it had its undisputed qualities – Connery's dark determination as Marko Ramius being uppermost – its aura belonged to the seventies. The *Monthly Film Bulletin* called it 'old-fashioned' and expressed profound disappointment in director McTiernan: 'Although he has demonstrated with the empty but actionful *Predator* and the marvellously-tooled *Die Hard* that he is one of the best action men around . . . he can hardly do much with this overlong, humourless suspense picture.'

Red October served Connery well enough. 'It gave him back his vocal confidence,' said Sheamus Smith. It also provided a shot in the arm for the Scottish Educational Trust when the movie had a Royal Première on 17 April 1990 before Prince Charles and Princess Diana, with proceeds divided between the Prince's Trust and Connery's charity. Subsequently the movie played to good box office everywhere.

Russia had always played a subtle, vital role in Connery's professional life. As Bond, he challenged its might. In 1969, filming *The Red Tent* there he had developed a fascination for a nation he found mysterious, misdirected, confused. On *Red October* he was intrigued by conversations with Soviet émigré extras like Herman Sinitzen, who played one of his naval subordinates and was in fact responsible for the recruiting of 25 former Soviet residents for the movie. Sinitzen had worked for Intourist, and had resided in LA for nine years, working as an interpreter for the LA court system. His, and others', descriptions of new Soviet life riveted the always-eager-to-learn Connery. Now, on the heels of McTiernan's film, he had again the chance to visit the country and see the effects of *glasnost* first hand. Connery jumped at the opportunity to do Fred Schepisi's *The Russia House* not just because of its Leningrad and Moscow locations, but because the story was a thoroughbred, adapted by Stoppard from John Le Carré's novel. Some saw his eagerness for the project as a gesture of conciliation towards Stoppard, who was allegedly still smarting over his directional début letdown. But Connery wasn't saying so. For Connery, the inducement was, pure and simple, 'the landmark opportunity of making an American movie in Russia'.

Director Schepisi describes his first scouting trip to Russia, which came after months of delicate diplomatic negotiations: 'It was incredible because I was there when they were making historic changes in the country. You could feel the excitement. There was uncertainty and worry. I thought John le Carré's book was a real look at *glasnost* and the end of the Cold War, and a look at the people who should know better . . . [The story was about] the spymasters of East and West [and they] are the people who should appreciate that the Cold War is over . . . but they seem to want to perpetuate it to keep their jobs going.'

Co-operation, none the less, was forthcoming and the movie started filming – co-starring Roy Scheider, Michele Pfeiffer and Klaus Maria Brandauer – in Leningrad's Palace Square on 2 October 1989, with enthusiastic local police support. Connery said: 'When I was there before [on *The Red Tent*], you never knew where you were. I had a different driver every day, so he knew me but I never knew him. I'd be standing there like the laundry, waiting to get picked up. The interpreters were invariably KGB people. I'm not saying they are not KGB now, but this time they're younger, very outgoing . . .

The shoot was as arduous as any Connery had endured. Unlike the six static weeks on a Paramount sound stage for *Red October*, *The Russia House* leapt all over the place. Connery described the schedule to Baz Bamigboye as flying 'from Malaga to Madrid to Amsterdam, then Madrid again, from there to Warsaw, Leningrad, Moscow, back to Leningrad, on to London, then Lisbon . . .' The Russian locations, however, were enthralling and opened his eyes to the varied glories of a suppressed wonderland. After Leningrad, the shoot moved to St Basil's Cathedral in Red Square, then Peredelkino, dacha home of countless writers and artists, then the City of Churches Zagorsk, then Kolomenskoye above the Moscow River, where the Czars had a vast country estate. Schepisi was greatly helped by his friend the Russian director Elem Klimov, who cut through the remnants of starchy bureaucracy. Connery, and Micheline, drank in the sights, listened to the stories, took what they could from the momentous experience. Schepisi circulated a memo to his cast and crew: 'In a small way you are a part of history. We are the first people to be making a film, in this way, in this country. The people here are bending over backwards to help us in ways that are alien to their upbringing. They are more than willing. They know that many high-level people are closely observing what is considered a bold experiment. In an era of *glasnost* I believe it is important to make this work . . .'

Australian Schepisi, whose most significant movie till then had been Steve Martin's self-penned, exquisite *Roxanne*, declared himself utterly satisfied with Connery, Pfeiffer and *The Russia House* experience. Others concurred, though Connery concedes that in some degree the end result proved disappointing.

In *The Russia House* Connery played weary, cynical publisher Barley Blair who becomes involved with Katya (Pfeiffer), a courier being manipulated by a scientist codenamed 'Dante' who is putting *glasnost* to the test by spiriting Soviet nuclear information to the West. Blair becomes embroiled in the moral dilemmas of Katya and 'Dante', but the main thrust of the story is his slow-hatching love for

264

Katya. The movie has a moody, low-key movement that lost the youth audience and caused hiccups at the box office. Reviewer Kim Newman defined its problem: 'Although sold as a thriller, the film boils down to a series of scenes in which two people talk enigmatically to each other. . . . In the end this is a movie that tries to be tense and exciting without a single incident of violence.'

Connery didn't sit around licking wounds. His regular throat tests were encouraging and he continued to push himself, taking small roles in *Highlander II* ('Whizz-bang pop videoesque sequel,' said *Film Review*) and, at Kevin Costner's personal request, *Robin Hood, Prince of Thieves*, one of 1990's top earners. For *Highlander II* Connery bagged $3½ million. For one day's work on Costner's film, $250,000, which went to the Educational Trust.

1990 found Connery uncompromising as ever in his attitudes to fame and fortune . . . and private as ever in his plans for the future. Celebrating his sixtieth year, he had wealth and security beyond his dreams but – triumph of all, untypically in the industry – his wit and objectivity were still intact. Old Oscar was something he never spoke of, hardly thought about unless it looked him in the eye from its shelf in the new en suite bathroom Micheline had designed for him in Marbella. The industry, he told friends, still fascinated him, drove him, but neither money nor fame *per se* were enough now. Other goals, artistic goals, business goals, were in sight. He had no time, he said, for the conventions of the industry, nor desire to live out a career to others' prescriptions.

Watershed birthday or no, Connery was still not in the business of public self-analysis. But in one interview during that year he offered a rare glimpse of his personal theory of actor motivation: 'I do think a lot of American actresses' indulgences are permitted by some producers. Somehow all their neuroses, or whatever they are, come out. They think nobody but they have problems. Therefore we all have to share their problems, or be tortured by them. This has produced people who are forced into internal ways of acting. But standing on a set for twenty-two takes, looking for "something inside", is not going to be inspirational. I'm against using only oneself as a total instrument of acting. How – if you are a stupid actor – do you play someone intelligent, for example?'

However, humour tempered the chauvinism. When an American journalist asked, 'Is it true that sixty-year-old men are more virile, Mr Connery?', Connery offered the measured, deadpan response: 'It's years since I've been to bed with a sixty-year-old.'

Turning sixty in August 1990 didn't bother Connery because, says Ian Bannen, 'Sean has always been old . . . I don't mean that in a derogatory way. I mean it in the sense that from the start, when I met him, he had the world on his shoulders. He was not one who went running home to mummy. He was out to fight to the top and do whatever had to be done. He never hid his age. He wasn't one of those Rank types where you read in the official bios that he was born last week. He grew grey, he went bald, so what?' Connery did indeed defy the gloom of ageing. As a young man, in his late twenties when it became apparent that he would go bald as his father and grandfather had, he panicked. 'I remember thinking, My God, what can be done? I'm finished!' Now, at sixty, Connery laughed at the ironies. He had made fun of his baldness after Bond, relished it. Unlike star players like Richard Harris or Burton who dyed their thinning manes and hinted at youthful yearnings, Connery – in the words of Robert Hardy – 'dashed into middle age'. 'It doesn't worry me,' he once said. 'It is inevitable, so what can one do but accept it.' He had no interest at all in 'letting eighteen hairs grow a foot and a half long and dressing in trendy jeans'. Instead: 'Being comfortable in your own skin is more important than anything else – and most of the time I feel pretty comfortable in mine.'

Connery 'entered the pension decade' absorbed on a new project in the depths of the Central American rain forest. *The Last Days of Eden* (later retitled *Medicine Man*) was hugely important to him because it marked the transition from actor to producer, a crucial and unheralded manoeuvre that seemed to be his new main objective. Directed by McTiernan, the *Red October* director, the movie was a first venture from Andy Vanja's Cinergi Productions and afforded Connery the kind of creative control he had previously exercised only on *Never Say Never Again*. In this instance the social and political relevance of the project, written by Tom Schulman, greatly appealed. This was not simply a romantic adventure – though much of the advance publicity indicated a kind of late-life *Romancing the Stone*; this film had a profound statement to deliver, about the destruction of the rain forests and its probable consequences. As senior executive – the equivalent of Broccoli's status on Bond – Connery had script and casting approval and chose Lorraine Bracco from *Goodfellas* as his co-star. 'She was my choice immediately. We needed someone who could be tough, dynamic and have a sense of humour about it. We simply couldn't risk attempting something like this with an actress who was concerned whether her hair was in place, or whether she was sweating. It calls for a certain kind of girl . . .'

Medicine Man was an obstacle course. McTiernan scoured the world's jungles for the perfect base for a story of an ageing ethnobiologist who has found the cure for cancer in the rare bromeliads nestling in the treetops – then loses it. Five years earlier McTiernan made his movie name with Arnold Schwarzenegger's *Predator*, filmed in Borneo's rain forest. When he returned to recce the area now, that rain forest was gone. 'It was an object lesson in the message we were trying to put across,' said McTiernan. 'The forests are vanishing: that is the reality of it.' McTiernan went on scouting – in Malaysia, Equatorial Guinea, Belize, Venezuela, Ecuador before deciding – and convincing Connery – that the best solution was to import Brazilian Indians to the accessible remains of a jungle landscape at Catemaco, in Mexico. Here Micheline and Sean were installed in a modern, but modest bungalow situated on a lake which, at twilight anyway, reminded Connery of home. 'It could be the Highlands,' he told Sue Russell of

the *Express*. 'And there are some wonderful fish in the lake
. . . although everything has to be specially cooked because
of the parasites.'

The weeks in Mexico and later, briefly, in Brazil, were
weeks of discomfort and danger. As Dr Robert Campbell,
Connery explores the jungle's upper growth, frantically
searching for the plant extracts that will defeat cancer. As
usual Connery insisted on doing his own stunt work which
involved being strapped into fragile harnesses and levered
hundreds of feet into the sky. Fortunately Connery didn't
suffer from vertigo. 'I prefer heights to [going] underwater,' he said. 'At least you get to breathe.' But other
factors distressed him, not least the plodding slowness of
film-making in the depths of nowhere.

For McTiernan, just forty, with a background in
commercials and just three major features to his credit,
Connery still, even after their shared work on *Red October*,
proved slightly intimidating. By his own admission McTiernan 'pussyfooted' around Connery on *Red October*; now,
however, he learned that the best way to inspire his star was
by pushing him. 'Not only could I get away with telling him
what I thought,' says McTiernan, 'he *wanted* me to tell him
what I thought. In fact the only sure way to get him
annoyed is if you *don't* speak your mind.'

After several weeks of parasites and scorching temperatures Connery was chronically 'grumpy' and 'gruff' – and
sick of the dubious Mexican food. Frequent illnesses
among the unit caused more delays but Connery maintained the passion of purpose . . . and rose to the demands
of executive producer when his actor energies tired. 'I am
not always happy at work' he told Sue Russell, 'but then
who is? I'm certainly happier working than not. [My pro-
fession] has given me a real education too.'

For those who wanted to explore the bad news vibes
from the Mexico location Connery offered disappointment. He was – genuinely – too moved by the implications
of 'a serious and important story'. Where once there were
nine million Brazilian Indians in the forests, now there
were 200,000. Tragically, as the forests and their parasite

species were destroyed, so was the unknown, untapped potential of a thousand plants. 'An acre of rain forest is destroyed every second,' said Connery passionately. 'Its potential for pharmaceuticals is enormous . . . and it's vanishing.'

Medicine Man, the screenplay, started life as one of Hollywood's million-dollar 'spec' scripts – written speculatively by Tom Schulman and sold to the highest bidder. Connery greatly believed in it and in the finished movie, but the critics were less kind. *The Times* called it 'aimless' and stood unimpressed by its too-obvious ecological lob. *The Monthly Film Bulletin* found it 'loosely constructed and . . . pointless'.

Connery didn't appear at all affected by the negative press. STV producer Ross Wilson visited the Casa Malibu with his documentary crew immediately after Connery's return from South America and found him 'edgy, exhausted, wound down and a bit underweight as a consequence of the dodgy food. He said it had been a particularly awful location situation, but he was well used to the adversity of bad locations by then. Let's face it, he had conquered the world in terms of film locations . . and what does one lousy film review mean anyway, after all those astounding years?'

Sure enough Sean Connery had paid his dues. In 35 years of cinematic adventure he had worked in the Arctic snows, in the desert wastes of Morocco, in the bustle of New York's Hell's Kitchen, in the wilds of County Wicklow, in the Steppes of Russia, in jam-packed Tokyo, aboard submarines, in helicopters, cargo planes, Victorian steam trains, under sea and in the air.

What peak could possibly remain?

The Freedom of Edinburgh award that brought Ross Wilson to Marbella signalled a demarcation point. Since the death of Effie, Connery's ties with his homeland seemed little by little to slip. Now, with a passion, he was ready to revisit the past and share his memories. Wilson found him 'full of memories and vivid opinions on many things – on society, art, politics' and yet curiously, paradoxically, restrained. 'I felt we had, by Sean's own choosing at that moment in his life, received an insight. I felt we achieved a sketch portrait of the man, something intimate and accurate. But I knew there was more . . .

Connery allowed the STV crew freedom of movement in and around the Casa Malibu, allowed them to film in his work bungalow, in the bedrooms, even in his private bathroom where Oscar resides. The crew was fed, humoured, encouraged. They had everything they wanted. Except time.

'The dilemma in talking to Connery,' says Ross Wilson, is that 'he operates to his own dictates, seemingly in everything. It is too easy to say his choices have been whimsical, or tactical. What is the point? Where is he headed? To get him to address that, to break into that internal dialogue – that is the challenge with Connery.'

Garth Pearce is one of the few journalists the Connerys trust, and tend to open to. In a detailed interview in the *Mail* Connery mused on past and future: 'Someone reminded me that three years ago I said I was not going to make any more pictures. I don't remember saying that, but I'll probably say the same thing tomorrow. The business is cyclical. I have had work. I haven't had work. And now I have work . . . [so] I think now I'll retire.'

'He was laughing as he said that,' wrote Pearce. 'It was all a huge joke . . . but then, with Connery, you never know.'

Ross Wilson tells of shooting his Spanish–Scottish documentary and returning to base in Edinburgh with the footage. 'It was extraordinary, on reflection. Everyone had the same basic question: What is he like? Despite all the countless magazine articles, the interviews, the TV specials . . . still they wanted to know *What is he like?* It made me think that this is the triumph of his achievement: to have become one of the most successful actors of all time and still leave the personal mystery, and the questions. To give all, and yet reveal so little. This in itself seems a measure of greatness.'

Postscript
Looking Forward

'In the house by the sea at Marbella we have an excellent garden and I find myself looking at it more. Perhaps it is trying to tell me something. To slow down? I don't know. . . . When I was twenty-five I thought everything would be perfect when I reached the age of forty. Now I'm putting my estate totally in order, and I don't know whether that's a preparation for living or dying . . .'

It might almost have been James Bond talking. Early in the Fleming novel *You Only Live Twice*, the penultimate work, James Bond sat in Queen Mary's Rose Garden in Regent's Park and contemplated: 'The state of your health, the state of the weather, the wonders of nature . . .' Only in middle age, Bond mused, does a man cease taking the world for granted.

As a throw-over from his rough beginnings, Connery had never taken anything for granted. He has, in his words, worked his ass off since he was a child in order to acquire security and a good professional reputation. He is now past middle age, though his genes conceal it, but he has visibly mellowed and, as witness his recent interviews and the access afforded to the likes of STV, chooses to ruminate and evaluate more than he used to. All those close to him observe that now more than ever he will entertain memories of the past, the errors, even dabble in speculation of future possibilities. 'I think, when he won that Oscar and

271

then they gave him the BAFTA Lifetime Achievement Award, he suddenly realised all he had been missing out on by locking himself away in Spain,' says Michael Caine. After BAFTA, it was true, Connery did review his success and seclusion.

With hindsight, maritally he had been very fortunate. Diane Cilento had been a good career navigator for the time she was around and Micheline, as different in personality as could be imagined, was the ideal companion for years that were both rockier and richer. 'Micheline is the best thing that's every happened to Sean Connery,' says Sheamus Smith. 'She is his anchor,' Andrew Fyall says. 'Theirs is something beyond the traditional husband-wife pairing. Between them there is a magical bond.' Unlike Cilento, Micheline's artistic ambitions were not home distractions: she liked to build her sunny nest and look after the children and cook meals. Stefan and Jason, temperamentally different themselves, grew close and secure under Micheline's protective guidance and today, though distanced in their respective thriving careers – Stefan in fine arts (having recently left Sotheby's) and Jason filming worldwide – remain brothers. In his way, Connery repaid Micheline's devotion. A talented artist, he actively encouraged her to broaden her range and exhibit her paintings. She had always been shy of publicity but, with his bold prompting, finally exhibited in Europe and America, and won high praise for her daring portraits of King Hussein, John Huston, Effie Connery and – her favourite subject – her husband.

Insulated by this serene domestic backcloth, Sean Connery has fought his wars for twenty rocky years, taking on all comers with unwavering resolve. Beating Bond took a decade of his life. Balancing his finances and securing true independence took another. Micheline was there to coach him throughout, and she was there to laugh alongside him as he crossed the demarcation zone into 'mature' character-playing. The immediate adjacent anxiety, common to all actors who, like Connery, know the relative ephemerality of their art, was that of surviving the transition from young lead to character actor. Connery hardly flinched. Responding to a friend's remark that 'the face still stands close inspection,' Connery agreed that 'Time has been good to me.' Unlike most star leads he has not in any way contrived to extend his natural life as a romantic lead. Writer Tony Crawley observed what he believes is the true watershed moment in Connery's career – 'the point where he proved his credentials, displayed his integrity and became a movie immortal': in Richard Brooks's *The Man With the Deadly Lens* Connery ritually revels in the moment when, as go-getting TV journalist Hale, shuttling from presidents to palaces to tell it as it is, he prepares to parachute from a plane – and at the last second whips off the scanty toupee that was almost unnoticeable in the first place. 'It's a moment of black comedy that evokes a laugh and a sigh, and it says more about Sean Connery the man and the actor than a million reviews could. It shows the courage, and that's what makes us look out for him and look forward to what he will do next . . . because we know wherever he takes us, he will dare leave his vanity and ego behind, and take a chance.'

Appropriately, Connery's daring yielded gold-dust. By eschewing the vanities he has seemingly won the Fountain of Youth. 'He is never paired with a peer,' said the *Express*, pointing out that Michelle Pfeiffer in *The Russia House* was 32 and Lorraine Bracco in *Medicine Man* 36. Connery only nods sagely: 'There's a real reluctance [for some actors] to go forward, to go into anything that smacks of character . . .'

Though often depressed by his failures, Connery never quits. Part of it seems obviously the undying compensation factor – the desire to bury for ever the deprivations of Fountainbridge. Part of it too, as he expressed to Sue Russell, is the hunger for education and intellectual stimulus. More than once he has stated that his schooling started with Robert Henderson's hit list, and has grown through sixty films. And, like a child at school, there lingers the call of duty, some obsessive attraction to pass the exam, to *qualify*. In many ways, through many genres of movie,

Connery has passed the test. But he wants more. He hungers most, says Ian Bannen, for a crowning picture that is solely *his* – a statement delivered honestly by himself and not some 'stupid producer' whose motives are commerce, or avarice, or worse.

Was Connery crazy to reprise Bond? Is his sideline fascination with art house movies indulgent and professionally damaging? Is there a case to answer in his sometimes heavy-handed involvement in script changes or casting choices? Is his power-hungry pursuit of executive producer status – the role he occupies once again in Philip Kaufman's *Rising Sun* – an artistic distraction? Unarguably, when he has had the power, he has fostered absolute duds and altered screenplays that failed badly. But who hasn't?

Those who know him were not surprised by his resurrection of Bond. His brother Neil wasn't. John Boorman wasn't. Lewis Gilbert wasn't. Robert Hardy wasn't. Guy Hamilton wasn't. All of them recognise in it an exercise in daring: Connery once again testing his capacities and going for gold. 'It wasn't [indulgent] at all,' says Guy Hamilton, 'because Sean looks for the newness in things each time. He is never static. In my book that risk [in revising Bond] demonstrates his worthiness as an actor.' It also rocketed his earning scale and set him up for the sometimes radical choices of the eighties that yielded pictures of enduring quality like *The Name of the Rose* and *The Untouchables*. In that simply obvious regard Connery didn't just create an enjoyable diversion in sixties Bond: he created, then *developed* a dramatic trick to broaden the range of his possibilities, test his limits and give us more.

When I published the first version of this text in 1983, Connery had just finished *Never Say Never Again* and was $5 million richer. In talking to his friends and co-workers I frequently prodded the theory that he now had ample money to wind down his acting career. After all, scores of top-liners before him crested, took the millions, and did just that. Elizabeth Taylor is a case in point. Paul Newman. Brando. A close friend told me, 'He says he still doesn't have the money to retire. And maybe that is true when you look at his lifestyle – any wealthy man's lifestyle. But that isn't all the story . . . Sean has a genuine *need* to act. He is an actor's actor, and he is a punters' actor. It is different from Brando because it is in his blood.'

In June of 1991 as Connery held a press conference in the august, panelled chambers of Edinburgh District Council and faced the faces of his childhood, he defined conclusively the man he is. He was there, proudly, to acknowledge the Freeman of Edinburgh award and informally thank his town. Almost immediately the inevitable question was thrown at him: he spoke so often, so lovingly, of Scotland; wasn't it time he came home? Connery sighed and dreamed. He was always excited to come home, he said, because the people made him feel good here, and he loved the local sense of humour. 'But the reality is I am still enthusiastic about the work I do. I don't live anywhere really. I am living where I am working . . .'

No one in the room challenged him. But then it would have seemed a travesty, because his honesty and his commitment were writ large in the pages of cinema history, and Edinburgh itself was acknowledging it here and now in making a milkman a Freeman, and putting him up there with Churchill, Ben Jonson, David Livingstone, Eisenhower and Lord Hume.

A little time before, John Brady, the football chum from the biggie, summed up the Big Tommy Connery he knew: 'Sean made it, didn't he? Fountainbridge is very far away to him now. But, no, he hasn't lost touch. I haven't seen him for quite a bit but my wife and I were thinking of dropping by when we were in America on holidays. There'd be no problem. Tommy doesn't change . . .'

Terence Young, the director responsible for lighting the Bond touchpaper, contends that, with the probable exception of Lassie, no actor has been changed so little by success as Sean Connery. Others, from Michael Hayes to Richard Lester, speak of his natural talent, his unwavering spirit, his lack of ego trappings, his honesty.

'What is he like as a friend?' I asked Michael Caine over paper cartons of tasteless tea on a noisy, floodlit film set.

'Ordinary.' The direct, rheumy eyes squinted plaintively and the large hands spread. 'I wish I could say more, or less,' Caine twinkled. 'But Sean's just an ordinary bloke who likes his job and gets on with it.'

Therein lies the story, beginning to end. In 1973, divorcing from Diane Cilento, Connery made a solemn vow never to talk to anyone about his personal life. His loyalties have been tried and tested enough to explain forever his resistance to press grilling. Evaluating his own talents he always grunts evasively: 'I may not be qualified to be an actor, but I'm damned sure not qualified to be anything else.' Future hopes, he told a German magazine during *Five Days One Summer*, might be reduced to 'a little living, a little work, support my children and die quickly and without pain.'

Ultimately, to those who know him, James Bond, past or future, is irrelevant – of as much consequence as the proverbial sparrow's tears. Sean Connery, the echoes swell, is just a decent bloke who made good. 'A nice wee lad,' Fountainbridgers will tell you. Somehow, walking down the cobbled byways of Auld Reekie, talking to the scattered few who were left behind as the tenements fell, even luminous Oscar pales. Sean Connery has seen the glories of the gutter and the gutters of glory. One imagines he hungers for no greater honours.

Filmography

NO ROAD BACK (Great Britain; RKO-Radio, 1956)
Director: Montgomery Tully. Producer: Steve Pallos. Screenplay: Charles A. Leeds and Montgomery Tully, from the play *Madame Tic Tac* by Falkland L. Cary and Philip Weathers. Photography: Lionel Banes. Editor: Jim Connock. Music: John Veale. Art director: John Stoll. Running time: 83 minutes. In black & white. Certificate A.
Production company: Gibralter Pictures.
John Railton – Skip Homeier; *Clem Hayes* – Paul Carpenter; *Beth* – Patricia Dainton; *Inspector Harris* – Norman Woodland; *Mrs Railton* – Margaret Rawlings; *Marguerite* – Eleanor Summerfield; *Rudge Harvey* – Alfie Bass; *Spike* – Sean Connery; *Sergeant Brooks* – Robert Bruce; *Garage Man* – Philip Ray; *Night Watchman* – Thomas Gallagher; *The dog Rummy* – Romulus of Welham.

HELL DRIVERS (Great Britain; Rank, 1957)
Director: Cy Endfield. Producer: S. Benjamin Fisz. Executive producer: Earl St John. Screenplay: John Kruse and Cy Endfield. Photography: Geoffrey Unsworth. Editor: John D. Guthridge. Music: Hubert Clifford. Art director: Ernest Archer. Running time: 108 minutes. In black & white and VistaVision. Certificate A.
Production company: Aqua Film Production.
Tom – Stanley Baker; *Gino* – Herbert Lom; *Lucy* – Peggy Cummins; *Red* – Patrick McGoohan; *Cartley* – William Hartnell; *Ed* – Wilfrid Lawson; *Dusty* – Sidney James; *Tinker* – Alfie Bass; *Scottie* – Gordon Jackson; *Jimmy* – David McCallum; *Johnny* – Sean Connery; *Pop* – Wensley Pithey; *Tub* – George Murcell; *Ma West* – Marjorie Rhodes; *Blonde* – Vera Day; *Mother* – Beatrice Varley; *Assistant manager* – Robin Bailey; *Spinster* – Jean St

Clair; *Chick* – Jerry Stovin; *Doctor* – John Horsley; *Nurse* – Marianne Stone; *Barber Joe* – Ronald Clarke.

TIME LOCK (Great Britain; British Lion, 1957)
Director: Gerald Thomas. Producer: Peter Rogers. Screenplay: Peter Rogers, from the play for television by Arthur Hailey. Photography: Peter Hennessy. Editor: John Trumper. Music: Stanley Black. Art director: Norman Arnold. Running time: 73 minutes. In black & white. Certificate A.
Production company: Romulus. A Beaconsfield Production.
Dawson – Robert Beatty; *Lucille Walker* – Betty McDowall; *Steven Walker* – Vincent Winter; *Colin Walker* – Lee Patterson; *Evelyn Webb* – Sandra Francis; *George Foster* – Alan Gifford; *Inspector Andrews* – Robert Ayres; *Howard Zeeder* – Victor Wood; *Max Jarvis* – Jack Cunningham; *Dr Foy* – Peter Mannering; *1st Police Officer* – Roland Brand; *2nd Police Officer* – David Williams; *Reporter* – Larry Cross; *Dr Hewitson* – Gordon Tanner; *Foreman* – John Paul; *Bank Customer* – Donald Ewer; *1st Welder* – Murray Kash; *2nd Welder* – Sean Connery.

ACTION OF THE TIGER (Great Britain; MGM, 1957)
Director: Terence Young. Producer: Kenneth Harper. Screenplay: Robert Carson, based on the book by James Wellard. Photography: Desmond Dickinson. Editor: Frank Clarke. Music: Humphrey Searle. Art director: Scott McGregor. Running time: 93 minutes. In Technicolor Cinemascope. Certificate U.
Production company: Claridge Film Production.
Carson – Van Johnson; *Tracy* – Martine Carol; *Trifon* – Herbert Lom; *Henri* – Gustavo Rocco; *Kol Stendho* – Jose Nieto; *The Countess* – Helen Haye; *Mara* – Anna Gerber; *Security Guard* – Anthony Dawson; *Mike* – Sean Connery; *Katina* – Yvonne Warren.

ANOTHER TIME, ANOTHER PLACE (Great Britain; Paramount, 1958)
Director: Lewis Allen. Producers: Lewis Allen and Smedley Aston. Executive producer: Joseph Kaufman. Screenplay: Stanley Mann, from the novel by Lenore Coffee. Photography: Jack Hildyard. Editor: Geoffrey Foot. Music: Douglas Gamley. Art director: Tom Morahan. Running time: 95 minutes. In black & white and VistaVision. Certificate A.
Production company: A Kaydor Production.

Sara Scott – Lana Turner; *Carter Reynolds* – Barry Sullivan; *Kay Trevor* – Glynis Johns; *Mark Trevor* – Sean Connery; *Jake Klein* – Sidney James; *Alan Thompson* – Terence Longdon; *Mrs Bunker* – Doris Hare; *Brian Trevor* – Martin Stephens.

DARBY O'GILL AND THE LITTLE PEOPLE (USA; Walt Disney, 1959)

Director: Robert Stevenson. Producer: Walt Disney. Screenplay: Lawrence Edward Watkin, suggested by H. T. Kavanagh's *Darby O'Gill* stories. Photography: Winton C. Hoch. Editor: Stanley Johnson. Special photographic effects: Peter Ellenshaw and Eustace Lycett. Technical advisor: Michael O'Herlihy. Music: Oliver Wallace. Songs: 'Wishing Song' by Lawrence Edward Watkin and 'Pretty Irish Girl' by Oliver Wallace. Assistant director: Robert G. Shannon. Running time: 90 minutes in original release; 89 minutes in 1978 re-release. In Technicolor. Certificate U.
Production company: Walt Disney Productions.
Darby O'Gill – Albert Sharpe; *Katie* – Janet Munro; *Michael McBride* – Sean Connery; *King Brian* – Jimmy O'Dea; *Pony Sugrue* – Kieron Moore; *Sheelah* – Estelle Winwood; *Lord Fitzpatrick* – Walter Fitzgerald; *Father Murphy* – Dennis O'Dea; *Tom Kerrigan* – J. G. Devlin; *Phadrig Oge* – Jack McGowran; *Paddy Scanlon* – Farrell Pelly; *Molly Malloy* – Nora O'Mahoney.

TARZAN'S GREATEST ADVENTURE (Great Britain; Paramount, 1959)

Director: John Guillermin. Producer: Sy Weintraub. Screenplay: Berne Giler and John Guillermin, from a story by Les Crutchfield, based on the characters created by Edgar Rice Burroughs. Photography: Skeets Kelly. Editor: Bert Rule. Art director: Michael Stringer. Running time: 84 minutes. In Technicolor. Certificate U.
Production company: Solar Films.
Tarzan – Gordon Scott; *Slade* – Anthony Quayle; *Angie* – Sara Shane; *Toni* – Scilla Gabel; *O'Bannion* – Sean Connery; *Kruger* – Niall MacGinnis; *Dino* – Al Mulock.

THE FRIGHTENED CITY (Great Britain; Anglo Amalgamated, 1961)

Director: John Lemont. Producers: John Lemont and Leigh Vance. Screenplay: Leigh Vance. Photography: Desmond Dickinson. Editor: Bernard Gribble. Music: Norrie Paramor. Songs:

'Marvellous Lie' and 'I laughed at Love'; lyrics by Bunny Lewis, music by Norrie Paramor. Assistant director: Basil Rayburn. Running time: 98 minutes. In black & white. Certificate A. Production company: A Zodiac Production.

Waldo Zhernikov – Herbert Lom; *Det. Inspector Sayers* – John Gregson; *Paddy Damion* – Sean Connery; *Harry Foulcher* – Alfred Marks; *Anya* – Yvonne Romain; *Sadie* – Olive McFarland; *Ogle* – Frederick Piper; *Hood* – John Stone; *Alf Peters* – David Davies; *Tanky Thomas* – Tom Bowman; *Nero* – Robert Cawdron; *Sanchetti* – George Pastell; *Supt. Carter* – Patrick Holt; *Avril* – Sheena Marsh; *Frankie Farmer* – Patrick Jordan; *Moffat* – Arnold Diamond; *Tyson* – Jack Stewart; *Security Officer* – Martin Wyldeck; *Warder* – John Baker; *Wally* – Kenneth Griffiths; *Salty Brewer* – Douglas Robinson; *Wingrove* – Robert Percival; *Barmaid (Riviera)* – Marianne Stone; *TV Announcer* – John Witty; *Informer* – J. G. Devlin; *Hatcheck girl* – Julie Shearing; *Pretty secretary (Wingrove)* – April Wilding; *Sophie Peters* – Vanda Godsell; *Asst. Commissioner* – Bruce Seton; *Myra* – Yvonne Ball; *Title scene thug* – Kenneth Warren; *Alf's 1st thug* – Stephen Cato; *Alf's 2nd thug* – James Fitzpatrick; *Head waiter (Taboo club)* – Neal Arden; *Miss Rush* – Joan Haythorne; *Publican* – Stuart Saunders; *Lippy Green* – John Maxin; *Lord Buncholme* – Tony Hawes; *Rover driver* – Joe Wadham; *Clarissa* – Penelope Service; *Billy Agnew* – Walter Brown; *Basher Preeble* – Maurice Bush; *Pianist (Taboo club)* – Norrie Paramor; *Choreographer (Taboo club)* – Malcolm Clare; *Pretty girl (Taboo club)* – Yvonne Buckingham; *Cigarette girl (Taboo club)* – Eve Eden.

ON THE FIDDLE (Great Britain; Anglo Amalgamated, 1961)
USA title: *Operation Snafu*
Director: Cyril Frankel. Producer: S. Benjamin Fisz. Screenplay: Harold Buchman, from the novel *Stop at a Winner* by R. F. Delderfield. Photography: Edward Scaife. Editor: Peter Hunt. Music: Malcolm Arnold. Art director: John Blezard. Running time: 97 minutes. In black & white. Certificate A.
Production company: S. Benjamin Fisz.

Pedlar Pascoe – Sean Connery; *Horace Pope* – Alfred Lynch; *Gp/Cpt Bascombe* – Cecil Parker; *Trowbridge* – Wilfred Hyde White; *Cooksley* – Stanley Holloway; *Mrs Cooksley* – Kathleen Harrison; *Flora McNaughton* – Eleanor Summerfield; *Doctor* – Eric Barker; *Air Gunner* – Terence Longdon; *T/Sgt Buzzer* – Alan King; *Iris* – Ann Beach; *Hixon* – John Le Mesurier; *1st Airman* – Victor Maddern; *Huxtable* – Harry Locke; *Sister* – Viola

Keats; *Pope* – Peter Sinclair; *Lil* – Edna Morris; *Sergeant* – Thomas Heathcote; *P.C.* – Jack Lambert; *Ticket Collector* – Cyril Smith; *Baldwin* – Simon Lack; *Sgt Ellis* – Graham Stark; *WAAF Corporal* – Jean Aubrey; *WAAF Sergeant* – Miriam Karlin; *Cpl. Gittens* – Bill Owen; *Lancing* – Ian Whittaker; *Cpl. Reeves* – Harold Goodwin; *Mavis* – Barbara Windsor; *Dusty* – Kenneth Warren; *Lady Edith* – Beatrix Lehmann; *US Snowdrop* – Gary Cockrell.

THE LONGEST DAY (USA; Twentieth Century-Fox, 1962)
Directors: Ken Annakin (British exteriors); Andrew Marton (American exteriors); Bernhard Wicki (German episodes); Darryl F. Zanuck (American interiors). Producer: Darryl F. Zanuck. Screenplay: Cornelius Ryan, based on his book. Additional episodes written by: Romain Gary, James Jones, David Pursall and Jack Seddon. Photography: Jean Bourgoin, Henri Persin and Walter Wottitz; Guy Tabary in charge of helicopter shots. Editor: Samuel E. Beetley. Music: Maurice Jarre. Thematic music: Paul Anka. Assistant directors: Bernhard Farrel, Louis Pitzélé, Gerard Renateau and Henri Sokal. Supervisor of special action: John Sullivan. Running time: 108 minutes. In black & white. Certificate A.
Production company: Darryl F. Zanuck.
RAF pilot – Richard Burton; *Capt. Maud* – Kenneth More; *Lord Lovat* – Peter Lawford; *Major John Howard* – Richard Todd; *Brig. General Parker* – Leo Genn; *British Padre* – John Gregson; *Private Flanagan* – Sean Connery; *Briefing Officer* – Jack Hedley; *Private Watney* – Michael Medwin; *Private Clough* – Norman Rossington; *Admiral Ramsey* – John Robinson; *Group Capt. Stagg* – Patrick Barr; *RAF officer* – Leslie Phillips; *RAF pilot* – Donald Houston; *Private Coke* – Frank Finlay; *Lieutenant Walsh* – Lyndon Brook; *Ronald Callen* – Bryan Coleman; *General Montgomery* – Trevor Reid; *Air Chief Marshal Leigh-Mallory* – Simon Lack; *Air Chief Marshal Tedder* – Louis Mounier; *Wren* – Sian Phillips; *Lt. Col. Vandervoort* – John Wayne; *Brig. General Cota* – Robert Mitchum; *Brig. General Roosevelt* – Henry Fonda; *Brig. General Gavin* – Robert Ryan; *Destroyer Commander* – Rod Steiger; *US Ranger* – Robert Wagner; *Private Dutch Schultz* – Richard Beymer; *Major-General Haines* – Mel Ferrer; *Sgt. Fuller* – Jeffrey Hunter; *US Ranger* – Paul Anka; *Private Martini* – Sal Mineo; *Private Morris* – Roddy McDowall; *Lieutenant Sheen* – Stuart Whitman; *Captain Harding* – Steve Forrest; *Col. Tom Newton* – Eddie Albert. *General R. O. Barton* – Edmond

O'Brien; *US Ranger* – Fabian; *Private John Steele* – Red Buttons; *Lieutenant Wilson* – Tom Tryon; *Major-General Smith* – Alexander Knox; *US Ranger* – Tommy Sands; *Captain Frank* – Ray Danton; *General Eisenhower* – Henry Grace; *Private Harris* – Mark Damon; *Private Wilder* – Dewey Martin; *Colonel Caffey* – John Crawford; *Joe Williams* – Ron Randell; *Lieutenant-General Bradley* – Nicholas Stuart; *Rear-Admiral Kirk* – John Moillon; *Janine Boitard* – Irina Demick; *Mayor of Colleville* – Bourvil; *Father Roulland* – Jean-Louis Barrault; *Commander Philippe Kieffer* – Christian Marquand; *Madame Barrault* – Arletty; *Mother Superior* – Madeline Renaud; *Sergeant de Montlaur* – Georges Riviere; *Rear-Admiral Jaujard* – Jean Servais; *Alexandre Renaud* – Georges Wilson; *Louis* – Fernand Ledoux; *Jean* – Maurice Poli; *Housekeeper* – Alice Tissot; *Naval captain* – Jo D'Avra; *Major-General Blumontritt* – Curt Jurgens; *Field-Marshal Rommel* – Werner Hinz; *Field-Marshal von Rundstedt* – Paul Hartmann; *Sergeant Kaffeeklatsch* – Gert Frobe; *Major Pluskat* – Hans Christian Blech; *Major-General Max Pemsel* – Wolfgang Preiss; *Lieutenant-Colonel Ocker* – Peter Van Eyck; *Colonel Priller* – Heinz Reincke; *General Erich Marcks* – Richard Munch; *General Hans von Salmuth* – Ernest Schroeder; *Captain Ernst During* – Karl Meisel; *Lieutenant-Colonel Meyer* – Heinz Spitner; *Aide to Lt.-Col. Meyer* – Robert Freytag; *Colonel General Jodl* – Wolfgang Luckschy; *Captain Hellmuth Lang* – Til Kiwe; *Major-General Dr. Hans Speidel* – Wolfgang Buttner; *Frau Rommel* – Ruth Hausmeister; *Manfred Rommel* – Michael Hinz; *Colonel Schiller* – Paul Roth; *Sergeant Bergsdorf* – Hartmut Rock; *Luftwaffe General* – Karl John; *Luftwaffe Major* – Dietmar Schonherr; *Lieutenant Fritz Theen* – Reiner Penkert.
Note: Sean Connery uncredited in some publicity handouts.

DR NO (Great Britain; United Artists, 1962)
Director: Terence Young. Producers: Harry Saltzman and Albert R. Broccoli. Screenplay: Richard Maibaum, Johanna Harwood and Berkely Mather, from the novel by Ian Fleming. Photography: Ted Moore. Editor: Peter Hunt. Production designer: Ken Adam. Art director: Syd Cain. Music: Monty Norman. 'James Bond Theme' played by The John Barry Orchestra. Assistant director: Clive Reed. Running time: 105 minutes. In Technicolor. Certificate A.
Production company: Eon Productions.
James Bond – Sean Connery; *Honey Rider* – Ursula Andress; *Dr No* – Joseph Wiseman; *Felix Leiter* – Jack Lord; *M* – Bernard Lee;

Professor Dent – Anthony Dawson; *Quarrel* – John Kitzmiller; *Miss Taro* – Zena Marshall; *Sylvia* – Eunice Gayson; *Miss Moneypenny* – Lois Maxwell; *Puss-Feller* – Lester Prendergast; *Major Boothroyd* – Peter Burton; *Strangways* – Tim Moxon; *Girl Photographer* – Margaret LeWars; *Jones* – Reggie Carter; *Duff* – William Foster-Davis; *Playdell-Smith* – Louis Blaazer; *Sister Rose* – Michele Mok; *Mary* – Dolores Keator; *Sister Lily* – Yvonne Shima.

FROM RUSSIA WITH LOVE (Great Britain; United Artists, 1963)
Director: Terence Young. Producers: Harry Saltzman and Albert R. Broccoli. Screenplay: Richard Maibaum and Johanna Harwood, from the novel by Ian Fleming. Photography: Ted Moore. Editor: Peter Hunt. Art director: Syd Cain. Set dresser: Freda Pearson. Music: John Barry Title song: Lionel Bart, sung by Matt Munro. Assistant director: David Anderson. Stunt work arranged by Peter Perkins. Running time: 116 minutes. In Technicolor. Certificate A.
Production company: Eon Productions.
James Bond – Sean Connery; *Tatiana Romanova* – Daniela Bianchi; *Kerim Bey* – Pedro Armendariz; *Rosa Klebb* – Lotte Lenya; *Red Grant* – Robert Shaw; *M* – Bernard Lee; *Sylvia* – Eunice Gayson; *Morzeny* – Walter Gotell; *Vavra* – Francis de Wolff; *Train Conductor* – George Pastell; *Kerim's girl* – Nadja Regin; *Miss Moneypenny* – Lois Maxwell; *Vida* – Aliza Gur; *Zora* – Martine Beswick; *Kronsteen* – Vladek Sheybal; *Belly dancer* – Leila; *Foreign agent* – Hasan Ceylan; *Krilencu* – Fred Haggerty; *Rolls chauffeur* – Neville Jason; *Benz* – Peter Bayliss; *Mehmet* – Mushet Auaer; *Rhoda* – Peter Brayham; *Boothroyd* – Desmond Llewelyn; *Grant's masseuse* – Jan Williams; *McAdams* – Peter Madden.

WOMAN OF STRAW (Great Britain; United Artists, 1964)
Director: Basil Dearden. Producer: Michael Relph. Screenplay: Robert Muller, Stanley Mann and Michael Relph, from the novel by Catherine Arley. Photography: Otto Heller, Editor: John D. Guthridge. Production designer: Ken Adam. Music: Muir Mathieson. Assistant director: Clive Reed. Miss Lollobrigida's clothes by Dior. Running time: 117 minutes. In Eastman Colour. Certificate A.
Production company: Novus Production.
Maria – Gina Lollobrigida; *Anthony Richmond* – Sean Connery;

Charles Richmond – Ralph Richardson; *Thomas* – Johnny Sekka; *Baines* – Laurence Hardy; *Fenton* – Danny Daniels; *Third Executive* – A. J. Brown; *Yacht Captain* – Peter Madden; *Lomer* – Alexander Knox; *First Executive* – Edward Underdown; *Second Executive* – Georg Curzon; *Judge* – Andre Morell; *Chauffeur* – Robert Bruce; *Wardress* – Peggy Marshall.

MARNIE (USA; Rank UK, 1964)
Director: Alfred Hitchcock. Producer: Alfred Hitchcock. Screenplay: Jay Presson Allen, from the novel by Winston Graham. Photography: Robert Burks. Editor: George Tomasini. Sets: Robert Boyle and George Milo. Music: Bernard Herrmann. Assistant director: James H. Brown. Running time: 130 minutes. In Technicolor. Certificate X.
Production company: Universal International.
Mark Ruthland – Sean Connery; *Marnie* – 'Tippi' Hedren; *Lil Mainwaring* – Diane Baker; *Sidney Strutt* – Martin Gabel; *Bernice Edgar* – Louise Latham; *Cousin Bob* – Bob Sweeney; *Mr Ruthland* – Alan Napier; *Sam Ward* – S. John Launer; *Susan Clabon* – Mariette Hartley; *Sailor* – Bruce Dern; *First detective* – Henry Beckman; *Rita* – Edith Evanson; *Mrs Turpin* – Meg Wyllie.

GOLDFINGER (Great Britain; United Artists, 1964)
Director: Guy Hamilton. Producers: Harry Saltzman and Albert R. Broccoli. Screenplay: Richard Maibaum and Paul Dehn, from the novel by Ian Fleming. Photography: Ted Moore. Editor: Peter Hunt. Production designer: Ken Adam. Art director: Peter Murton. Music: John Barry. Title song: lyrics by Leslie Bricusse and Anthony Newley, music by John Barry, sung by Shirley Bassey. Assistant director: Frank Ernst. Action sequences by Bob Simmons. Running time: 109 minutes. In Technicolor. Certificate A.
Production company: Eon Productions.
James Bond – Sean Connery; *Pussy Galore* – Honor Blackman; *Goldfinger* – Gert Frobe; *Jill Masterson* – Shirley Eaton; *Tilly Masterson* – Tania Mallet; *Oddjob* – Harold Sakata; *M* – Bernard Lee; *Solo* – Martin Benson; *Felix Leiter* – Cec Linder; *Simmons* – Austin Willis; *Miss Moneypenny* – Lois Maxwell; *Midnight* – Bill Nagy; *Capungo* – Alf Joint; *Old lady* – Varley Thomas; *Bonita* – Nadja Regin; *Sierra* – Raymond Young; *Smithers* – Richard Vernon; *Brunskill* – Denis Cowles; *Kisch* – Michael Mellinger;

Mr Ling – Bert Kwouk; *Strap* – Hal Galili; *Henchman* – Lenny Rabin; *Q* – Desmond Llewelyn.

THE HILL (Great Britain; MGM, 1965)
Director: Sidney Lumet. Producer: Kenneth Hyman. Screenplay: Ray Rigby, based on the original play by Ray Rigby and R. S. Allen. Photography: Oswald Morris. Editor: Thelma Connell. Technical advisor: George Montford. Assistant directors: Frank Ernst and Pedro Vidal. Running time: 123 minutes. In black & white. Certificate X.
Production company: A Kenneth Hyman Production.
Joe Roberts – Sean Connery; *R. S. M. Wilson* – Harry Andrews; *Harris* – Ian Bannen; *George Stevens* – Alfred Lynch; *Jacko King* – Ossie Davis; *Monty Bartlett* – Roy Kinnear; *Jock McGrath* – Jack Watson; *Williams* – Ian Hendry; *M.O.* – Sir Michael Redgrave; *Commandant* – Norman Bird; *Burton* – Neil McCarthy; *Walters* – Howard Goorney; *Martin* – Tony Caunter.

THUNDERBALL (Great Britain; United Artists, 1965)
Director: Terence Young. Producer: Kevin McClory. Screenplay: Richard Maibaum and John Hopkins, based on the original treatment by Jack Whittingham, Kevin McClory and Ian Fleming. Photography: Ted Moore. Editor: Peter Hunt. Production designer: Ken Adam. Art director: Peter Murton. Music: John Barry. Title song: lyrics by Don Black, music by John Barry, sung by Tom Jones. Assistant director: Gus Agosti. Underwater sequences: Ivan Tors Underwater Studios Ltd. Underwater director: Ricou Browning. Underwater cameraman: Lamar Boren. Action sequences by Bob Simmons. Running time: 130 minutes. In Technicolor Panavision. Certificate A.
Production company: Eon Productions.
James Bond – Sean Connery; *Domino* – Claudine Auger; *Largo* – Adolfo Celi; *Fiona* – Luciana Paluzzi; *Felix Leiter* – Rik Van Nutter; *M* – Bernard Lee; *Paula* – Martine Beswick; *Count Lippe* – Guy Doleman; *Patricia* – Molly Peters; *Q* – Desmond Llewelyn; *Miss Moneypenny* – Lois Maxwell; *Foreign Secretary* – Roland Culver; *Pinder* – Earl Cameron; *Palazzi* – Paul Stassino; *Madame Boiter* – Rose Alba; *Vargas* – Philip Locke; *Kutee* – George Pravda; *Janni* – Michael Brennan; *Group Captain* – Leonard Sachs; *Air Vice Marshal* – Edward Underdown; *Kenniston* – Reginald Beckwith.

A FINE MADNESS (USA; Warner-Pathe, 1966)
Director: Irvin Kershner. Producer: Jerome Hellman. Screenplay: Elliott Baker, based upon his novel. Photography: Ted McCord. Editor: William Ziegler. Music: John Addison. Assistant director: Russell Llewellyn. Running time: 104 minutes. In Technicolor. Certificate A.
Production company: A Pan Arts Production.
Samson Shillitoe – Sean Connery; *Rhoda* – Joanne Woodward; *Lydia West* – Jean Seberg; *Dr Oliver West* – Patrick O'Neal; *Dr Vera Kropotkin* – Colleen Dewhurst; *Dr Menken* – Clive Revill; *Dr Vorbeck* – Werner Peters; *Daniel K. Papp* – John Fiedler; *Mrs Fish* – Kay Medford; *Mr Fitzgerald* – Jackie Coogan; Ms Tupperman – Zohra Lampert; *Miss Walnicki* – Sue Anne Langdon; *Leonard Tupperman* – Sorrell Booke; *Mrs Fitzgerald* – Bibi Osterwald; *Chairwoman* – Mabel Albertson.

YOU ONLY LIVE TWICE (Great Britain; United Artists, 1967)
Director: Lewis Gilbert. Producers: Harry Saltzman and Albert R. Broccoli. Screenplay: Roald Dahl. Additional story material: Harold Jack Bloom. Based on the novel by Ian Fleming. Photography: Freddie Young. Editor: Thelma Connell. Production designer: Ken Adams. Art director: Harry Pottle. Music: John Barry. Title song: lyrics by Leslie Bricusse, music by John Barry, sung by Nancy Sinatra. Second Unit director: Peter Hunt. Technical advisor: Kikumaru Okuda. Underwater cameraman: Lamar Boren. Aerial camerman: John Jordan. Action sequences by Bob Simmons. Assistant director: William P. Cartlidge. Running time: 116 minutes. In Technicolor Panavision. Certificate A.
Production company: Eon–Danjaq.
James Bond – Sean Connery; *Aki* – Akiko Wakabayashi; *Tiger Tanaka* – Tetsuro Tamba; *Kissy Suzuki* – Mie Hama; *Osato* – Teru Shimada; *Helga Brandt* – Karin Dor; *Miss Moneypenny* – Lois Maxwell; *Q* – Desmond Llewelyn; *Henderson* – Charles Gray; *Chinese girl* – Tsai Chin; *M* – Bernard Lee; *Blofeld* – Donald Pleasence; *American President* – Alexander Knox; *President's aide* – Robert Hutton; *SPECTRE 3* – Burt Kwouk; *SPECTRE 4* – Michael Chow.

SHALAKO (Great Britain; Warner-Pathe, 1968)
Director: Edward Dmytryk. Producer: Euan Lloyd. Screenplay: J. J. Griffith, Hal Hopper and Scot Finch, from the screen story by Clarke Reynolds, based on the novel by Louis L'Amour. Photography: Ted Moore. Editor: Bill Blunden. Special effects:

Michael Collins. Music: Robert Farnon. Musical director: Muir Mathieson. Title song: lyrics by Jim Dale. Art director: Herbert Smith. Running time: 113 minutes. In Technicolor Franscope. Certificate A.
Production company: Kingston Films. A Dimitri de Grunwald Production.
Shalako – Sean Connery; *Irina Lazaar* – Brigitte Bardot; *Bosky Fulton* – Stephen Boyd; *Sir Charles Daggett* – Jack Hawkins; *Frederick von Hallstatt* – Peter Van Eyck; *Lady Daggett* – Honor Blackman; *Chato* – Woody Strode; *Mako* – Eric Sykes; *Henry Clarke* – Alexander Knox; *Elena Clarke* – Valerie French; *Rojas* – Julian Mateos; *Buffalo* – Donald Barry; *Chato's father* – Rodd Redwing; *Loco* – 'Chief' Elmer Smith; *Hans* – Hans De Vries; *Peter Wells* – Walter Brown; *Marker* – Charles Stinaker; *Luther* – Bob Cunningham; *Hockett* – John Clark; *Johnson* – Bob Hall.

THE MOLLY MAGUIRES (USA; Paramount, 1969)
Director: Martin Ritt. Producers: Martin Ritt and Walter Bernstein. Screenplay: Walter Bernstein, suggested by a book by Arthur H. Lewis. Photography: James Wong Howe. Editor: Frank Bracht. Script supervisor: Marvin Weldon. Second Unit director: Oscar Rudolph. Second Unit photography: Morris Hartzband. Technical advisor Mine Operations: Joseph Lawrence. Music: Henry Mancini. Songs: 'Eileen Aroon', 'Cockles and Mussels and Gary Owen', all traditional Irish songs. Assistant director: James Rosenberger. Running time: 125 minutes. In Technicolor. Certificate A.
Production company: A Martin Ritt Production.
James McParlan – Richard Harris; *Jack Kehoe* – Sean Connery; *Mary Raines* – Samantha Eggar; *Davies* – Frank Finlay; *Dougherty Anthony Zerbe; Mrs Kehoe* – Bethel Leslie; *Frazier* – Art Lund; *Frank McAndrew* – Anthony Costello; *Father O'Connor* – Philip Bourneuf; *Mr Raines* – Brendan Dillon; *Mrs Frazier* – Frances Heflin; *Jenkins* – John Alderson; *Bartender* – Malachy McCourt; *Mrs McAndrew* – Susan Goodman.

THE RED TENT (Italy/USSR; Paramount, 1969)
Director: Mickail K. Kalatozov. Producer: Franco Cristaldi. Screenplay: Ennio De Concini and Richard Adams. Photography: Leonid Kalashnikov. Editor: John Shirley. Second Unit director: Igor Petrov. Music: Ennio Morricone. Assistant director: Valerj Sirovsky. Running time: 121 minutes. In Technicolor. Certificate U.

Production company: A Vides Cinematografica, Rome-
Mosfilm, Moscow Coproduction.
General Nobile – Peter Finch; *Amundsen* – Sean Connery;
Valeria – Claudia Cardinale; *Lundborg* – Hardy Kruger; *Biagi*
– Mario Adorf; *Romagna* – Massimo Girotti; *Zappi* – Luigi
Vannucchi; *Malmgren* – Edward Marzevic; *Viglieri* – Boris
Kmelnizki; *Trioani* – Juri Solomin; *Behounek* – Juri Vizbor;
Mariano – Donatas Banionis; *Cecioni* – Otar Koberidze;
Samoilovich – Grigori Gaj; *Chuknovsky* – Nikita Mikhalkov;
Kolka – Nicolai Ivanov
Note: Original Italian release title: *La Tenda Rossa*.

THE ANDERSON TAPES (USA; Columbia–Warner, 1971)
Director: Sidney Lumet. Producer: Robert M. Weitman.
Screenplay: Frank R. Pierson, based on the novel by Lawrence
Sanders. Photography: Arthur J. Ornitz. Editor: Joanne Burke.
Technical consultant: Robert G. Battie, Script supervisor: Nick
Sgarro. Music: Quincy Jones. Assistant director: Alan
Hopkins. All electronic devices are authentic and provided by
The Wiliam J. Burns International Detective Agency, Inc.
Video and tape recorders, cameras and related equipment by
Ampex Corporation. Running time: 99 minutes. In Techni-
color. Certificate AA. Production company: A Robert M.
Weitman Production.
Anderson – Sean Connery; *Ingrid* – Dyan Cannon; *Haskins* –
Martin Balsman; *Delaney* – Ralph Meeker; *Angelo* – Alan
King; *The Kid* – Christopher Walken; *Parelli* – Val Avery;
Spencer – Dick Wiliams; *Everson* – Garrett Morris; *Pop* – Stan
Gottlieb; *Jimmy* – Paul Benjamin; *Psychologist* – Anthony Hol-
land; *Werner* – Richard B. Schull; *Dr Rubicoff* – Conrad Bain;
Miss Kaler – Margaret Hamilton; *Mrs Hathaway* – Judith
Lowry; *Bingham* – Max Showalter; *Mrs Bingham* – Janet
Ward; *Jerry Bingham* – Scott Jacoby; *Longene* – Norman Rose;
Mrs Longene – Meg Miles; *O'Learly* – John Call; *D'Medico* –
Ralph Stanley; *Vanessi* – John Braden; *Nurse* – Paula Trueman;
First Agent – Michael Miller; *Johnson* – Michael Prince; *Papa
Angelo* – Frank Macetta; *Eric* – Jack Doroshow; *Eric's friend* –
Michael Clary; *Receptionist* – Hildy Brooks; *Doctor* – Robert
Dagny; *TV watcher* – Bradford English; *Judge* – Reid
Cruckshanks; *Syc man* – Tom Signorelli; *Detective A* – Carmine
Caridi; *Sergeant Claire* – Michael Fairman; *Detective B* –
George Patelis; *Detective C* – William Da Prato; *Private
Detective* – Sam Coppola.

DIAMONDS ARE FOREVER (Great Britain; United Artists, 1971)
Director: Guy Hamilton. Producers: Harry Saltzman and Albert R. Broccoli. Screenplay: Richard Maibaum and Tom Mankiewicz. Based on the novel by Ian Fleming. Photography: Ted Moore. Editors: Bert Bates and John W. Holmes. Production designer: Ken Adams. Art directors: Jack Maxsted and Bill Kenney. Music: John Barry. Title song: lyrics by Don Black, music by John Barry, sung by Shirley Bassey. Stunt arrangers: Bob Simmons and Paul Baxley, Assistant directors: Derek Cracknell and Jerome M. Siegel. Miss St. John's costumes by Donfeld. Running time: 120 minutes. In Technicolor Panavision. Certificate A.
Production company: Eon Productions.
James Bond – Sean Connery; *Tiffany case* – Jill St. John; *Blofeld* – Charles Gray; *Plenty O'Toole* – Lana Wood; *Willard Whyte* Jimmy Dean; *Saxby* – Bruce Cabot; *Mr Kidd* – Putter Smith; *Mr Wint* – Bruce Glover; *Leiter* – Norman Burton; *Dr Metz* – Joseph Furst; *M* – Bernard Lee; *Q* – Desmond Llewelyn; *Shady Tree* – Leonard Barr; *Miss Moneypenny* – Lois Maxwell; *Mrs Whistler* – Margaret Lacey; *Peter Franks* – Joe Robinson; *'Bambi'* – Donna Garratt; *'Thumper'* – Trina Parks; *Doctor* – David de Keyser; *Sir Donald Munger* – Lawrence Naismith; *Mr Slumber* – David Bauer.

THE OFFENCE (Great Britain; United Artists, 1972)
Director: Sidney Lumet. Producer: Denis O'Dell. Screenplay: John Hopkins based on his own stage play. Photography: Gerry Fisher. Editor: John Victor Smith. Music: Harrison Birtwhistle. Assistant director; Ted Sturgis. Running time: 112 minutes. In colour. Certificate X.
Production company: Tantallon Films.
Det. Sergeant Johnson – Sean Connery; *Cartwright* – Trevor Howard; *Maureen* – Viven Merchant; *Baxter* – Ian Bannen; *Jessard* – Derek Newark; *Panton* – John Hallam; *Cameron* – Peter Bowles; *Lawson* – Ronald Radd; *Hill* – Anthony Sagar; *Lambeth* – Howard Goorney; *Garrett* – Richard Moore; *Janie* – Maxine Gordon.

ZARDOZ (Great Britain; Fox–Rank, 1974)
Director: John Boorman. Producer: John Boorman. Screenplay: John Boorman. Photography: Geoffrey Unsworth. Editor: John Merritt. Production designer: Anthony Pratt. Design and story

associate: Bill Stair. Speical effects: Jerry Johnston. Music: David
Munrow. Assistant director: Simon Reph. Costumes by Christel
Kruse Boorman, made by La Tabard Boutique, Dublin. Running
time: 104 minutes. In DeLuxe Panavision. Certificate X. (Origi-
nal running time: 105 minutes.)
Production company: John Boorman Productions.
Zed – Sean Connery; *Consuella* – Charlotte Rampling; *May* –
Sara Kestleman; *Avalow* – Saley Anne Newton; *Friend* – John
Alderton; *Arthur Frayn* – Niall Buggy; *George Saden* – Bosco
Hogan; *Apathetic* – Jessica Swift; *Star* – Bairbre Dowling; *Old
scientist* – Christopher Casson; *Death* – Reginald Jarman.

RANSOM (Great Britain; British Lion, 1974)
USA title: *The Terrorists*
Director: Caspar Wrede. Producer: Peter Rawley. Screenplay:
Paul Wheeler. Photography: Sven Nykvist. Editor: Thelma Con-
nell. Art director: Sven Wickman. Music: Jerry Goldsmith. Assis-
tant director: Beranrd Hanson. Running time: 94 minutes. In
Eastman Colour. Certificate A.
Production company: A Peter Rawley Production.
Nils Tahlvik – Sean Connery; *Petrie* – Ian McShane; *Captain
Denver* – Norman Bristow; *Bert* – John Cording; *Mrs Palmer* –
Isabel Dean; *Ferris* – William Fox; *Joe* – Richard Hampton;
Palmer – Robert Harris; *Lookout pilot* – Harry Landis; *Hislop* –
Preston Lockwood; *Bernhard* – James Maxwell; *Shepherd* – John
Quentin; *Barnes* – Jeffry Wickham; *Second pilot* – Sven Aune;
Matson – Knut Hansson; *Donner* – Kaare Kroppan; *Police
inspector* – Alf Malland; *Female housekeeper* – Noeste Schwab;
Male housekeeper – Kare Wicklund; *Poison* – Knut Wigert; *Air
hostesses* – Froeydis Damslora, Inger Heidal, Brita Rogde.

MURDER ON THE ORIENT EXPRESS (Great Britain; EMI,
1974)
Director: Sidney Lumet. Producers: John Brabourne and
Richard Goodwin. Screenplay: Paul Dehn, from the novel by
Agatha Christie. Photography: Geoffrey Unsworth. Editor:
Anne V. Coates. Production designer and costumes by: Tony
Walton. Art Director: Jack Stephens. Music: Richard Rodney
Bennett. Orchestra of the Royal Opera House, Covent Garden,
conducted by: Marcus Dods. Assistant director: Ted Sturgis.
Running time: 127½ minutes. In Technicolor. Certificate A.
Production company: A John Brabourne–Richard Goodwin
Production.

Hercule Poirot – Albert Finney; *Mrs Hubbard* – Lauren Bacall; *Bianchi* – Martin Balsam; *Greta* – Ingrid Berman; *Countess Andrenyi* – Jacqueline Bisset; *Pierre* – Jean-Pierre Cassel; *Col. Arbuthnott* – Sean Connery; *Beddoes* – John Gielgud; *Princess Dragomiroff* – Wendy Hiller; *McQueen* – Anthony Perkins; *Mary Debenham* – Vanessa Redgrave; *Hildegarde* – Rachel Roberts; *Ratchett* – Richard Widmark; *Count Andrenyi* – Michael York; *Hardman* – Colin Blakely; *Doctor* – George Coulouris; *Foscarelli* – Denis Quilley; *Conceirge* – Vernon Dobtcheff; *A.D.C.* – Jeremy Lloyd; *Chief attendant* – John Moffatt.

THE WIND AND THE LION (USA; Columbia, 1975)
Director: John Milius. Producer: Herb Jaffe. Screenplay: John Milius, based loosely on actual events. Photography: Billy Williams. Editor: Bob Wolfe. Production designer: Gil Parrondo. Special effects: Alex Weldon. Music: Jerry Goldsmith. Assistant director: Miguel A. Gil. Running time: 119 minutes. In Metrocolor Panavision. Certificate A.
Production company: A Herb Jaffe Production. Production services by Claridge Associates/Persky-Bright.
Raisuli – Sean Connery; *Eden* – Candice Bergen; *T. Roosevelt* – Brian Keith; *Hay* – John Huston; *Gummere* – Geoffrey Lewis; *Jerome* – Steve Kanaly; *Chadwick* – Roy Jenson; *Bashaw* – Vladek Sheybal; *Dreighton* – Darrell Fetty; *Wazan* – Nadim Sawalha; *Sultan* – Mark Zuber; *Von Roerkel* – Antoine St. John; *William* – Simon Harrison; *Jennifer* – Polly Gottesman; *Alice Roosevelt* – Deborah Baxter; *Gayaan* – Luis Bar Boo; *Ugly Arab* – Aldo Sambrell; *Edith* – Shirley Rothman; *Lodge* – Larry Cross; *Sketch artist* – Ben Tatar; *Japanese General* – Akio Mitamura; *1st aide* – Frank Gassman; *2nd aide* Leon Liberman; *3rd aide* – Allen Russell; *Secretary* – Michael Damian; *Root* – Alex Weldon; *Diplomat* – Howard Hagan; *1st Secret Serviceman* – Arthur Larkin; *2nd Secret Serviceman* – James Cooley; *3rd Secret Serviceman* – M. Ciudad; *Marine sergeant* – Rusty Cox; *Quentin* – Jack Cooley; *Kermit* – Chris Aller; *Mountain man* – Rupert Crabb; *1st reporter* – Charles Stalnaker; *2nd reporter* – David Lester; *3rd reporter* – Paul Rusking; *1st station man* – Carl Rapp; *Gummere's aide* – Jim Mitchell; *Station woman* – Anita Colby; *Torres* – Ricardo Palacois; *UK military advisor* – Robert Case; *Pock-faced Arab* – Felipe Solano; *Miss Hitchcock* – Audrey San Felix; *Decapitated Arab* – Charley Bravo; *Philippe* – Eduardo Bea; *Chef* – Juan Cazalilla.

THE MAN WHO WOULD BE KING (USA, Columbia–Warner, 1975)
Director: John Huston. Producer: John Foreman. Screenplay: John Huston and Gladys Hill, based on the short story by Rudyard Kipling. Photography: Oswald Morris: Editor: Russell Lloyd. Second Unit Director: Michael Moore. Production designer: Alexander Trauner. Art director: Tony Inglis. Special effects: Dick Parker. Sculptor: Giulio Srubek Tomassy. Music: Maurice Jarre. Assistant directors: Bert Batt, Michael Cheyko and Christopher Carreras. Costumes: Edith Head. Running time: 129 minutes. In colour Panavision. Certificate A.
Production company: Perskey–Bright/Devon. For Allied Artists/ Columbia.
Daniel Dravot – Sean Connery; *Peachy Carnehan* – Michael Caine; *Rudyard Kipling* – Christopher Plummer; *Billy Fish* – Saeed Jaffrey; *Kafu-Selim* – Karroum Ben Bouih; *District Commissioner* – Jack May; *Ootah* – Doghmi Larbi; *Roxanne* – Shakira Caine; *Babu* – Mohammed Shamsi; *Mulvaney* – Paul Antrim; *Ghulam* – Albert Moses; *Sikh soldier* – Kimat Singh; *Sikh soldier 2* – Gurmuks Singh; *Dancers* – Yvonne Ocampo, Nadia Atbib; *Officer* – Graham Acres. With the Blue Dancers of Goulamine.

ROBIN AND MARIAN (USA; Columbia–Warner, 1976)
Director: Richard Lester. Producer: Denis O'Dell. Executive producer: Richard Shephard. Screenplay: James Goldman. Photography: David Watkin. Editor: John Victor Smith. Production designer: Michael Stringer. Art director: Gil Perondo. Music: John Barry. Assistant director: Jose Lopez Rodero. Fight arrangers: William Hobbs and Ian McKay. Stunt sequences by Miguel Pedregosa, Joaquin Parra. Running time: 107 minutes. In colour. Certificate A.
Production company: Raster. For Columbia.
Robin Hood – Sean Connery; *Maid Marian* – Audrey Hepburn; *Sheriff of Nottingham* – Robert Shaw; *King Richard* – Richard Harris; *Little John* – Nicol Williamson; *Will Scarlett* – Denholm Elliott; *Sir Ranulf* – Kenneth Haigh; *Friar Tuck* – Ronnie Barker; *King John* – Ian Holm; *Mercadier* – Bill Maynard; *Old Defender* – Esmond Knight; *Sister Mary* – Veronica Quilligan; *Surgeon* – Peter Butterworth; *Jack* – John Barrett; *Jack's apprentice* – Kenneth Cranham; *Queen Isabella* – Victoria Merida Roja; *1st Sister* – Montserrat Julio; *2nd Sister* – Victoria Hernandez Sanguino; *3rd Sister* – Margarita Minguillon.

THE NEXT MAN (USA; Harris Films, 1976)
Director: Richard C. Sarafian. Producer: Martin Bregman. Executive producer: Emanuel L. Wolf. Screenplay: Mort Fine, Alan R. Trustman, David M. Wolf and Richard C. Sarafian, from a story by Alan R. Trustman and David M Wolf. Photography: Michael Chapman. Editor: Aram Avakian and Robert Q. Lovett. Production designer: Gene Callahan. Art director: Stuart Wurtzel. Music: Michael Kamen. Songs: 'The Next Man Theme', by Michael Kamen; French lyrics by Rosko Mercer, sung by Robert Fitoussi; 'Stay with Me' sung by Tasha Thomas. Stunt co-ordinator: Louie Elias. Running time: 107 minutes. (16 mm film.) In Technicolor.
Production company: Artists Entertainment Complex.
Khalil Abdul-Muhsen – Sean Connery; *Nicole Scott* – Cornelia Sharpe; *Hamid* – Albert Paulsen; *Al Sharif* – Adolfo Celi; *Justin* – Marco St. John; *Frank Dedario* – Ted Beniades; *Fouad* – Charles Cioffi; *New York Security Men* – Jaime Sanchez, James Bullett; *Ghassan Kaddara* – Salem Ludwig; *Yassin* – Roger Omar Serbagi; *Hafim Othman* – Tom Klunis; *Abdel-Latif Khaldoun* – Armand Dahan; *Atif Abbas* – Charles Randall; *Devereaux* – Ian Collier; *Salazar* – Michael Storm; *Conglomerate Chairman* – Maurice Copeland; *Zolchev* – George Pravda; *Russian Economics Minister* – Alex Jadokimov; *Andy Hampsas* – Stephen D. Newman; *TV interviewer* – Holland Taylor; *Mrs Scott* – Peggy Feury; *Mr Scott* – Patrick Bedford; *Japanese diplomat* – Toru Nagai; *Japanese UN delegate* – Ryokei Kanogogi; *Federal Security Agents* – Bill Snickowski, Lance Hendrickson; *UN reporters* – Camille Yarborough, Thomas Ruisinger, Edward Setrakian, Jack Davidson; *Press Room reporters* – Robert Levine, William Mooney; *Waldorf manager* – John McKay; *Auctioneer* – Robert Wooley; *London assassin* – Bob Simmons; *Ibn Sidki* – Tony Ellis; *Ibn Sidki's wife* – Jamila Massey; *London street dancer* – Jim Norris; *Arab at Parke Bernet* – Joe Zaloom; *Khalil's driver* – Richard Zakka; *British attaché* – Jamie Ross; *Nicole's Irish chauffeur* – David Kelly; *Customs man* – Bill Golding; *Socialite* – Diane Peterson; *Assassin in Saudi Arabia* – Mohammed Sedrihini; *Le Club* – Patrick Shields; *Junkanoo dancer* – Tony Carroll.

A BRIDGE TOO FAR (USA; United Artists, 1977)
Director: Richard Attenborough. Producers: Joseph E. Levine and Richard P. Levine. Screenplay: William Goldman, based on the book by Cornelius Ryan. Photography: Geoffrey Unsworth. Editor: Antony Gibb. Production designer: Terence Marsh. Art

293

directors: Stuart Craig, Alan Tomkins and Roy Stannard. Second Unit director: Sidney Hayers. Aerial photography: Robin Browne. Parachute cameramen: Dave Waterman and John Partington-Smith. Chief technical advisor: Kathryn Morgan Ryan. Military advisers: Colonel J. L. Waddy O.B.E. and Colonel Frank A. Gregg, USA. Music: John Addison. Assistant directors: Steve Lanning, Roy Button, Peter Waller and Geoffrey Ryan. Running time: 180 minutes. In Technicolor Panavision. Certificate A.

Production company: Joseph E. Levine Production.

Underground leader – Siem Vroom; *Underground leader's wife* – Marlies Van Alcmaer; *Underground leader's son* – Eric Van't Wout; *Field Marshal Von Rundstedt* – Wolfgang Preiss; *General Blumentritt* – Hans Von Borsody; *Café waitress* – Josephine Peeper; *Lieutenant General Browning* – Dirk Bogarde; *Major General Maxwell Taylor* – Paul Maxwell; *Major General Urquhart* – Sean Connery; *Brig. General Gavin* – Ryan O'Neal; *Major General Sosabowski* – Gene Hackman; *Field Marshal Model* – Walter Kohut; *Capt 'Harry' Bestebreurtje* – Peter Faber; *German sentry* – Hartmut Becker; *Major Fuller* – Frank Grimes; *RAF Briefing Officer* – Jeremy Kemp; *Lieutenant Colonel Mackenzie* – Donald Pickering; *Brigadier Lathbury* – Donald Douglas; *Lieutenant Cole* – Peter Settelen; *Major Steele* – Stephen Moore; *Lt. General Horrocks* – Edward Fox; *Lt. Col. J.O.E. Vandeleur* – Michael Caine; *Lt. Col. Giles Vandeleur* – Michael Byrne; *Lt. Col. Frost* – Anthony Hopkins; *Private Wicks* – Paul Copley; *Captain Glass* – Nicholas Campbell; *Staff Sergeant Dohun* – James Caan; *Colonel Sims* – Gerald Sim; *US Private* – Harry Ditson; *Organist* – Erik Chitty; *Vicar* – Brian Hawksley; *Corporal Hancock* – Colin Farrell; *Major Carlyle* – Christopher Good; *Private Morgan* – Norman Gregory; *Corporal Davies* – Alun Armstrong; *Private Dodds* – Anthony Milner; *Private Clark* – Barry McCarthy; *Sergeant Matthias* – Lex Van Delden; *Lieutenant General Bittrich* – Maximilian Schell; *Major General Ludwig* – Hardy Kruger; *Irish Guards Lieutenant* – Sean Mathias; *German Private* – Tim Beekman; *British Padre* – Edward Seckerson; *Kate Ter Horst* – Liv Ullmann; *Jan Ter Horst* – Tom Van Beek; *Colonel Stout* – Elliott Gould; *Lieutenant Cornish* – Keith Drinkel; *Old Dutch lady* – Mary Smithuysen; *Hans, her son* – Hans Croiset; *Captain Grabner* – Fred Williams; *German Lieutenant* – John Peel; *Sergeant Clegg* – John Judd; *Trooper Binns* – Ben Cross; *British Medical Officer* – Hilary Minster; *Private Andrews* – David English; *Sergeant Towns* – Ben Howard; *Captain Cleminson* –

294

Michael Graham Cox; *RAF Met. Officer* – Denholm Elliott; *US Sergeant* – Peter Gordon; *US Medical Colonel* – Arthur Hill; *Lieutenant Rafferty* – Garrick Hagon; *US Engineer* – Brian Gwaspari; *Grenadier Guards Lieutenant* – Stephen Rayment; *British Corporal* – Tim Morand; *Private Gibbs* – James Wardroper; *Colonel Barker* – Neil Kennedy; *Private 'Ginger' Marsh* – John Salthouse; *Glider Pilot* – Jonathan Hackett; *Regimental Sergeant Major* – Stanley Lebor; *Private Vincent* – Jack Galloway; *Private Long* – Milton Cadman; *'Taffy' Brace* – David Aucker; *Doctor Spaander* – Laurence Olivier; *Colonel Weaver* – Richard Kane; *Private Stephenson* – Toby Salaman; *British Staff Colonel* – Michael Bangerter; *Grenadier Guards Colonel* – Philip Raymond; *Boat truck driver* – Myles Reithermann; *Major Cook* – Robert Redford; *US Captain* – Anthony Pullen; *US Padre* – John Morton; *US Lieutenant* – John Ratzenberger; *German Lieutenant* – Patrick Ryecart; *Captain Krafft* – Dick Rienstra; *Sergeant Whitney* – Ian Liston; *Private Gordon* – Paul Rattee; *Sergeant Tomblin* – Mark Sheridan; *Sergeant Macdonald* – George Innes; *Grenadier Guards Major* – John Stride; *British Medical Orderlies* – Nial Padden, Michael Graves; *Private Simmonds* – Simon Chandler; *Private Archer* – Edward Kalinski; *Corporal Robbins* – Shaun Curry; *Sergeant Treadell* – Sebastian Abineri; *Corporal Merrick* – Chris Williams; *Flute player* – Andrew Branch; *British Staff Major* – Anthony Garner; *Dutch priest* – Feliks Arons; *Dutch villagers* – Bertus Botterman, Henny Alma; *Elderly Dutch couple* – Johan Te Slaa, Georgette Reyevski; *Young Dutch couple* – Pieter Groenier, Adrienne Kleiweg.

THE FIRST GREAT TRAIN ROBBERY (Great Britain; United Artists, 1978)
USA title: *The Great Train Robbery*
Director: Michael Crichton. Producer: John Foreman. Screenplay: Michael Crichton, based on his own novel. Photography: Geoffrey Unsworth. Editor: David Bretherton. Production designer: Maurice Carter. Art director: Bert Davey. Music: Jerry Goldsmith. Assistant directors: Anthony Waye, Gerry Gavignan and Chris Carreras. Running time: 110 minutes. In Technicolor Panavision. Certificate AA.
Production company: Starling Productions. Presented by Dino De Laurentiis.
Edward Pierce – Sean Connery; *Agar* – Donald Sutherland; *Miriam* – Lesley-Anne Down; *Edgar Trent* – Alan Webb; *Henry*

Fowler – Malcolm Terris; *Sharp* – Robert Lang; *Clean Willy* – Wayne Sleep; *Burgess* – Michael Elphick; *Emily Trent* – Pamela Salem; *Elizabeth Trent* – Gabrielle Lloyd; *Harranby* – James Cossins; *McPherson* – John Bett; *Station dispatcher* – Peter Benson; *Maggie* – Janine Duvitski; *Woman on platform* – Agnes Bernelle; *Police constable* – Frank McDonald; *Trent's butler;* – Brian De Salvo; *Rail guard* – Joe Cahill; *Shepherd* – Pat Layde; *Executioner* – Derek Lord; *Elderly woman on train* – Rachel Burrows

Note: Film dedicated to the memory of the late Geoffrey Unsworth.

METEOR (USA: Columbia–EMI–Warner, 1979)
Director: Ronald Neame. Producers: Arnold Orgolini and Theodore Parvi. Executive producers: Sandy Howard and Gabriel Katzka. Screenplay: Stanley Mann and Edmund H. North, from a story by Edmund H. North. Photography: Paul Lohmann. Editor: Carl Kress. Production designer: Edward Carfagno. Art director: David Constable. Special effects: Glen Robinson and Robert Staples. Technical Advisor (Jet Propulsion Laboratories): John Small. Technical Advisor (NASA): Doug Ward. Music: Laurence Rosenthal. Stunt co-ordinator: Roger Creed. Assistant director: Daniel J. McCauley. Running time: 107 minutes. In color Panavision. Certificate A.
Production company: A Sandy Howard/Gabriel Katzka/Sir Run Run Shaw Presentation.
Dr. Paul Bradley – Sean Connery; *Tatiana Donskaya* – Natalie Wood; *Harold Sherwood* – Karl Malden; *Dr. Alexei Dubov* – Brian Keith; *General Barry Adlon* – Martin Landau; *Sir Michael Hughes* – Trevor Howard; *Secretary of Defence* – Richard Dysart; *The President* – Henry Fonda; *Easton* – Joseph Campanella; *Jan* – Katherine DeHetre; *Alan* – James Richardson; *Manheim* – Bo Brundin; *Hunter* – Roger Robinson; *Mrs Bradley* – Bibi Besch; *Watson* – John McKinney; *Mason* – Michael Zaslow; *Tom Easton* – John Findlater; *Bill Frager* – Paul Tulley; *Michael McKendrick* – Allen Williams; *Russian Premier* – Gregory Gay; *Hawk-faced Party Member* – Zitto Kazann; *Yamashiro* – Clyde Kusatsu; *Coastguard Officer* – Burke Byrnes.

CUBA (USA; United Artists, 1979)
Director: Richard Lester. Producers: Arlene Sellers and Alex Winitsky. Executive producer: Denis O'Dell. Screenplay: Charles Wood. Photography: David Watkin. Editor: John Victor Smith. Production designer: Gil Parrondo. Art director: Denis

Gordon Orr. Second Unit photography: Robert Stevens. Music: Patrick Williams. Assistant directors: David Tringham, Roberto Parra, Steve Lanning, Javier Carrasco. Running time: 122 minutes. In Technicolor Panavision. Certificate AA.
Production company: An Alex Winitsky-Arlene Sellers Production.
Robert Dapes – Sean Connery; *Alexandra Pulido* – Brooke Adams; *Gutman* – Jack Weston; *Ramirez* – Hector Elizondo; *Skinner* – Denholm Elliott; *General Bello* – Martin Balsam; *Juan Pulido* – Chris Sarandon; *Faustino* – Alejandro Rey; *Therese* – Lonette McKee; *Julio* – Danny De La Paz; *Miss Wonderly* – Louisa Moritz; *Press agent* – Dave King; *Don Pulido* – Walter Gotell; *Colonel Rosell Y Leyva* – Earl Cameron; *Dolores* – Pauline Peart; *Maria* – Anna Nicholas; *Jesus* – David Rappaport; *Carillo* – Tony Matthews; *Cecilia* – Leticia Garrado; *Gary* – John Morton; *Spencer* – Anthony Pullen Shaw; *Ramon* – Stefan Kalipha; *Painter* – Raul Newney; *Girl in arcade* – Eva Louise.

TIME BANDITS (Great Britain; HandMade Films, 1981)
Director: Terry Gilliam. Producer: Terry Gilliam. Executive producers: George Harrison and Denis O'Brien. Screenplay: Michael Palin and Terry Gilliam. Photography: Peter Biziou. Editor: Julian Doyle. Production designer: Millie Burns. Art director: Norman Garwood. Special effects supervisor: John Bunker. Models: Val Charlton, (asst.) Carol De Jong, Jean Ramsey, Alix Harwood and Behira Thraves. Sculptors: Geoff Rivers Bland and Laurie Warburton. Special optical effects: Kent Houston, Paul Whitbread, (asst.) Tim Ollive, Dennis De Groot, Peerless Camera Co. Second Unit director: Julian Doyle. Music: Mike Moran. Greek dance music: Trevor Jones. Songs and additional material: George Harrison. Song: 'Me and My Shadow' by Rose Jolson, Dreyer, arranged by Trevor Jones. Assistant directors: Simon Hinkley, Guy Travers, Mark Cooper and Chris Thompson. Costumes: Jim Acheson and Hazel Côté. Running time: 113 minutes. In Technicolor. Certificate A.
Production company: HandMade Films.
Robin Hood – John Cleese; *King Agamemnon* – Sean Connery; *Pansy* – Shelley Duvall; *Mrs Ogre* – Katherine Helmond; *Napoleon* – Ian Holm; *Vincent* – Michael Palin; *Evil Genius* – David Warner; *Supreme Being* – Ralph Richardson; *Ogre* – Peter Vaughan; *Randall* – David Rappaport; *Fidgit* – Kenny Baker; *Wally* – Jack Purvis; *Og* – Mike Edmonds; *Strutter* – Malcolm Dixon; *Vermin* – Tiny Ross; *Kevin* – Craig Warnock; *Kevin's*

father – David Baker; *Kevin's mother* – Sheila Fearn; *Compere* –
Jim Broadbent; *Reginald* – John Young; *Beryl* – Myrtle Devenish;
Hussar – Brian Bowes; *1st refugee* – Leon Lissek; *Lucien* –
Terence Bayler; *Neguy* – Preston Lockwood; *Theatre manager* –
Charles McKeown; *Puppeteer* – David Leland; *The Great
Rumbozo* – John Hughman; *Robber leader* – Derrick O'Connor;
2nd robber – Declan Mulholland; *3rd robber* – Neil McCarthy;
Arm wrestler – Peter Jonfield; *Robert* – Derek Deadman; *Benson*
– Jerold Wells; *Cartwright* – Roger Frost; *Baxi Brazilia III* –
Martin Carroll; *Horseflesh* – Marcus Powell; *Bull-headed warrior*
– Winston Dennis; *Greek fighting warrior* – Del Baker; *Greek
Queen* – Juliette James; *Giant* – Ian Muir; *Troll father* – Mark
Holmes; *Fireman* – Andrew McLachlan; *Voice of TV announcer* –
Chris Grant; *Voice of Supreme Being* – Tony Jay; *Supreme
Being's face* – Edwin Finn.

OUTLAND (USA; Columbia–EMI–Warner, 1981)
Director: Peter Hyams. Producer: Richard A. Roth. Executive
producer: Stanley O'Toole. Screenplay: Peter Hyams. Photo-
graphy: Stephen Goldblatt. Editor: Stuart Baird. Production
designer: Philip Harrison. Art director: Malcolm Middleton.
Special effects: John Stears. Optical effects supervision: Roy
Field. Music Jerry Goldsmith. Assistant directors: David
Tringham and Bob Wright. Running time: 109 minutes. In
Technicolor Panavision. Certificate AA.
Production company: The Ladd Company.
O'Niel – Sean Connery; *Sheppard* – Peter Boyle; *Lazarus* –
Frances Sternhagen; *Montone* – James B. Sikking; *Carol* – Kika
Markham; *Ballard* – Clarke Peters; *Sagan* – Steven Berkoff;
Tarlow – John Ratzenberger; *Pau O'Nile* – Nicholas Barnes;
Lowell – Manning Redwood; *Mrs Spector* – Pat Starr; *Nelson* –
Hal Galili; *Hughes* – Angus MacInnes; *Walters* – Stuart Milligan;
Cane – Eugene Lipinski; *Slater* – Norman Chancer; *Fanning* –
Ron Travis; *Morton* – Anni Domingo; *Hill* – Bill Bailey; *Caldwell*
– Chris Williams; *Spota* – Marc Boyle; *Yario* – Richard Hammat;
Rudd – James Berwick; *Worker* – Gary Olsen; *Nurse* – Isabelle
Lucas; *Prostitute* – Sharon Duce; *Man 1* – P. H. Moriarty; *Mainte-
nance woman* – Angelique Rockas; *Female prostitute (Leisure
Club)* – Judith Alderson; *Male prostitute (Leisure Club)* – Rayner
Bourton; *Man 2* – Doug Robinson; *Dancers at Leisure Club* –
Julia Depyer, Nina Francoise, Brendon Hughes, Philip Johnston
and Norri Morgan.

THE MAN WITH THE DEADLY LENS (USA; Columbia, 1982)
USA title: *Wrong is Right*
Director: Richard Brooks. Producer: Richard Brooks. Executive
producer: Andrew Fogelson. Screenplay: Richard Brooks, based
on the novel *The Better Angels* by Charles McCarry. Photo-
graphy: Fred J. Koenekamp. Editor: George Grenville. Pro-
duction designer: Edward Carfagno. Art director: Karl Hueglin.
Music: Artie Kane. Assistant director: Alan Hopkins. Running
time: 117 minutes. In Metrocolor. Certificate A.
Production company: Richard Brooks Production.
Patrick Hale – Sean Connery; *President Lockwood* – George
Grizzard; *General Wombat* – Robert Conrad; *Sally Blake* –
Katherine Ross; *Philindros* G. D. Spradlin; *Homer Hubbard* –
John Saxon; *Rafeeq* – Henry Silva; *Mallory* – Leslie Nielsen;
Harvey – Robert Webber; *Mrs Ford* – Rosalind Cash; *Helmut
Unger* – Hardy Kruger; *Hacker* – Dean Stockwell; *King Awad* –
Ron Moody; *Erika* – Cherie Michan; *Abu* – Tony March.

FIVE DAYS ONE SUMMER (USA; Warner Bros, 1982)
Director: Fred Zinnemann. Producer: Fred Zinnemann. Execu-
tive producer: Peter Beale. Screenplay: Michael Austin, based on
the short story by Kay Boyle. Photography: Giuseppe Rotunno.
Editor: Stuart Baird. Production designer: Willy Holt. Art direc-
tors: Gérard Viard and Bob Cartwright. Second Unit director:
Norman Dyhrenfurth. Mountain consultant: Hamish McInnes.
Music: Elmer Bernstein. Assistant director: Anthony Waye.
Costumes by Emma Porteous. Running time: 100 minutes
approx. In colour.
Production company: A Ladd Company Production.
Douglas – Sean Connery; *Kate* – Betsy Brantley; *Johann* – Lam-
bert Wilson; *Sarah* – Jennifer Hilary; *Kate's mother* – Isabel
Dean; *Brendel* – Gerard Buhr; *Jennifer Pierce* – Anna Massey;
Gillian Pierce – Sheila Reid; *Dieter* – Georges Claisse; *Georg* –
Terry Kingley; *Old woman* – Emilie Lihou; *Van Royen* – Jerry
Brouwer; *French students* – Marc Duret, Francois Caron, Benoist
Ferreux; *Maclean* – Alexander John; *Horse taxi driver* – Michael
Burrell; *1st hut guardian* – Frank Duncan; *Choreographer* –
D'Dee.

NEVER SAY NEVER AGAIN (USA; Warner Bros, 1983)
Director: Irvin Kershner. Producer: Jack Schwartzman. Execu-
tive producer: Kevin McClory. Based on *Thunderball*, by Ian
Fleming, Jack Whittingham and Kevin McClory. Photography:

Douglas Slocombe. Editor: Ian Crafford. Production designer: Philip Harrison. Art director: Michael White with Les Dilley. Computer video electronics supervisor: Rob Dickenson. Special effects supervisor: Ian Wingrove. Assistant director: David Tomblin. Sean Connery's make-up artiste: Ilona Herman. Music: Michel Legrand. Running time: 100 minutes approx. In colour. Production company: Woodcote Productions.

James Bond – Sean Connery; *Domino* – Kim Basinger; *Ernst Blofeld* – Max Von Sydow; *Largo* – Klaus Maria Brandauer; *Fatima Blush* – Barbara Carrera; *Felix Leiter* – Bernie Casey; *M* – Edward Fox; *Moneypenny* – Pamela Salem; *Armourer* – Alec McGowan.

SWORD OF THE VALIANT – THE LEGEND OF GAWAIN AND THE GREEN KNIGHT (Great Britain; Cannon, 1983)
Director: Stephen Weeks. Producer: Menahem Golan and Yorum Globus. Executive producers: Philip M. Green and Michael Kagan. Screenplay: Stephen Weeks, Howard C. Pen, Philip M. Breen. Story consultant: Roger Towne. Photography: Freddie Young and Peter Hurst. Editor: Richard Marden and Barry Peters. Production designers: Maurice Fowler and Derek Nice. Assistant directors: David Bracknell, Ken Tuohy, Zsuzsanna Mills, Michael Mercy, Rod Lomax and Jerry Daly. Music: Ron Geesin. Running time: 102 minutes. Scope. Certificate PG.
Production company: London Cannon Films in association with Stephen Weeks Company.

Sir Gawain – Myles O'Keefe; *King Arthur* – Trevor Howard; *Green Knight* – Sean Connery; *Seneschal* – Peter Cushing; *Oswald* – Ronald Lacey; *Linet* – Cyrielle Claire; *Morgan le Fay* – Emma Sutton; *Black Knight* – Douglas Wilmer; *Lady of Lyonesse* – Lila Kedrova; *Humphrey* – Leigh Lawson; *Baron Forntinbras* – John Rhys-Davies.

HIGHLANDER (Great Britain; Columbia–Cannon–Warner, 1986)
Director: Russell Mulcahy. Producers: Peter S. Davis and William N. Panzer. Executive producer: E. C. Monell. Screenplay: Gregory Widen, Peter Bellwood and Larry Ferguson. Story by: Greogry Widen. Photography: Gerry Fisher and Tony Mitchell. Editor: Peter Honess. Production designer: Allan Cameron. Art directors: Tim Hutchinson and Martin Atkinson. Music:

Michael Kamen. Running time: 116 minutes. In Technicolor. Certificate 15.
Production company: Highlander Productions.
Conner MacLeod – Christopher Lambert; *Brena Wyatt* – Roxanne Hart; *Kurgan* – Clancy Brown; *Ramirez* – Sean Connery; *Heather* – Beatie Edney; *Lt Frank Moran* – Alan North; *Rachel Ellenstein* – Sheila Gish; *Det Walter Bedsoe* – Jon Polito; *Sunda Kastagir* – Hugh Quarshie; *Kirk Matunas* – Christopher Malcolm; *Fasil* – Peter Diamond; *Dugal MacLeod* – Billy Hartman; *Angus Macleod* – James Cosmo.

THE NAME OF THE ROSE (West Germany–Italy–France; Rank, 1986)

Director: Jean-Jacques Annaud. Producer: Bernd Eichinger. Executive producers: Thomas Schuhly and Jake Eberts. Screenplay: Andrew Birkin, Gerard Brach, Howard Franklin and Alain Godard. Based on the novel *Il nomme dela rosa* by Umberto Eco. Photography: Tonino Delli Colli. Editor: Jane Seitz. Production designer: Dante Ferretti. Music: James Horner. Costume design: Gabriella Pescucci. Running time: 131 minutes in English version. Eastman Colour. Certificate 18.
Production company: Neue Constantin (West Berlin)/Cristaldifilm (Rome)/Films Ariane (Paris). In association with ZDF. A Bernd Eichinger–Bernd Schaefers production.
William of Baskerville – Sean Connery; *Adso of Melk* – Christian Slater; *Remigio de Varagine* – Helmut Qualtinger; *Severinus* – Elya Baskin; *Abbot* – Michael Lonsdale; *Malachia* – Volker Prechtel; *Jourge de Burgos* – Feodor Chaliapin Jnr; *Ubertino de Casale* – William Hickey; *Berengar* – Michael Habeck; *Venantius* – Urs Althaus; *Girl* – Valentina Vargas; *Bernardo Gui* – F. Murray Abraham.

THE UNTOUCHABLES (USA; UIP, 1987)

Director: Brian De Palma. Producer: Art Linson. Screenplay: David Mamet, suggested by the TV series and based on works by Oscar Fraley with Eliot Ness and with Paul Robsky. Photography: Stephen H. Burum. Editors: Jerry Greenberg and Bill Pankow. Associate editor: Ray Hubley. Production designers: E. C. Chen, Steven P. Sardinis, Gil Clayton and Nichlas Laborczy. Music: Ennio Morricone. Musical extracts: 'Vesti la Guibba' from *I Pagliacci* by Ruggeriero Leoncavallo, performed by Mario Del Monaco; 'Mood Indigo' by Duke Ellington, Irving Mills and Barney Bigard, arranged by Bob Wilber. Costume design:

Marilyn Vance-Straker. Wardrobe: Giorgio Armani. Running time: 120 minutes. In Panavision Technicolor. Certificate 18. Production company: Paramount.

Eliot Ness – Kevin Costner; *Jim Malone* – Sean Connery; *Oscar Wallace* – Charles Martin Smith; *George Stone* – Andy Garcia; *Al Capone* – Robert De Niro; *Mike* – Richard Bradford; *Payne* – Jack Kehoe; *George* – Brad Sullivan; *Frank Nitti* – Stevn Drago; *Lt. Anderson* – Peter Aylward; *Preeuski* – Don Harvey; *Mountie Captain* – Robert Swan; *Bartender* – John J. Walsh; *Alderman* – Del Close; *Mrs Blackmer* – Colleen Bade; *Rangemaster* – Greg Noonan; *Cop Cousin* – Sean Grennan; *Italian waiter* – Larry Viverito Sr; *Williamson* – Kevin Michael Doyle; *Overcoat hood* – Mike Bacarella; *Ness's Clerk* – Michael P. Byrne; *Ness's Daughter* – Kaitlin Montgomery; *Blackmer girl* – Aditra Kohl; Reporters – Charles Keller Whatson, Larry Brandenburg, Chelcie Ross, Tim Gamble; *Bailiffs* – Sam Smiley, Pat Billingsley; *Fat Man* – Jack Bracci; *Woman in elevator* – Jennifer Anglin; *Butler* – Eddie Minasian; *Judge* – Tony Mockus Sr; *Defence Attorney* – Will Zahrn; *Barber* – Louis Lanciloti; *Bodyguards* – Vince Viverito, Valentino Cimmo, Joe Greco, Clem Caserta, Bob Martana, Joseph Scianablo, George S. Spataro.

FAMILY BUSINESS (USA; MGM/UA, 1989)
Director: Sidney Lumet. Producer: Lawrence Gordon. Executive producers: Jennifer Ogden and Burtt Harris. Screenplay: Vincent Patrick, based on his novel. Photography: Andrzej Bartkowiak. Editor: Andrew Mondshein. Production designer: Philip Rosenburg. Costumes: Ann Roth. Music: Cy Coleman. Running time: 109 minutes. Colour. Certificate PG.
Production company: Tri-Star Pictures in association with A. Milchan Investment Group.

Jessie – Sean Connery; *Vito* – Dustin Hoffman; *Adam* – Matthew Broderick; *Elaine* – Rosana de Soto; *Margie* – Janet Carroll; *Christine* – Victoria Jackson; *Doheny* – Bill McCutcheon; *Michelle Dempsey* – Deborah Rush; *Rose* – Marilyn Cooper; *Nat* – Salem Ludwig; *Ray Garvey* – Rex Everhart; *Judge* – James S. Tolkan; *Marie* – Marilyn Sokol; *Neary* – Thomas A. Carlin; *Phil* – Tony Di Benedetto; *Judge* – Isabell Monk; *Prosecutor* – Wendell Pierce.

THE PRESIDIO (USA; UIP, 1989)
Director: Peter Hyams. Producer: D. Constantine Conte. Co-producer: Fred Caruso. Executive producer: Jonathan A. Zimbert. Screenplay: Larry Ferguson. Photography: Peter Hyams.

Editor: James Mitchell, with Diane Adler and Beau Barthel-Blair. Production designer: Albert Brenner. Music: Bruce Broughton. Running time: 98 minutes. In Technicolor. Certificate 15.
Production company: A. D. Constantine Conte Production.
Lt Col. Alan Caldwell – Sean Connery; *Jay Austin* – Mark Harmon; *Donna Caldwell* – Meg Ryan; *Maclure* – Jack Warden; *Peale* – Mark Blum; *Lawrence* – Dana Gladstone; *Patti Jean* – Jenette Goldstein; *M. P. Zeke* – Marvin J. McIntyre; Howard Buckley – Don Calfa; *Det. Marvin Powell* – John Di Santi; *Mueller* – Robert Lesser; *Spota* – James Hooks Reynolds; *Garfield* – Curtis W. Sims; *Bully in bar* – Rick Zumwalt; *Lawrence's secretary* – Rosalyn Marshall; *Pilot at Travis A.F.B.* – Jessie Lawrence Ferguson.

INDIANA JONES AND THE LAST CRUSADE (USA; UIP, 1989)
Director: Steven Spielberg. Producer: Robert Watts. Executive Producers: George Lucas and Frank Marshall. Production executive (2nd Unit) Kathleen Kennedy. Screenplay: Jeffrey Boam. Story: George Lucas and Menno Meyjes. Based on characters created by George Lucas and Philip Kaufman. Photography: Douglas Slocombe. Additional photography: Paul Beeson. 2nd Unit photography: Robert Stevens, Rex Metz. Aerial photography: Peter Allwork. Editor: Michael Kahn. Associate editor: Colin Wilson. Production designer: Elliot Scott. Art designers: Fred Hole and Stephen Scott with Richard Berger, Benjamin Fernandez and Guido Salsilli. Visual effects: supervised by Michael J. McAlister for Industrial Light & Magic (producer: Patricia Blau). Music: John Williams. Songs: 'You're a Sweet Little Headache' by Leo Robin and Ralph Rainger, performed by Benny Goodman; 'Just A Gigolo' by Leonello Casucci and Julius Brammer. Running time: 127 minutes. In Eastman Colour DeLuxe. Certificate PG.
Production Company: Lucasfilm for Paramount.
Indian Jones – Harrison Ford; *Dr Henry Jones* – Sean Connery; *Marcus Brody* – Denholm Elliott; *Dr Elsa Schneider* – Alison Doody; *Sallah* – John Rhys-Davies; *Walter Donovan* – Julian Glover; *Young Indy* – River Phoenix; *Vogel* – Michael Byrne; *Kazim* – Kevork Malikyan; *Grail Knight* – Robert Eddison; *Fedora* – Richard Young; *Sultan* – Alexi Sayle; *Young Henry* – Alex Hyde-White; *Panama Hat* – Paul Maxwell; *Mrs Donovan* – Mrs Glover; *Butler* – Vernon Dobtcheff; *Herman* – J. J. Hardy;

Roscoe – Bradley Gregg; *Half-breed* – Jeff O'Haco; *Rough rider* – Vince Deadrick; *Sheriff* – Marc Miles; *Deputy Sheriff* – Ted Grossman; *Young Panama hat* – Tim Hiser; *Scout master* – Larry Sanders; *Scouts* – Will Miles, David Murray; *World War I ace* – Frederick Jaeger; *Professor Stanton* – Jerry Harte; *Dr Mulbray* – Billy J. Mitchell; *Man at Hitler rally* – Martin Gordon; *Gestapo* – Pat Roach; *Film director* – Suzanne Roquette; *Flower girl* – Nina Almond.

THE HUNT FOR RED OCTOBER (USA; UIP, 1990)

Director: John McTiernan. Producer: Mace Neufeld. Executive Producers: Larry DeWaay and Jerry Sherlock. Screenplay: Larry Ferguson and Donald Stewart. Based on the novel by Tom Clancy. Photography: Jan de Bont. Editors: Juno J. Ellis, Jay Kamen and Shelley Rae Buck. Music: Basl Poledouris. Songs: 'The Anthem of the Soviet Union' by A. V. Alexsandrov, G. A. El Reghistan and S. V. Mikhailov; 'Payoff' by Basil Poledouris. Running time: 135 minutes. Technicolor Panavision. Certificate PG.
Production company: Paramount. A Mace Neufeld–Jerry Sherlock Production.
Marko Ramius – Sean Connery; *Jack Ryan* – Alec Baldwin; *Bart Mancuso* – Scott Glenn; *Captain Borodin* – Sam Neill; *Admiral Greer* – James Earl Jones; *Lysenko* – Joss Ackland; *Jeffrey Pelt* – Richard Jordan; *Ivan Putin* – Peter Firth; *Dr. Petrov* – Tim Curry; *Seaman Jones* – Courtney B. Vance; *Tupolev* – Stellan Skarasgard; *Skip Tyler* – Jeffrey Jones; *Steiner* – Timothy Carhart; *Chief of boat* – Larry Ferguson; *Admiral Painter* – Fred Dalton Thompson; *Davenport* – Daniel Davis; *Thompson* – Anthony Peck; *Red October officers and crew* – Ronald Guttman, Michael George Benko, Anatoly Davydov, Ivan Michael Welden, Boris Krutonog, Kenton Kovell, Radu Gavor, Ivan Ivanov, Ping Wu, Herman Sinitzyn; *Konovalov officers and crew* – Christopher Janczar, Vlado Benden, George Winston; *Helicopter pilot* – Don Oscar Smith; *Navigator* – Rick Ducommun; *DSRV officer* – George H. Billy; *Curry* – Reed Popovich; *Amalric* – Andrew Divoff; *Moore* – Peter Zinner; *General at briefing* – F. J. O'Neill; *Caroline Ryan* – Gates McFadden; *Sally Ryan* – Louise Borras; *Himself* – Stanley.

THE RUSSIA HOUSE (USA; UIP, 1990)

Director: Fred Schepisi. Producers: Paul Maslansky and Fred Schepisi. Screenplay: Tom Stoppard. Based on the novel by John Le Carré. Photography: Ian Baker. Music: Jerry Goldsmith.

Songs: 'What is this Thing Called Love?' by Cole Porter; 'The Sheik of Araby' by T. Snyder, F. Wheeler and H. B. Smith; 'Ain't Misbehavin'' by Thomas 'Fats' Waller, Harry Brooks and Andy Razaf. Production designer: Richard MacDonald. Running time: 123 minutes. In Technicolor. Certificate 15.
Production company: Pathe Entertainment.
Barley Blair – Sean Connery; *Katya* – Michelle Pfeiffer; *Russell* – Roy Scheider; *Ned* – James Fox; *Brady* – John Mahoney; *Clive* – Michael Kitchen; *Quinn* – J. T. Walsh; *Walter* – Ken Russell; *Wicklow* – David Threlfall; *'Dante'* – Klaus Maria Brandauer; *Bob* – 'Mac' MacDonald; *Landau* – Nicholas Woodeson; *Brock* – Martin Clunes; *Merrydew* – Ian McNeice; *Henziger* – Colin Stinton; *Paddy* – Denys Hawthorne; *Cy* – George Roth; *US Scientist* – Peter Mariner; *Anna* – Ellen Hurst; *Sergey* – Peter Knupffer; *Uncle Matvey* – Nikolai Pastukhov; *Johnny* – Jason Salkey; *Nasayan* – Eric Anzumonyin; *Zapadny* – Daniel Wazniak; *Yuri* – Georgi Andzhaparidze; *Tout* – Vladek Nikiforov; *Larry* – Christopher Lawford; *Todd* – Mark La Mura; *Merv* – Blu Mankuma; *Stanley* – Tuck Milligan; *Spiky* – Jay Benedict; *George* – David Timson; *Anastasia* – Elena Stroyeva; *Watchers* – Fyodor Smirnov, Pavel Sirotin; *Misha* – Paul Jutkevich; *Woman interpreter* – Margot Pinvidic; *Junior Minister in Whitehall* – David Henry; *Scientist* – Martin Wenner; *Army officer* – Paul Rattee; *Psychoanalyst* – Simon Templeman.

HIGHLANDER II (USA; 1991)
Director: Russell Mulcahy. Producers: Peter S. Davis and William Panzer. Executive Producers: Guy Collins and Mario Sotela. Co-producers: Alejandro Sessa and Robin Clark. Screenplay: Peter Belwood. Story by: Brian Clemens, William Panzer. Based on characters by: Gregory Widen. Photography: Phil Meheux. Additional photography: Jamie Thompson. Animation supervisor: Chris Cassidy. Editors: Hubert C. de la Bouillerie and Anthony Redman. Associate editor: Silvia Ripoll. Music: Stewart Copeland. Music extracts: From *Götterdammerung* by Richard Wagner. Production designer: Roger Hall. Art directors: Cliff Robinson, John Frankish and Leon Dourage. Costume designer: Deborah Everton. Running time: 100 minutes. Eastman Colour. Certificate PG.
Production Company: Lamb Bear Entertainment.
Conner MacLeod – Christopher Lambert; *Ramirez* – Sean Connery; *Louise Marcus* – Virginia Madsen: *Katana* – Michael Ironside; *Alan Neyman* – Alan Rich; *Blake* – John C. McGinley;

Cabbie – Phil Brock; *Drunk* – Rusty Schwimmer; *Jimmy* – Ed Trucco; *Hamlet* – Stephen Grives; *Horatio* – Jimmy Murray; *Corda* – Pete Antico; *Reno* – Peter Buccossi; *Joe* – Peter Bromilow; *Doctor* – Jeff Altman; *Virginia* – Diana Rossi; *Max Guard* – Randall Newsome; *Brenda* – Karin Drexler; *Charlie* – Max Berliner; *Holt* – Eduardo Sapac; *Kids* – Michael Peyronel, Sebastian Morgan; *Zeist* – Bruno Cuichelli; *2nd Justice* – Daniel Trovo; *3rd Justice* – Diego Leske; *Terrorist* – Matt Johnson; *Voices* – Julio Breshnev.

ROBIN HOOD – PRINCE OF THIEVES (USA; Warner Bros, 1991)
Director: Kevin Reynolds. Producers: John Watson, Pen Densham and Richard B. Lewis. Executive Producers: James G. Robinson, David Nicksay and Gary Barber. Co-producer: Michael J. Kagan. Screenplay: Pen Densham and John Watson. Story: Pen Densham. Photography: Douglas Milsome. Editors: Peter Boyle, with Marcus Manton, Carmel Davis, Peter Hollywood and Michael Kelly. Music: Michael Kamen. Songs: '(Everything I Do) I Do For You' by M. Kamen, B. Adams and R. J. Lange; 'Wild Times' by M. Kamen, Jeff Lynne. Costume designer: John Bloomfield. Swordmaster: Terry Walsh. Horsemaster: Tony Smart. Running time: 143 minutes. In Technicolor. Certificate PG.
Production company: Morgan Creek.
Robin of Locksley – Kevin Costner; *Azeem* – Morgan Freeman; *Marian* – Mary Elizabeth Mastrantonio; *Will Scarlett* – Christian Slater; *Sheriff of Nottingham* – Alan Rickman; *King Richard* – Sean Connery; *Mortianna* – Geraldine McEwan; *Friar Tuck* – Micheal McShane; *Lord Locksley* – Brian Blessed; *Guy of Gisborne* – Michael Wincott; *Little John* – Nick Brimble; *Fanny* – Soo Drouet; *Wulf* – Daniel Newman; *Bull* – Daniel Peacock; *Duncan* – Walter Sparrow; *Bishop* – Harold Innocent; *Much* – Jack Wild; *Kenneth* – Michael Goldie; *Peter Dubois* – Liam Halligan; *Turk Interrogator* – Marz Zuber; *Old woman* – Aerelina Kendall; *Sarah* – Imogen Bain; *Farmer* – Jimmy Gardner; *Villager* – Bobby Parr; *Courier* – John Francis; *Red-headed baron* – John Hallam; *Grey-bearded baron* – Douglas Blackwell; *Celtic chieftain* – Pat Roach; *Ox* – Andy Hockley; *Broth* – John Dallimore; *Kneelock* – Derek Deadman; *Hal* – Howard Lew Lewis; *Scribe* – John Tordoff; *Sergeant* – Andrew Lawden; *Lady in coach* – Susannah Corbett; *Small girl* – Sarah Alexandra; *Soldier* – Christopher Adamson; *Executioner* – Richard Strange.

MEDICINE MAN (USA; Guild, 1992)
Director: John McTiernan. Producers: Andrew G. Vajna and
Donna Dubrow. Executive producer: Sean Connery. Line pro-
ducer: Beau Marks. Screenplay: Tom Schulman and Sally Robin-
son. Story: Tom Schulman. Photography: Donald McAlpine.
Editors: Michael R. Miller, with Mary Jo Markey. Production
designer: John Krenz Reinhart Jr. Art directors: Don Diers, Jesus
Buenrostro and Marlisi Storchi. Special effects tree climbing:
Socorro Carvajal. Costume design: Marilyn Vance-Straker; for
Brazilian Indians, Rita Murtimho. Music: Jerry Goldsmith.
Authentic ritual music: Xavante Nation. Song: 'That Old Black
Magic' by Johnny Mercer and Harold Arlen. Running time: 105
minutes. In Technicolor. Certificate PG.
Production company: Cinergi.
Dr Robert Campbell – Sean Connery; *Dr Rae Crane* – Lorraine
Bracco; *Dr Miguel Ornega* – Jose Wilker; *Tanaki* – Rodolfo de
Alexandre; *Jahausa* – Francisco Tsirene Tscre Rereme; *Palala* –
Elias Monteiro da Silva; *Kalana* – Edinei Maria Serrior Dos
Santos; *Imana* – Bec-Kana-Re Dos Santos Kaiapo; *Medicine man*
– Angelo Barra Moreira; *Government man* – Jose Lavat.

RISING SUN (USA; Twentieth Century-Fox, 1993)
Director: Philip Kaufman. Producer: Peter Kaufman. Line pro-
ducer: Ian Bryce. Executive producer: Sean Connery. Screen-
play: David Mamet and Philip Kaufman. Original screenplay
(from his own novel): Michael Crichton. Photography: Michael
Chapman. Production designer: Dean Tavoularis. Editors:
Stephen A. Rotter and William Scharf. Running time: approx.
100 minutes. In Technicolor.
Production company: Walrus & Associates.
John Connor – Sean Connery; *Web Smith* – Wesley Snipes; *Lt
Tom Graham* – Harvey Keitel; *Jingo* – Tia Carrere; *Bob Richmond*
– Kevin Anderson; *Yoshida* – Mako; *Eddie Sakamura* – Cary-
Hiroyuki Tagawa; *Ishihara* – Stan Egi; *Senator Morton* – Ray
Wise.

Index

313

315